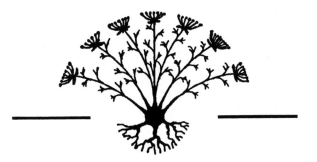

USING HERBS
IN THE LANDSCAPE

*How to Design and Grow Gardens of Herbal
Annuals, Perennials, Shrubs, and Trees*

Debra Kirkpatrick

STACKPOLE
BOOKS

Historical designs from Paterson, Catherine Childs, ed. *Medieval Gardens*. New York: Hacker Art Books, reprint, 1966.
Design page 183: Copyright © 1984 by the Trustees of Dartmouth College
Reprinted from Herb Garden Design by Faith H. Swanson and Virginia B. Rady by permission of the University Press of New England.
Design page 221: Adapted from the garden of Becky Talbot, used with permission.

Published by
STACKPOLE BOOKS
Cameron and Kelker Streets
P.O. Box 1831
Harrisburg, PA 17105

Cover design by Tracy Patterson
Cover photo by Judy Glattstein

Printed in the United States of America

First Edition

10 9 8 7 6 5 4 3 2 1

Library of Congress Cataloging-in-Publication Data

Kirkpatrick, Debra
    Using herbs in the landscape : how to design and grow gardens of herbal annuals, perennials, shrubs, and trees / Debra Kirkpatrick. —
1st ed.
        p.   cm.
Includes bibliographical references and index.
    ISBN 0-8117-1187-0
    1. Herb gardening.   2. Herb gardens—Design.
3. Landscape gardening.   I. Title.
SB351.H5K57   1992
716—dc20   91-90155
                                                    CIP

CONTENTS

ACKNOWLEDGMENTS

Putting this book together has been an interesting adventure as well as a long and involved process. Along the way many people have helped. Tremendous thanks go to my brother, Richard Kirkpatrick, for his patient assistance, expertise, and all-around brilliance. I am also indebted to Dorothy Kirkpatrick, my ever-optimistic and energetic mother, for sharing her ideas and insights, sensitivity to the art and beauty of gardens, and sense of humor, which helped keep the book a fun and rewarding project.

Special thanks to my friend and colleague, Holly Harmar Shimizu, for her encouragement and assistance in horticultural editing.

I am also grateful to Wiley McKellar for his contributions in the writing craft, and to Jan Hahn for her artistic eye and the feedback she offered as I prepared the drawings for the book. I would also like to acknowledge others who helped and supported me along the way, including Bertha Reppert, Faith Swanson, Steve Harris, Leora Kirkpatrick, Peter Seidel, Bob Galaskas, Tom Hedenberg, Tricia Boothby-Melchert, David Melchert, and the talented editorial staff at Stackpole Books.

My appreciation is extended to the Herb Society of America and their Scholarship and Research Grants Program Committee for their part in supporting my work on *Using Herbs in the Landscape.*

INTRODUCTION

Herbs have a mystique. Perhaps this special quality stems from their rich historical legacy; perhaps it is attributable to their association with the power to heal; perhaps we are drawn to herbs by their innate beauty. Highly ornamental, they are especially valued for their interesting leaf textures, foliage colors, and softly beautiful flowers. Many herbs offer the unique pleasure of fragrance. These delightful plants deserve sensitive placement in the landscape—sites that allow people to appreciate them. Herbal plantings are appropriate anywhere people congregate, meditate, pause, or pass by. An outstanding virtue of herbs is their ability to lend an intimacy and gentle, restful ambience to the hurried and often impersonal atmosphere of cities and suburban developments. Herbs can animate lifeless areas and stimulate the senses with their beauty and lovely aromatic qualities.

Opportunities abound for enriching developed areas with herb gardens and herb plantings. The traditional geometrical herb garden motif can be easily translated to many situations within the architectural fabric of a city, for example. The historical knot-garden designs can be restated or reinterpreted in courtyards, townhouse plots, and terraces to create interesting patterns that are especially spectacular when viewed from above.

Residential and public spaces can be enlivened by herbs in street-level plantings, raised beds, window boxes, and containers. Parks and residential properties are excellent settings for naturalized plantings using the many native American herbs—a refreshing alternative to the annuals commonly used for seasonal-interest beds. The use of herbs in garden designs is a potential waiting to be explored, particularly in urban and suburban locations. Properly sited and well-chosen herbs can adapt with relative ease to these environments.

In this book residential gardeners, horticulturists, and landscape design professionals will find useful guidance for including herbs in their design repertoire. Though this book addresses the special needs of herbs in the city, it applies to a wide range of design environments. It offers practical information about choosing sites, selecting and growing the plants, and designing traditional and nontraditional herb gardens. It is my hope that this publication will promote herbs to a more prominent position in gardeners' plant palettes and, ultimately, to a more visible place in the landscape.

Herb
Culture

*H*erbs, broadly defined, are plants that are valued for their usefulness to cooks and chemists, doctors and dyers. Though not every gardener today grows herbs for the purpose of preparing medicinal decoctions or dyeing and weaving homespun linen, it is for such uses that herbs were cultivated in the past.

Providing good growing conditions is no less important now than it was when the gardener depended on a steady supply of useful leaves, flowers, and roots, even if the plants' value is primarily aesthetic: well-grown plants are attractive plants, with good form and good color in both leaf and flower. Good herb culture begins with an understanding of the needs of these plants.

Many of the popular herbs in American gardens trace their origins to the hot, dry, gravelly slopes of Mediterranean Europe. These conditions can be approximated in many urban and suburban environments in the United States and Canada. Although many herbs do thrive in heat and bright light, gardeners tend to overlook the ability of other herb species to perform remarkably well in various levels of shade. Many native American woodland herbs, for example, perform well in deep shade.

The importance of well-drained soils cannot be overemphasized. Herbs will not perform well in compacted soils. They are not nearly so particular about soil fertility and soil reaction, but these factors should also be considered when locating herbs, as well as other garden plants.

Temperature, too, is a consideration, especially since many of the popular shrubby perennial herbs are borderline hardy in colder climates. Special attention should be given to providing winter protection and sheltering them from drying winds.

Microclimate refers to the various environmental factors that are specific to a particular planting site. Creating amiable growing conditions in certain microclimates can be a challenge. Trees and buildings may obstruct direct sunlight. Wind turbulence patterns will affect a plant's success. Paved areas may create problems with drainage and moisture availability. Frost pockets and stagnant air spaces can form in the canyons of the city or even around townhouse courtyards. Chemical pollutants leave the soil in poor condition. Urban soils may even need to be replaced. But with careful site analysis, proper plant selection, and adequate soil preparation, herbs will adapt well and become both a practical and a beautiful landscaping option.

The terms *prefer* and *accept* are used to evaluate an herb's response to certain

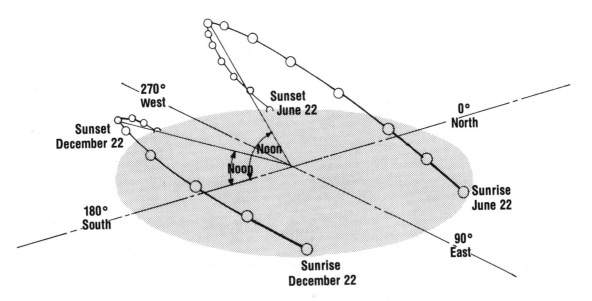

The sun's seasonal and daily movement in the sky determines the light levels reaching your planting area. This information will help you choose the right plant for the right place.

cultural conditions. *Prefer* describes the ideal conditions for optimal plant growth, vigor, health, fragrance, taste, and appearance, including blooming. *Accept* refers to less than the ideal conditions for optimal growth. Acceptable conditions will usually produce satisfactory plants, although the plants may bloom sparsely, have less vigor, and be smaller or leggy in form.

LIGHT

Herbs thrive in a wide range of light conditions, from direct all-day sun to light or partial shade. A few even grow in total absence of direct light. To determine which plants will do well in which spots, light analysis of a potential planting site is very important.

Understanding the sun's daily and seasonal movement is essential for an accurate assessment of the amount and intensity of sunlight reaching a site. For instance, the summer sun rises in the northeast and sets in the northwest, whereas the winter sun rises in the southeast and sets in the southwest. Thus, a northwest location, which may not receive any direct sunlight in winter, could receive intense, potentially harmful late-afternoon sun in the summer.

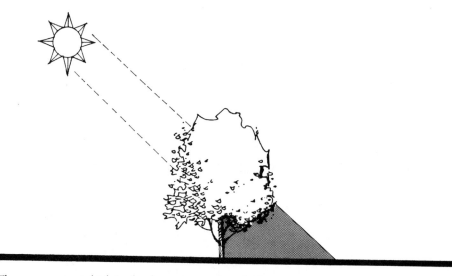

The summer sun is high in the sky and casts short shadows.

Also, remember that the altitude of the noonday sun in summer is different from the altitude of the noonday sun in winter. The sun is high in the summer sky and will cast a relatively short shadow from a building or tree. The angle of the sun is low in the sky during the winter months, however, and a shadow cast from an obstruction is significantly longer. For further instruction on how to determine more exact light calculations, refer to the diagrams in *Architectural Graphic Standards.*

The intensity of light that falls on a site is just as important to assess as the length of time it receives light. Direct noonday and afternoon sun is much more intense than morning sun. Thus, a plant that prefers partial shade may be able to thrive where it receives a few hours of direct morning sun, but the same number of hours of direct afternoon sun may be too much for it. The intensity and heat of afternoon sun are reduced when its direct rays are filtered by tall vegetation or other structures.

When assessing a site's light conditions, pay careful attention to the nature of any obstructions in or near the planting area. Buildings, tree canopies, walls, hedges, and trellises all can affect how much light gets through. A fine-foliaged tree or a trellised vine with small leaves and an open branching habit will allow more light through than canopies with larger leaves and a dense branching habit. And of course a building structure will totally block direct sunlight.

Buildings can, however, be a valuable source of reflected light in cities and towns, and even alongside suburban homes. Texture, color, and surface material

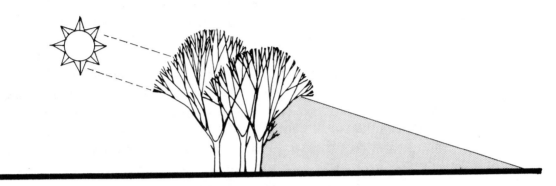

The winter sun is low in the sky and casts longer shadows.

affect the amount of light absorbed and reflected. Dark, highly textured surfaces absorb light; smooth, light-colored surfaces are better for reflection. Sometimes the patterns of reflected light produce a beautifully subtle effect. Harmful, glaring reflected light in garden spaces should be avoided.

In the list that follows, the terms *shade, partial shade*, and *full sun* represent approximate categories of the many situations possible within the spectrum of outdoor light levels.

Shade can describe a site receiving dappled, filtered sunlight from a moderately to densely canopied tree for the entire day. A shady site might receive a few hours of direct, unobstructed sunlight each day with building or canopy shade for the remainder of the day. A plant that prefers shade will generally do better with a few hours of morning light than with more intense afternoon sun, especially if it prefers cooler temperatures as well.

Full sun describes a planting site that receives a minimum of six hours of direct, unobstructed sunlight per day during the growing season. Plants that prefer full sun usually perform very well in a partially shaded site as long as they receive their minimum daily requirement of direct sunlight.

Partial shade describes the various conditions that fall between those of shade and full sun. It refers to sites that receive less than six hours of direct sunlight per day, with shade or filtered light for the remainder of the day. A partially shaded location might receive dappled, filtered sunlight through an airy canopy all day. *Partial shade* could also describe a site that receives a combination of direct and filtered or diffused light. Again, plants that prefer partial shade tolerate morning sun better than they do afternoon sun.

Keep in mind that those terms represent approximations and should be used as guides. The process of selecting a plant for a particular site is not like following a recipe or using a scientific formula. Use good judgment and don't be afraid to experiment. Finding an exception to a rule in plant culture is a frequent occurrence.

Since a plant's health and vigor are influenced by several conditions, its flexibility with regard to any particular one depends on all the others. Light, moisture, and temperature, as well as other factors, are intrinsically related. For example, a plant that receives a little more light than is optimal may perform just fine if it is watered more frequently. This same overexposed plant may also do well if the microclimate is cool, but may suffer from heat buildup in heavily paved areas. Use a holistic approach to site analysis.

The plant lists that follow categorize herbs according to the conditions that they prefer or accept. Plant names may appear in two lists; this means both conditions produce optimal results. Use the lists as an easy guide for selecting the proper plant for the light level of your planting site. And although there is no substitute for a conscientious site analysis, allow yourself to make occasional mistakes. Your gardening endeavors will be an ongoing learning process.

Prefers Shade

Alchemilla alpina	Alpine lady's mantle	*Helleborus* spp.	Hellebores
Alchemilla mollis	Lady's mantle	*Hydrastis canadensis*	Goldenseal
Angelica archangelica	Angelica	*Myrrhis odorata*	Sweet cicely
Anthriscus cerefolium	Sweet chervil	*Oenothera biennis*	Evening primrose
Arisaema triphyllum	Jack-in-the-pulpit	*Panax quinquefolius*	Ginseng
Asarum canadense	Wild ginger	*Pulmonaria officinalis*	Lungwort
Chelidonium majus	Celandine poppy	*Sanguinaria canadensis*	Bloodroot
Chimaphila umbellata	Pipsissewa	*Viola odorata*	Sweet violet
Convallaria majalis	Lily-of-the-valley		
Galium odoratum	Sweet woodruff		
Gaultheria procumbens	Wintergreen or teaberry		

Accepts Shade

Anthriscus cerefolium	Sweet chervil
Chrysanthemum balsamita	Costmary or alecost
Colchicum autumnale	Autumn crocus
Crocus sativus	Saffron crocus
Digitalis purpurea	Foxglove
Levisticum officinale	Lovage
Melissa officinalis	Lemon balm
Mentha × *gentilis* 'Variegata'	Ginger mint
Mentha × *piperita*	Peppermint
Mentha × *piperita* var. *citrata*	Lemon or bergamot mint
Mentha pulegium	Pennyroyal
Mentha requienii	Creme-de-menthe or Corsican mint
Mentha suaveolens	Apple mint
Mentha suaveolens 'Variegata'	Pineapple mint
Mentha spicata	Spearmint
Mentha spicata 'Crispii' or 'Crispata'	Curly mint
Nepeta cataria	Catnip
Petroselinum crispum	Parsley
Petroselinum crispum 'Curly Parsley'	Curly parsley
Petroselinum crispum var. *neapolitanum*	Italian parsley
Valeriana officinalis	Valerian

Prefers Partial Shade

Alchemilla alpina	Alpine lady's mantle
Alchemilla mollis	Lady's mantle
Angelica archangelica	Angelica
Anthriscus cerefolium	Sweet chervil
Calamintha nepeta	Calamint
Colchicum autumnale	Autumn crocus
Crocus sativus	Saffron crocus
Digitalis purpurea	Foxglove
Heliotropium arborescens	Heliotrope
Hypericum perforatum	St. John's wort
Laurus nobilis	Sweet bay
Levisticum officinale	Lovage
Melissa officinalis	Lemon balm
Melissa officinalis 'Variegata'	Golden lemon balm
Mentha × *gentilis* 'Variegata'	Ginger mint
Mentha × *piperita*	Peppermint
Mentha × *piperita* var. *citrata*	Lemon or bergamot mint
Mentha pulegium	Pennyroyal
Mentha requienii	Creme-de-menthe or Corsican mint
Mentha suaveolens	Apple mint
Mentha suaveolens 'Variegata'	Pineapple mint
Mentha spicata	Spearmint
Mentha spicata 'Crispii' or 'Crispata'	Curly mint
Monarda citriodora	Lemon bergamot or lemon bee balm
Monarda didyma and cultivars	Bee balm

Prefers Partial Shade, continued

Nepeta cataria	Catnip
Pelargonium tomentosum	
	Peppermint-scented geranium
Perilla frutescens 'Atropurpurea'	
	Purple perilla
Petroselinum crispum	Parsley
Petroselinum crispum 'Curly Parsley'	
	Curly parsley
Petroselinum crispum var. *neapolitanum*	
	Italian parsley
Poterium sanguisorba	Burnet
Stachys officinalis	Betony

Symphytum caucasicum	Small blue comfrey
Symphytum officinale	Comfrey
Symphytum officinale 'Variegatum'	
	Variegated comfrey
Symphytum × *uplandicum*	Russian comfrey
Tanacetum vulgare	Tansy
Tanacetum vulgare var. *crispum*	
	Curly or fern-leaf tansy
Valeriana officinalis	Valerian
Viola odorata	Sweet violet

Accepts Partial Shade

Agastache foeniculum	
	Anise hyssop or giant blue hyssop
Agastache rugosa	Korean anise hyssop
Allium schoenoprasum	Chives
Althaea officinalis	Marsh mallow
Artemisia absinthium 'Lambrook Silver'	
	'Lambrook Silver' artemisia
Artemisia annua	Sweet annual wormwood
Artemisia dracunculus var. *sativa*	
	French tarragon
Artemisia pontica	Roman wormwood
Artemisia stellerana	Beach wormwood
Asarum canadense	Wild ginger
Borago officinalis	Borage
Chamaemelum nobile	Roman chamomile
Chamaemelum nobile 'Treanague'	
	Flowerless chamomile
Chelidonium majus	Celandine poppy
Chimaphila umbellata	Pipsissewa

Chrysanthemum balsamita	
	Costmary or alecost
Chrysanthemum parthenium	Feverfew
Convallaria majalis	Lily-of-the-valley
Coriandrum sativum	
	Coriander, cilantro, or Chinese parsley
Foeniculum vulgare	Fennel
Foeniculum vulgare var. *rubrum*	
	Bronze fennel
Galium odoratum	Sweet woodruff
Galium verum	Yellow bedstraw
Gaultheria procumbens	
	Wintergreen or teaberry
Helleborus spp.	Hellebores
Hydrastis canadensis	Goldenseal
Hyssopus officinalis	Hyssop
Hyssopus officinalis 'Alba'	
	White-flowering hyssop
Hyssopus officinalis 'Rubra'	
	Rose-flowering hyssop

Accepts Partial Shade, continued

Iris × germanica var. florentina	Orris or Florentina iris
Marrubium vulgare	Horehound
Matricaria recutita	German chamomile
Myrrhis odorata	Sweet cicely
Myrtus communis	Sweet myrtle
Nepeta cataria 'Blue Wonder'	'Blue Wonder' catnip
Nepeta cataria 'Citriodora'	Lemon-scented catnip
Nepeta × faassenii	Catmint
Nepeta mussinii	Catmint
Oenothera biennis	Evening primrose
Origanum majorana	Sweet marjoram
Origanum vulgare	Common oregano or wild marjoram
Panax quinquefolius	Ginseng
Pulmonaria officinalis	Lungwort
Rosmarinus officinalis	Rosemary
Rosmarinus officinalis 'Albus'	White-flowering rosemary
Rosmarinus officinalis 'Arp'	Hardy rosemary
Rosmarinus officinalis 'Benedin Blue'	'Benedin Blue' rosemary
Rosmarinus officinalis 'Collingwood Ingram'	Graceful rosemary
Rosmarinus officinalis 'Lockwood de Forest'	Prostrate rosemary
Rosmarinus officinalis 'Prostratus'	Prostrate rosemary
Rosmarinus officinalis 'Tuscan Blue'	Columnar rosemary
Ruta graveolens	Rue
Sanguinaria canadensis	Bloodroot
Satureja hortensis	Summer savory
Satureja montana	Winter savory

Satureja montana pygmaea	Dwarf winter savory
Teucrium canadense	Wood sage or American germander
Teucrium chamaedrys	Germander
Teucrium chamaedrys 'Prostratum'	Prostrate germander
Teucrium chamaedrys 'Variegatum'	Variegated germander
Teucrium fruticans	Tree germander
Thymus × citriodorus	Lemon thyme
Thymus herba-barona	Caraway thyme
Thymus nitidus	Tiny-leaf thyme
Thymus praecox arcticus	Mother-of-thyme or creeping thyme
Thymus praecox arcticus 'Albus'	White-flowering creeping thyme
Thymus praecox arcticus 'Coccineus'	Red-flowering creeping thyme
Thymus pseudolanuginosus	Woolly thyme
Thymus pulegioides	Oregano-scented thyme
Thymus vulgaris	Common thyme
Thymus vulgaris 'Argenteus'	Silver thyme
Thymus vulgaris 'Broad-leaf'	English thyme
Thymus vulgaris 'Narrow-leaf'	French thyme

Prefers Full Sun

Plants in this list will also perform well in light shade as long as they receive six hours of direct sunlight per day.

Agastache foeniculum
            Anise hyssop or giant blue hyssop
Agastache rugosa   Korean anise hyssop
Allium christophii   Stars-of-Persia
Allium neapolitanum   Flowering onion
Allium pulchellum   Flowering allium
Allium sativum   Garlic
Allium schoenoprasum   Chives
Allium senescens var. *glaucum*
                        Flowering allium
Allium tuberosum   Oriental chives
Aloysia triphylla   Lemon verbena
Althaea officinalis   Marsh mallow
Anethum graveolens   Dill
Anethum graveolens 'Dill Bouquet'
                        Dwarf dill
Artemisia abrotanum   Southernwood
Artemisia absinthium 'Lambrook Silver'
            'Lambrook Silver' artemisia
Artemisia annua Sweet annual wormwood
Artemisia dracunculus var. *sativa*
                        French tarragon
Artemisia ludoviciana var. *albula*
'Silver Queen and Silver King' artemisia
Artemisia pontica   Roman wormwood
Artemisia schmidtiana 'Nana'
                'Silver Mound' artemisia
Artemisia stellerana   Beach wormwood
Borago officinalis   Borage
Capsicum annuum Cayenne or chili pepper
Capsicum frutescens   Tabasco pepper
Carum carvi   Caraway

Chamaemelum nobile   Roman chamomile
Chamaemelum nobile 'Treanague'
                Flowerless chamomile
Chrysanthemum balsamita
                Costmary or alecost
Chrysanthemum coccineum Pyrethrum daisy
Chrysanthemum parthenium   Feverfew
Chrysanthemum parthenium 'Aureum'
            Golden-feather feverfew
Coriandrum sativum
    Coriander, cilantro, or Chinese parsley
Foeniculum vulgare   Fennel
Foeniculum vulgare var. *azoricum*
            Florence fennel or finocchio
Foeniculum vulgare var. *rubrum*
                Bronze fennel
Galium verum   Yellow bedstraw
Hyssopus officinalis   Hyssop
Hyssopus officinalis 'Alba'
            White-flowering hyssop
Hyssopus officinalis 'Rubra'
            Rose-flowering hyssop
Iris × *germanica* var. *florentina*
            Orris or Florentina iris
Lavandula angustifolia subsp. *angustifolia*
                English lavender
Lavandula angustifolia 'Alba'
            White-flowering lavender
Lavandula angustifolia 'Hidcote'
                'Hidcote' lavender
Lavandula angustifolia 'Munstead'
                'Munstead' lavender
Lavandula dentata   French lavender

Prefers Full Sun, continued

Lavandula × *intermedia* 'Dutch'
                                           'Dutch' lavender

Lavandula × *intermedia* 'Grosso'
                                           'Grosso' lavender

Lavandula multifida   Fern-leaf lavender

Lavandula stoechas   Spanish lavender

Marrubium vulgare   Horehound

Matricaria recutita   German chamomile

Myrtus communis   Sweet myrtle

Nepeta cataria 'Blue Wonder'
                                     'Blue Wonder' catnip

Nepeta cataria 'Citriodora'
                                 Lemon-scented catnip

Nepeta × *faassenii*   Catmint

Nepeta mussinii   Catmint

Ocimum basilicum   Sweet basil

Ocimum basilicum 'Citriodorum'
                                          Lemon basil

Ocimum basilicum 'Crispum'
                                     Lettuce-leaf basil

Ocimum basilicum 'Minimum'   Dwarf basil

Ocimum basilicum 'Purpurascens'
                          Purple-leaf or dark opal basil

Origanum aureum crispum
                         Golden puckered marjoram

Origanum compactum   Dwarf oregano

Origanum dictamnus   Dittany-of-Crete

Origanum majorana   Sweet marjoram

Origanum onites   Pot marjoram

Origanum pulchellum   Flowering marjoram

Origanum vulgare
               Common oregano or wild marjoram

Origanum vulgare 'Aureum'
                                    Golden oregano

Origanum vulgare subsp. *hirtum*
                                      Italian oregano

Pelargonium crispum and cultivars
                          Lemon-scented geranium

Pelargonium graveolens and cultivars
                          Rose-scented geranium

Pelargonium odoratissimum
                          Apple-scented geranium

Perilla frutescens 'Atropurpurea'
                                      Purple perilla

Perovskia atriplicifolia   Russian sage

Petroselinum crispum   Parsley

Petroselinum crispum 'Curly Parsley'
                                      Curly parsley

Petrosilinum crispum var. *neapolitanum*
                                      Italian parsley

Rosmarinus officinalis   Rosemary

Rosmarinus officinalis 'Albus'
                           White-flowering rosemary

Rosmarinus officinalis 'Arp' Hardy rosemary

Rosmarinus officinalis 'Benedin Blue'
                             'Benedin Blue' rosemary

Rosmarinus officinalis 'Collingwood
Ingram'   Graceful rosemary

Rosmarinus officinalis 'Lockwood de Forest'
                                   Prostrate rosemary

Rosmarinus officinalis 'Prostratus'
                                   Prostrate rosemary

Rosmarinus officinalis 'Tuscan Blue'
                                  Columnar rosemary

Ruta graveolens   Rue

Ruta graveolens 'Blue Beauty'
                                      'Blue Beauty' rue

Ruta graveolens 'Blue Mound'
                                       Compact rue

Ruta graveolens 'Jackman Blue'
                                       Compact rue

Ruta graveolens 'Variegata'   Variegated rue

Salvia elegans   Pineapple sage

Salvia officinalis   Garden sage

Salvia officinalis 'Albiflora'
                           White-flowering garden sage

Prefers Full Sun, continued

Salvia officinalis 'Icteriana' or 'Aurea'
Golden sage

Salvia officinalis 'Purpurascens' Purple sage

Salvia officinalis 'Tricolor'   Tricolor sage

Salvia sclarea   Clary sage

Santolina chamaecyparissus
Lavender cotton or gray santolina

Santolina chamaecyparissus 'Nana'
Dwarf lavender cotton

Santolina chamaecyparissus 'Plumosus'
Lacy lavender cotton

Santolina ericoides Compact green santolina

Santolina neapolitana   a variety of santolina

Santolina virens   Green santolina

Satureja hortensis   Summer savory

Satureja montana   Winter savory

Satureja montana pygmaea
Dwarf winter savory

Solidago canadensis   Canada goldenrod

Solidago odora   Fragrant goldenrod

Stachys byzantina   Lamb's-ears

Stachys byzantina 'Alba'
White-flowering lamb's-ears

Stachys byzantina 'Silver Carpet'
'Silver Carpet' lamb's-ears

Symphytum caucasicum Small blue comfrey

Symphytum officinale   Comfrey

Symphytum officinale 'Variegatum'
Variegated comfrey

Symphytum × *uplandicum*
Russian comfrey

Teucrium canadense
Wood sage or American germander

Teucrium chamaedrys   Germander

Teucrium chamaedrys 'Prostratum'
Prostrate germander

Teucrium chamaedrys 'Variegatum'
Variegated germander

Teucrium fruticans   Tree germander

Thymus × *citriodorus*   Lemon thyme

Thymus herba-barona   Caraway thyme

Thymus nitidus   Tiny-leaf thyme

Thymus praecox arcticus
Mother-of-thyme or creeping thyme

Thymus praecox arcticus 'Albus'
White-flowering creeping thyme

Thymus praecox arcticus 'Coccineus'
Red-flowering creeping thyme

Thymus pseudolanuginosus   Woolly thyme

Thymus pulegioides
Oregano-scented thyme

Thymus vulgaris   Common thyme

Thymus vulgaris 'Argenteus'   Silver thyme

Thymus vulgaris 'Broad-leaf'
English thyme

Thymus vulgaris 'Narrow-leaf'
French thyme

Accepts Full Sun

Angelica archangelica	Angelica	*Mentha suaveolens*	Apple mint
Calamintha nepeta	Calamint	*Mentha suaveolens* 'Variegata'	Pineapple mint
Colchicum autumnale	Autumn crocus	*Mentha spicata*	Spearmint
Crocus sativus	Saffron crocus	*Mentha spicata* 'Crispii' or 'Crispata'	Curly mint
Digitalis purpurea	Foxglove	*Monarda citriodora*	Lemon bergamot or lemon bee balm
Heliotropium arborescens	Heliotrope	*Monarda didyma* and cultivars	Bee balm
Hypericum perforatum	St. John's wort	*Nepeta cataria*	Catnip
Laurus nobilis	Sweet bay	*Pelargonium tomentosum*	Peppermint-scented geranium
Levisticum officinale	Lovage	*Poterium sanguisorba*	Burnet
Melissa officinalis	Lemon balm	*Stachys officinalis*	Betony
Melissa officinalis 'Variegata'	Golden lemon balm	*Tanacetum vulgare*	Tansy
Mentha × *gentilis* 'Variegata'	Ginger mint	*Tanacetum vulgare* var. *crispum*	Curly or fern-leaf tansy
Mentha × *piperita*	Peppermint	*Valeriana officinalis*	Valerian
Mentha × *piperita* var. *citrata*	Lemon or bergamot mint	*Viola odorata*	Sweet violet
Mentha pulegium	Pennyroyal		
Mentha requienii	Creme-de-menthe or Corsican mint		

TEMPERATURE

As you might expect, there are two temperature factors that the herb gardener must consider: extremes of heat and extremes of cold. The more moderate your climate, the more flexibility you'll have in your designs. Even extreme climates, however, can be tolerated by many herbs, as long as you plan carefully. And although climate determines your temperature conditions in general, remember that the amount and intensity of light reaching a planting site also affect the temperature. Even in cooler climates, a site that receives full afternoon sun or strong reflected light requires plants that can tolerate heat.

Many herbs, such as the artemisias, santolinas, and rosemaries, actually prefer hot, dry weather. These plants are excellent choices for hot sites facing south, southwest, or west. They can be especially useful where heat buildup from pavement and buildings creates problems for other plants.

Heat retention in soils adjacent to driveways, sidewalks, and streets also causes plants to dry out faster than those with more ground area around their roots. The same principle applies to raised beds, containers, and especially window boxes, which tend to dry out quickly from exposure. Using generously sized containers and beds can moderate the adverse effects of temperature extremes. Insulation on the inside of a raised container also helps minimize moisture loss.

Some herbs, such as lavenders, thymes, and savories, do not tolerate the combination of heat and high humidity and sometimes develop root and foliage fungus problems. There is, however, a wide selection of herbs that accept humid conditions, including oreganos, basils, and fennels. The mints are tolerant of humidity but prefer cooler temperatures.

Cold is a more serious problem in herb culture than heat, and in climates where temperatures drop below freezing, hardiness is an important design consideration. Although the hardiness range for many herbs is 20 degrees F to −10 degrees F, their hardiness behavior is notoriously variable.

Winter protection measures often enable borderline-hardy herbs to succeed in very cold regions. Maintenance should include these procedures: mulch the soil, use antidesiccant foliar sprays, withhold fertilizer late in the season, water thoroughly before the ground freezes, and avoid planting in stagnant cold pockets and windy areas. The traditional use of evergreen boughs as mulch material in herb gardens is effective.

Herbs planted in containers, raised beds, and window boxes are much more susceptible to winter injury and winterkill than the same plants growing in the natural insulation of the ground. Excessive freezing and thawing from exposure to temperature and winds can do a lot of harm. For permanent above-ground containers, choose herbs that are rated hardy to one or two zones colder than your own.

Some perennial herbs deemed tender in a particular climatic zone often behave as hardy perennials and live for years if they are provided with protection or grown in protected areas. Those perennials that are definitely tender, as well as hardy annuals, can be lifted from their containers or beds and overwintered indoors or in a greenhouse kept above 40 degrees F. This is a common practice in cold regions and is well worth the effort for the many shrubby herbs. Rosemary, sweet bay, and myrtle are attractive in containers and have traditionally been grown this way for ornament.

In warmer climates, the herb gardener has a tremendous range of plants to choose from, as most of the perennial herbs are hardy and remain evergreen. Many hardy annuals continue to grow year-round. Rosemary is a valuable landscape plant in these regions, used extensively as a ground cover or shrubby evergreen ornamental. Many of the beautiful sages, tender in colder areas, are evergreen in Texas and Florida.

WIND

Wind causes damage to plants by increasing water loss through transpiration. Since many perennial and subshrub herbs are borderline hardy in colder regions of the country, the influence of wind often becomes a critical factor in determining whether these plants survive the winter. Strong winds can cause plant tissue to dry up, and during winter months, the water lost through the foliage may not be adequately replaced by the roots' uptake of soil moisture. During the growing season, plants in windy spots may need twice as much watering as they would in a sheltered spot. Strong winds can also loosen and uproot plants, particularly newly planted trees and shrubs.

For obvious reasons, then, it is important to understand the way wind patterns may affect your planting site. Observe the site on windy days. Hilltops and wide-open plains are often scoured by unrelenting winds in both summer and winter months. In the city, gusts can accelerate to high velocities as they funnel through skyscraper corridors. Forceful eddies may swirl around tall buildings and into courtyards. Rooftop gardens, plazas of high buildings, courtyard gardens, and street corridors are particularly vulnerable to the adverse effects of winds.

A strategically placed wall, hardy hedge, or some other structure, such as an arbor covered with a hardy vine, will deflect winds from a planting site. Such a barrier serves as a windbreak, lifting the wind up and over the obstruction and carrying it away from the site. The taller the barrier, the more the wind is diverted. The protected area thus created at the base of the wall or hedge becomes an excellent location for herbs.

If creating a windbreak is not possible, you may have to take other measures to protect your plants. Many herbs exposed to wind may benefit from antidesiccant foliar sprays in areas where they are susceptible to winter injury or winterkill. Tall herbs, such as fennel and angelica, may require staking on windswept sites. For herbal shrubs and trees, pruning should help prevent wind damage.

SOILS

Herbs require high-quality, well-drained soils. The soil texture and structure should provide excellent drainage and an adequate organic content for moisture retention. Unfortunately, many urban and suburban soils are compacted, acidic, and high in soluble salts. These soils tend to be dry, depleted of nutrients, and full of building debris; the topsoil layer may be shallow or absent altogether. Any of these conditions can make plant cultivation difficult.

Another common problem is hardpan. If you think your shovel has hit a rock but it hasn't, then you may have struck hardpan. Hardpan is formed by the interaction of soluble salts or chemicals with the subsoil. This produces a very hard substance, often close to the surface, that is impermeable to roots. Hardpan also causes excessive heaving in winter. It should be removed completely and replaced with a good-quality soil.

Soil analysis can help you determine whether your existing soil needs to be amended. Local county extension offices have soil test kits and instructions for their use. These tests are well worth the inexpensive fee. Before planting, test existing soil, new mix, or amended media for the major nutrients (nitrogen, phosphorus, and potassium) and for soluble salt levels. For sites where you suspect soil compaction or contamination, specify a full range of tests, including micronutrient levels and heavy metal content, as well as the standard tests for major nutrients and pH. Special tests are available that evaluate soil texture and structure by determining percentages of silt, sand, and loam.

You may need to replace your soil with fresh topsoil. Quality topsoil is often expensive and hard to find, but it is invaluable to gardening success. A good topsoil is usually sandy loam, loam, or silty loam. It should be friable (easily crumbled) with at least 4 percent organic matter and a maximum pH range of 5.0 to 7.5. The topsoil should be free of debris, hardpan material, and noxious weed seeds.

The pH can be adjusted by following the liming recommendations supplied by the soil test report. A convenient measure for increasing the pH is to add five pounds of finely ground limestone to each 100 square feet of planting surface. This will raise the pH by .5 to 1. To lower the pH by an equal amount, add one-half pound of ground sulfur or three pounds of iron sulfate (or its equivalent) to 100 square feet of surface. (Ground sulfur is slower to react but lasts longer in the soil.)

Compacted soils must be amended to improve drainage for herb culture. Mixing large particles with the soil increases permeability. Coarse builder's sand is a commonly used material, but it tends to compact, especially in clay soils, thus losing its effectiveness over time. Chicken grit is the preferred drainage material for herbs because it provides excellent drainage and because it does not compact in the soil.

Clay soils tend to be heavy, sticky, and compacted. Working with them is difficult and unpleasant. In clay soils, drainage materials should always be mixed with organic material to be effective. Gypsum also helps improve clay soils.

Sandy soils are usually too acidic for many herbs and may need to be limed. They will benefit from the addition of organic material to improve moisture- and nutrient-holding capacity. Chalky soils usually drain well, but they also need more organic matter.

SOIL FERTILITY

Herbs have the reputation for growing in poor, infertile soils, and indeed, many can tolerate this condition. But to promote healthy, attractive foliage and flower production, moderate supplementary fertilization is necessary, especially when herbs are grown for their ornamental value. Excessive fertilization, however, can cause leggy, rank growth, thus requiring extra pruning to keep plants attractive. Some references maintain that excessive fertilization also diminishes the aroma of some herbs; however, moderate fertilization promotes general health, and a healthy aromatic plant is fragrant.

Since urban soils typically are low in nutrients, adding humus to the soil is beneficial. Herbs grown in beds benefit from two to three applications of granular fertilizer each year. Use a complete fertilizer that has a high phosphorus content, such as 15-30-15. Because herbs grown in containers, raised beds, or window boxes cannot replenish nutrients naturally, they should be fed regularly with a complete liquid fertilizer. Slow-release fertilizers can be worked into the soil medium when larger plants are installed. These slow-release pellets, however, may cause injury to small transplants, especially if applied improperly.

MOISTURE

Ensuring the proper amount of water is critical to your herb garden's success. Too much and too little water are equally detrimental to plants. Pay careful attention to the features that will affect the moisture your site receives. Buildings, overhangs, and densely canopied trees can significantly reduce the amount of rainfall reaching a plant below. Assess the drainage patterns around your site, since they may send excessive drainage water into it, especially if paving is sloped into the planted areas. And remember that upslope sites will lose water to runoff.

In sites that receive little natural water, plant herbs that are drought tolerant. Work the soil deeply so that roots can obtain moisture during dry periods; the deeper and more generous the root space, the greater the moisture availability. Mulching also helps keep moisture in the soil. Trickle irrigation methods are outstanding for dry areas because they conserve up to 80 percent of the water lost to evaporation. A simple soaker hose is an inexpensive and effective way to water herbs.

Irrigation systems are increasing in popularity for use in both residential and public gardens. Flood bubblers and pop-up heads are useful irrigation devices. The bubblers require a fairly high water pressure to run a large number of heads, but they are especially useful with herbs that are more susceptible to foliar fungus when their leaves are wet. The pop-up heads can be adjusted to various heights and distribute water over smaller plants or spray water under larger plants. Inevitably, some areas of a densely planted bed will be missed and require spot watering.

In predominantly paved areas, water runoff from natural rainfall is much more rapid than in open ground. Water penetration into a planting bed or pit in paved areas is often insufficient to maintain plant growth. In addition, the heat retention from the concrete can build up and bake the soil. Furthermore, a planting pit in a paved area can be thought of as a container, since its root space is typically small and confined. The plant cannot replenish itself in the same way as a plant growing in natural conditions because the roots don't have as much area to grow in search of moisture.

Plants show a marked improvement in size, health, and performance when they are planted in large openings in the pavement with ample common root space, in contrast to single plants grown in single planting pits. The surface ground area can catch more natural rainfall, and roots can develop more fully to better anchor a plant and find water and nutrient replenishment. Trees in urban areas are more often being planted this way, but the same principle applies to herb plantings in residential terraces, for example.

In all cases, good drainage is an essential requirement of herbs, whether they are growing in open ground, near paved areas, or in containers. Wet, poorly drained soils aggravate winterkill for the perennial herbs that are borderline hardy and result in poor growth for most, if not all, herbs. Without proper drainage, the root area can fill up with water, which replaces the soil air spaces and suffocates the plants. You need to amend poorly drained soils if they exist in your planting area.

Many traditional garden designs made use of raised beds. The higher soil level allowed for better drainage and prevented the roots from becoming damaged by the wet, cold climate of northern Europe, for example. Today, growing herbs in raised beds serves practical and design purposes. If your soils are poorly drained or compacted, a raised bed allows you to import a better soil medium. An elevated bed also enables people to get close enough to enjoy the fragrance of the plants. You might even design the wall of a raised bed wide enough to function as a seat, so that you can be comfortable as you prune, plant, and harvest.

Note that overwatering usually occurs from watering too frequently rather than applying too much water at one time (unless the soil does not drain properly, of course). Thorough, deep watering helps the plant develop deep roots. If only small amounts of water are given, then only the top inch or two of the soil will become moistened and the roots remain close to the moist surface. Furthermore, soluble salts (especially from fertilizers) build up in the soil of container-grown plants and need to be flushed out periodically. Thorough watering will help leach out these potentially damaging salts. To prevent overwatering of container plants, empty the excess water in the saucers promptly.

As a rule, a majority of herbs prefer soils that are allowed to approach dryness between waterings; many are drought tolerant. Refer to the Plant Profiles.

Moisture Descriptions

Drier. These plants can withstand drier soil and less frequent watering. Drought tolerance is achieved and enhanced by working the soil to allow roots to penetrate deep for water.

Moderately moist. These plants prefer soil that approaches dryness between thorough, deep watering.

Moist. These plants prefer soil that is pleasantly moist, but never excessively wet.

Prefers or Requires Drier Soil

Allium christophii   Star-of-Persia

Allium tuberosum   Oriental chives

★*Artemisia abrotanum*   Southernwood

Artemisia absinthium 'Lambrook Silver'
          'Lambrook Silver' artemisia

Artemisia annual
               Sweet annual wormwood

Artemisia dracunculus var. *sativa*
                    French tarragon

★*Artemisia ludoviciana* var. *albula*
          'Silver Queen' and 'Silver King'

Artemisia pontica   Roman wormwood

★*Artemisia schmidtiana* 'Nana'
               Silver mound artemisia

★*Artemisia stellerana*   Beach wormwood

Borago officinalis   Borage

★*Chamaemelum nobile*   Roman chamomile

★*Chamaemelum nobile* 'Treanague'
               Flowerless chamomile

Chrysanthemum balsamita
               Costmary or alecost

Chrysanthemum coccineum
               Pyrethrum daisy

★*Chrysanthemum parthenium*   Feverfew

★*Chrysanthemum parthenium* 'Aureum'
          Golden feather feverfew

Hyssopus officinalis   Hyssop

Hyssopus officinalis 'Alba'
               White-flowering hyssop

Hyssopus officinalis 'Rubra'
               Rose-flowering hyssop

★*Iris* × *germanica* var. *florentina*
               Orris or Florentina iris

Lavandula angustifolia subsp. *angustifolia*
               English lavender

Lavandula angustifolia 'Alba'
               White-flowering lavender

Lavandula angustifolia 'Hidcote'
               'Hidcote' lavender

Lavandula angustifolia 'Munstead'
               'Munstead' lavender

Lavandula angustifolia 'Rosea'
               Pink-flowering lavender

Lavandula dentata   French lavender

Lavandula × *intermedia* 'Dutch'
               'Dutch' lavender

Lavandula × *intermedia* 'Grosso'
               'Grosso' lavender

Lavandula multifida   Fern-leaf lavender

Lavandula stoechas   Spanish lavender

Marrubium vulgare   Horehound

Matricaria recutita   German chamomile

Melissa officinalis   Lemon balm

★*Origanum aureum crispum*
               Golden puckered marjoram

Origanum compactum   Dwarf oregano

★*Origanum majorana*   Sweet marjoram

★*Origanum onites*   Pot marjoram

Origanum pulchellum
               Flowering marjoram

★*Origanum vulgare*
          Common oregano or wild marjoram

★*Origanum vulgare* 'Aureum'
               Golden oregano

★*Origanum vulgare* subsp. *hirtum*
               Italian oregano

Pelargonium crispum and cultivars
               Lemon-scented geranium

Pelargonium graveolens and cultivars
               Rose-scented geranium

★Drought tolerant

Prefers or Requires Drier Soil, **continued**

Pelargonium odoratissimum
Apple-scented geranium

Pelargonium tomentosum
Peppermint-scented geranium

Perovskia atriplicifolia   Russian sage

Poterium sanguisorba   Burnet

Rosmarinus officinalis   Rosemary

Rosmarinus officinalis 'Albus'
White-flowering rosemary

Rosmarinus officinalis 'Arp'
Hardy rosemary

Rosmarinus officinalis 'Benedin Blue'
'Benedin Blue' rosemary

Rosmarinus officinalis
'Collingwood Ingram'
Graceful rosemary

Rosmarinus officinalis 'Lockwood de Forest'
Prostrate rosemary

Rosmarinus officinalis 'Prostratus'
Prostrate rosemary

Rosmarinus officinalis 'Tuscan Blue'
Columnar rosemary

★*Ruta graveolens*   Rue

★*Ruta graveolens* 'Blue Beauty'
'Blue Beauty' rue

★*Ruta graveolens* 'Blue Mound'
Compact rue

★*Ruta graveolens* 'Jackman Blue'
Compact rue

★*Salvia azurea*   Azure sage

★*Salvia farinacea* 'Victoria'
Annual blue salvia

★*Salvia greggii*   Autumn sage

★*Salvia leucantha*   Mexican bush plant

★*Salvia officinalis*   Garden sage

★*Salvia officinalis* 'Albiflora'
White-flowering garden sage

★*Salvia officinalis* 'Icterina' or 'Aurea'
Golden sage

★*Salvia officinalis* 'Purpurascens'
Purple sage

★*Salvia sclarea*   Clary sage

★*Santolina chamaecyparissus*
Lavender cotton or gray santolina

★*Santolina chamaecyparissus* 'Nana'
Dwarf lavender cotton

★*Santolina chamaecyparissus* 'Plumosus'
Lacy lavender cotton

★*Santolina ericoides*
Dwarf green santolina

★*Santolina neapolitana*
a variety of santolina

★*Santolina virens*   Green santolina

★*Satureja hortensis*   Summer savory

★*Satureja montana*   Winter savory

★*Thymus* × *citriodorus*   Lemon thyme

★*Thymus herba-barona*   Caraway thyme

★*Thymus nitidus*   Tiny-leaf thyme

★*Thymus praecox arcticus*
Mother-of-thyme or creeping thyme

★*Thymus praecox arcticus* 'Albus'
White-flowering creeping thyme

★*Thymus praecox arcticus* 'Coccineus'
Red-flowering creeping thyme

★*Thymus pseudolanuginosus*   Woolly thyme

★*Thymus pulegioides*
Oregano-scented thyme

★*Thymus vulgaris*   Common thyme

★*Thymus vulgaris* 'Argenteus'
Silver thyme

★*Thymus vulgaris* 'Broad-leaf'
English thyme

★*Thymus vulgaris* 'Narrow-leaf'
French thyme

★Drought tolerant

Prefers or Requires Moderately Moist Soil

Agastache foeniculum
Anise hyssop or giant blue hyssop

Agastache rugosa   Korean anise hyssop

Alchemilla alpina   Alpine lady's mantle

Alchemilla mollis   Lady's mantle

Allium neapolitanum
Flowering onion or daffodil garlic

Allium pulchellum   Flowering allium

Allium sativum   Garlic

Allium schoenoprasum   Chives

Allium senescens var. *glaucum*
Flowering allium

Anethum graveolens   Dill

Anethum graveolens 'Dill Bouquet'
Dwarf dill

Borago officinalis   Borage

Foeniculum vulgare   Fennel

Foeniculum vulgare var. *azoricum*
Florence fennel or finocchio

Foeniculum vulgare var. *rubrum*
Bronze fennel

Stachys byzantina   Lamb's-ears

Stachys byzantina 'Alba'
White-flowering lamb's-ears

Stachys byzantina 'Silver Carpet'
'Silver Carpet' lamb's-ears

Stachys officinalis   Betony

Tanacetum vulgare   Tansy

Tanacetum vulgare var. *crispum*
Curly or fern-leaf tansy

Teucrium chamaedrys   Germander

Teucrium chamaedrys 'Prostratum'
Prostrate germander

Teucrium chamaedrys 'Variegatum'
Variegated germander

Prefers or Requires Moist Soil

Angelica archangelica	Angelica
Anthriscus cerefolium	Sweet chervil
Calamintha nepeta	Calamint
Galium odoratum	Sweet woodruff
Glycyrrhiza glabra	Licorice
Laurus nobilis	Sweet bay
Levisticum officinale	Lovage
Melissa officinalis	Lemon balm
Melissa officinalis 'Variegata'	Golden lemon balm
Mentha × *piperita*	Peppermint
Mentha piperita var. *citrata*	Lemon mint
Mentha pulegium	Pennyroyal
Mentha requienii	Creme-de-menthe or Corsican mint
Mentha spicata	Spearmint
Mentha spicata 'Crispii' or 'Crispata'	Curly mint
Mentha suaveolens	Apple mint
Mentha suaveolens 'Variegata'	Pineapple mint
Monarda didyma	Bee balm
Monarda didyma 'Alba'	White-flowering bee balm
Monarda didyma 'Croftway Pink'	Pink-flowering bee balm
Monarda didyma 'Violacea'	Violet-flowering bee balm
Myrrhis odorata	Sweet cicely
Nepeta cataria	Catnip
Nepeta cataria 'Blue Wonder'	'Blue Wonder' catnip
Nepeta cataria 'Citriodora'	Lemon-scented catnip
Nepeta × *faassenii*	Catmint
Nepeta mussinii	Catmint

Ocimum basilicum	Sweet basil
Ocimum basilicum 'Citriodorum'	Lemon basil
Ocimum basilicum 'Crispum'	Lettuce-leaf basil
Ocimum basilicum 'Minimum'	Dwarf basil
Ocimum basilicum 'Purpurascens'	Purple or 'Dark Opal' basil
Petroselinum crispum	Parsley
Petroselinum crispum 'Curly Parsley'	Curly parsley
Petroselinum crispum var. *neapolitanum*	Italian parsley
Symphytum caucasicum	Small blue comfrey
Symphytum officinale	Comfrey
Symphytum officinale 'Rubrum'	Rose-flowering comfrey
Symphytum officinale 'Variegata'	Variegated comfrey
Symphytum × *uplandicum*	Russian comfrey
Tanacetum crispum	Curly tansy
Tanacetum vulgare	Tansy
Valeriana officinalis	Valerian

PLANTING

The correct planting procedure for herbaceous and shrubby herbs is important. Nursery plants should be hardened off for a couple of weeks before installation. This treatment acclimates the plants, especially those that are greenhouse-grown, to the outdoor environment. Gradually increase direct sunlight and reduce moisture and fertilizer. All plants should be leached and watered before transporting and transplanting.

The planting pit should be at least two times as wide and deep as the plant's container or root ball. Amend the soil in the immediate planting area as required. Use drainage material such as chicken grit, organic material such as weed- and disease-free manure or compost, and good-quality topsoil. For herb culture, these amendments are superior to the peat moss and sand combination commonly used. Thoroughly mix the amendments with the existing soil. This creates an amiable soil environment that allows the plant to adjust to the shock of transplanting and encourages the roots to extend into the existing soil after the plant becomes established.

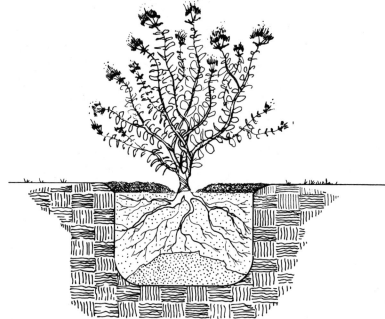

The correct planting process makes a big difference in the health and growth of the plant. By mounding up lightly compacted soil at the bottom of a planting pit, you will prevent the newly planted herb from sinking too deeply into the soil; such settling often leads to stem rot.

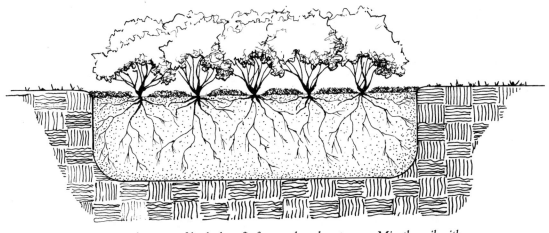

Group plantings of herbs benefit from a shared root space. Mix the soil with amendments to improve drainage or increase its water- and nutrient-holding capacity. Prevent crown or stem rot by not allowing the mulch to touch the plant base.

Plant herbs in the ground at the same level they were in their growing containers. The outer roots of container-grown plants, particularly those that are potbound, should be gently loosened before planting. Pull mulch away from the stem or base of the plant to prevent rotting.

Water the plant thoroughly immediately after transplanting. If settling occurs, gently reposition and firm the plant in the soil. A mound of tamped earth at the bottom of the planting pit will minimize settlement.

Plant Profiles

*T*he plant profiles are alphabetized by Latin name, followed by common name. The nomenclature for plants listed is according to *Hortus Third: A Concise Dictionary of Plants Cultivated in the United States and Canada*, revised edition, 1976.

Remember that there are discrepancies in the naming of herb plants in the nursery industry. A certain variety may go by different names in each of a dozen catalogues. The problem is well recognized, and the industry is making an effort to improve the accuracy and consistency of plant nomenclature. It is wise to use the botanical name and the common name of an herb when ordering from a nursery, especially if you want a specific plant or variety.

Family

The Latin family name is given for each plant.

Varieties

The plant profiles include ornamentally significant varieties, related species, and cultivars. Selections are also based on their fragrance and potential for use in herb garden designs.

Species is the basic unit in botanical classification. Species are combined into genera (genus), and variations or subordinate forms of them may be distinguished as subspecies, variety (varietas), and form (forma) in descending order of botanical hierarchy. Genus is written with a capitalized first letter, and species is always lowercase. A variety is the category below species. As defined in *Hortus Third*, a cultivar is a horticultural variety or race that has originated and persisted under cultivation, not necessarily as a botanical species, and is of sufficient botanical or horticultural importance as to require a name. The term *cultivar* is derived from *culti*vated *vari*ety. In this book, cultivars are denoted by single quotation marks, for example, *Lavandula angustifolia* 'Alba'.

Type

Herbs are identified as subshrub or herbaceous, as well as annual, biennial, or perennial.

An *annual* is a plant that normally completes its life cycle within one year—from germination to seedling to maturity to death. Horticulturally, the term denotes a plant that blooms the first year from seed and is treated like an annual, whether or not it completes its cycle by dying. Some herbs reseed naturally from year to year, especially if grown in a protected area. Other herbs may be perennials in the tropics but in colder regions are treated as annuals and started each year from seed. *Biennials* live two years from seed, blooming only or mostly the second year. If seed is planted in a greenhouse during early winter, however, some biennials may bloom the first year.

A *perennial* plant lives three or more years. Although many perennial herbs and flowers live a long time, others may reach their peak the third year and then gradually decline. The majority of herb plants are perennials, either herbaceous or subshrub plants.

An *herbaceous* plant is one that is not woody, at least above the ground. Many herbs are herbaceous perennials: they are leafy, not woody, and they endure for years. Typically in cold regions, many die back to the ground in winter, then put out new growth in spring. Herbs termed *subshrub* show some woody growth on the more mature, older stems. Subshrub and shrubby herbs are typically small.

Origin

By understanding the native habitat of a plant, the gardener is able to recreate the conditions for best growth. Information on where a plant has naturalized in this country is also provided.

Use

The herbal use of each plant is listed. (Many books listed in the bibliography also contain information on herbal uses.) Designers of public gardens may want to offer information about a plant's herbal use in educational or thematic herb gardens. The information engraved on a label in a thematic garden often includes the botanical name and common name with a word or phrase explaining the plant's herbal use.

Texture

The overall texture of a plant—fernlike, for example, or feathery—depends primarily on leaf size. Texture is more subtly influenced by the spacing, arrangement, and density of the leaves. The descriptions of plant texture refer to the foliage. The flower texture is described if it is different from the foliage texture and if it is a prominent feature.

Form

A description of the form of each plant is given. The illustrations are drawn to scale (1½ inches = 1 foot).

Fragrance

The type and intensity of a plant's fragrance may make it appropriate to use in potpourri, infusions, and fresh bouquets. In the garden, the fragrant atmosphere from the aromatic plants adds a unique and lovely dimension. When the foliage is touched, the essential oils in the leaves are released, producing an even stronger aroma. In many herbs the stems, flowers, seeds, and roots are also aromatic.

Foliage

An herb's foliage color is one of its prized ornamental features and should be used to full advantage in the planting design.

Flower

The dates shown represent the approximate starting period and duration of flowering. These dates vary slightly from year to year depending on such factors as the amount of rainfall, the number of sunny days, and other climatic variations. The dates given apply to the mid–Atlantic region, but can be adapted to other regions of the country. Add two to six weeks to the dates shown if you live north of Washington, D.C., and figure starting dates two to six weeks earlier if you live in southern areas. In southern Florida, the Southwest, and southern California, blooming periods are usually much longer than specified and repeated blooming periods are common.

Height, width, and spacing

Minimum and maximum height and width ranges for each plant are listed. These dimensions can vary from a few inches for a small plant to a foot or more for a large plant. These variations are influenced also by such climatic factors as sunlight, temperature, and wind, as well as by differences in soil texture, soil fertility, and soil moisture, which determine the size of a plant.

In designing an herb garden, the exact spacing distances will depend on how soon you want a mature effect and on your budget. It is usually advisable to space trees and shrubs according to their mature span, but perennial herbs may be spaced more closely together if you want to achieve interest the first year and a mature effect the second or third year. The annual herbs and those tender perennials grown as annuals should be spaced close enough to provide a mature planting the first growing season. Choose the smallest spacing distance given for these. Where otherwise tender perennials are hardy and evergreen and grow larger over the years—the Southwest, California, and Texas, for example—use the maximum spacing distance.

Both the spacing distance and the starting size of a plant determine the time a mature effect is achieved.

Starting size

Recommendations for container-grown starting sizes are given. In general, good-sized plants mature more quickly and will create a uniform, handsome effect.

Where a garden will be constantly before the public eye, the usual backyard propagation and planting techniques may be inappropriate. Starting some plants from seed and buying others in various-sized containers, for example, can give a spotty, less-than-professional appearance. In home gardens, however, using a variety of growing and propagation methods is part of the fun. In general, herbs grow fast. Herbaceous annuals, such as dill or basil, typically grow quickly and easily from seed. Many of the shrubby perennial herbs, such as lavender, rosemary, and santolina, grow relatively slowly from stem cuttings, and seed germination is often slow. These subshrubs should be purchased in at least a 4-inch container if you desire a full, showy effect the first year.

Availability

The availability ratings for herbs are based on the frequency with which they appear in the herb nursery catalogues from the list in the back of this book. The profiles rate the commercial availability for each herb as common, moderately common, or specialty.

Although the average local nursery is increasing its inventory of herbs in spring selections, it still falls short of offering the varieties and sizes that can be obtained from the specialty herb nurseries. The larger field-grown herbs are usually available from only a few nurseries.

Plan your herb planting design far in advance of the planting date so that you can obtain the plants you want. To help your local nursery find the herbs that it may not routinely carry, provide the buyer with an herb nursery source list, such as the one in the back of this book. You may need to order herbs from several sources to complete your design. Place your spring orders to herb nurseries in the fall, since selections may be limited if you order too late.

Zone

Hardiness zone maps show the average annual minimum temperature for the horticulturally important areas of the country. Plants are listed according to the coldest zone in which they normally grow. They can, however, be expected to grow in warmer areas. (For example, if Zone 5 is listed, the plant can be presumed to thrive in Zone 6 as well.) When known, the range of zones is listed. It indicates not only the coldest areas in which a plant will grow, but also the warmest zone limit it can survive. The ranges for every plant have not yet been determined by botanists.

Bear in mind that these zones are approximations and should be read as guides rather than exact cutoffs. Since the demarcation lines are at best an abstract graphic device, it is wise to investigate the climatic variables in your locality. Specific

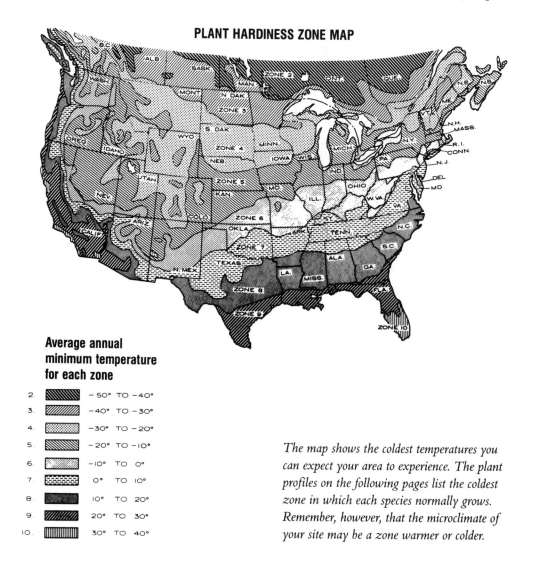

PLANT HARDINESS ZONE MAP

Average annual minimum temperature for each zone

2.		−50° TO −40°
3.		−40° TO −30°
4.		−30° TO −20°
5.		−20° TO −10°
6.		−10° TO 0°
7.		0° TO 10°
8.		10° TO 20°
9.		20° TO 30°
10.		30° TO 40°

The map shows the coldest temperatures you can expect your area to experience. The plant profiles on the following pages list the coldest zone in which each species normally grows. Remember, however, that the microclimate of your site may be a zone warmer or colder.

information can be obtained from county agricultural extension offices, nurseries, county and state climate records, and garden club publications.

Take precautions and provide winter protection for those herbs in the border-line hardiness zones, especially if your region has had more than a few uncharacteristically cold, harsh winters in the past decade.

Soil and moisture

The requirements for soil drainage, fertility, pH, and moisture are listed for each plant. Also refer to the discussion on soils and moisture under Herb Culture. Cultivate the plants according to their needs:

Moist. Allow soil to remain pleasantly moist, but never wet.

Moderately moist. Allow soil to approach dryness between thorough, deep waterings.

Drier. Allow soil to become a little drier than above between thorough, deep waterings.

Light and temperature

Information on the light and temperature preferences for each plant is provided. Also refer to the discussions of light and temperature in Herb Culture.

Planting and maintenance

For some herbs you should follow special planting procedures. Others may be susceptible to certain common pests and diseases, for which preventive and control measures are suggested. Information on fertilization, pruning, watering, soil preparation, and propagation methods is provided to maximize your gardening success and pleasure. Herbs in general are not high-maintenance plants, but they do require your attention.

Ornamental value

The ornamental characteristics and virtues of each plant are highlighted, followed by suggestions for appropriate use in planting design.

Agastache foeniculum
Anise hyssop or giant blue hyssop

(Actually not an anise or hyssop)
Family: Labiatae.
Varieties:

Agastache rugosa, Korean anise-hyssop
Aromatic medicinal, very similar to
Agastache foeniculum.

Type: Perennial.
Origin: Eastern Asia and dry areas of
north central United States.
Use: Beverage, culinary, dried flower,
good nectar plant for honeybees.
Texture: Medium; round, rough-
textured leaves.
Form: Upright.
Fragrance: Anise-scented leaves and
flowers.
Foliage: Dark green.
Flower: Lavender; June to August,
into autumn.
Height: 2½ to 4 feet.
Width: 2 to 3 feet.
Spacing: 2 to 4 feet.

Starting size: 4-inch to 2-gallon
containers.
Availability: Specialty.
Zone: 4 to 8.

Soil and moisture: Prefers fertile, well-drained soil. Tolerates wide range of pH,
optimum is 7. Prefers moderate moisture and can withstand dry soil.
Light and temperature: Prefers full sun and partial shade; accepts partial sun.
May become leggy and weak-stemmed in too much shade. Prefers moderate
temperatures; accepts heat well.
Planting and maintenance: A fast, vigorous grower. Easy to grow. Requires
pruning to maintain neat form. May need staking in windy areas. Doesn't spread
by runners, as do other members of the mint family. Self-sows readily. Propagation is by seed, cuttings, or root division in spring or fall.
Ornamental value: A tall, robust, attractive plant. Plants begin branching at
about one foot high. Great back-of-the-border plant. Especially valued for its

long-lasting, bluish lavender flowers. Blooms in mid-to-late summer when few other garden plants are flowering. Flowers form in abundance on spikes at branch terminals and attract bees. Flowers stand out when planted in front of a dark evergreen background.

Alchemilla mollis
Lady's mantle

Family: Rosaceae.
Varieties:
Alchemilla alpina, alpine lady's mantle
  Delicate foliage, yellow flowers,
  grows to 8 inches.
Type: Perennial.
Origin: Mountain areas of North America and Eurasia.
Use: Cut flower, medicinal, dye plant.
Texture: Medium coarse. Deeply lobed, large, rounded leaves. Flowers are lacy and frothy.
Form: Sprawling. Low, loose mound.
Fragrance: None.
Foliage: Gray-green.
Flower: Chartreuse; June through July.

Height: 12 to 20 inches.
Width: 15 to 24 inches.
Spacing: 1 to 2 feet.
Starting size: 4-inch to 1-gallon containers.
Availability: Common.
Zone: 3 to 8.

Soil and moisture: Lady's mantle requires good drainage. Prefers loose, loamy soil with high amount of organic material. Prefers moist to moderately moist soil and moderate fertility. Tolerates a wide pH range and lower fertility. Intolerant of very dry soil.
Light and temperature: Prefers partial shade or shade and cool temperatures.

Alchemilla mollis, continued

Accepts dense shade. Performs best when planted in a location that receives afternoon shade. Extra moisture needed when planted in higher light locations.

Planting and maintenance: Easy to grow. Fast spreader and low maintenance once established. Older plants may need to be divided every several years to renew. Tightly spaced plants may flower less profusely and produce tired-looking foliage. Cut off spent flowers before they have a chance to reseed, also to maintain a tidy appearance. Propagate by division or seed. Essentially no pest or disease problems, although may get spider mites in dry, hot weather.

Ornamental value: Lady's mantle is a handsome plant with large, fan-shaped leaves. The chartreuse flowers create a lacy, foamy, frothy effect. Flowers form well above the foliage. Great ground cover, especially useful in the hard combination of dry shade, although it prefers partial shade and a moderately moist soil. Use where the plant can spill over a raised edge or wall. Nice in containers or baskets. Leaves hold moisture and glisten in sunlight. Interesting plant for woodland edge or ground cover plantings in parks and larger residential properties, especially when designing with a native herbal theme.

Allium schoenoprasum
Chives

Family: Amaryllidaceae.

Varieties:

Allium christophii, stars-of-Persia
  Pink-lilac, starlike flowers have an 8- to 12-inch diameter; grows to 2½ feet.

A. flavum, A. moly
  Yellow flowers.

A. neapolitanum, flowering onion, daffodil garlic
  Ornamental white flowers, Zone 7.

Cultivars include 'Roseum' (pink flowers), 'Grandiflorum' (white flowers, 18 inches).

A. pulchellum, flowering allium
Grows 1 to 2 feet, showy lavender flowers, blue-green leaves.

A. sativum, garlic
White flowers.

A. senescens var. *glaucum*
Blue-green leaves, rose-pink flowers, sickle-shaped new growth.

A. tuberosum, Oriental chives
White starlike flowers in autumn, broad straplike foliage. 12-inch plant, 2-inch flowers.

Type: Perennial.

Origin: N. Hemisphere; Eurasia.

Use: Culinary, medicinal, natural insect deterrent.

Texture: Fine. Linear, grasslike tapered leaves.

Form: Upright, grasslike clump.

Fragrance: Pungent, oniony leaves.

Foliage: Blue-green.

Flower: Lavender-pink (varieties: white, yellow, pink); June (some varieties: August and September).

Height: 12 to 15 inches.

Width: 12 to 15 inches.

Spacing: 1 to 2 feet.

Starting size: 1-gallon pot.

Availability: Very common; varieties: specialty.

Zone: 3.

Soil and moisture: Prefers moderately rich, moist soil. Requires good drainage. pH range 6 to 7. Accepts less than ideal soil conditions, but leaves turn brown and become limp in very dry areas.

Light and temperature: Most *Allium* varieties prefer full sun. Accepts partial shade but may not flower as profusely. Tolerates heat.

Planting and maintenance: Start with at least a full 1-gallon container, since *Allium* varieties are slow growing when young. Small plants will get lost in the garden. The seeds of *A. tuberosum* self-sow readily and can become a persistent weed problem; to avoid this, remove the spent flowers of Oriental chives before the plant sets seed. Other alliums tend not to have this problem. Propagate by division in the spring. Renew plants by division every three to four years.

Ornamental value: Chives' distinctive blue-green, grasslike foliage and round, lavender-pink flowers make it a useful ornament. The flowering *Allium* family contains many unusual and ornamental species. Once established, alliums are very durable plants, requiring little maintenance. Compact clumps and graceful flowers make chives a useful edging or low border plant. The dried seed heads of most alliums are interesting ornamental features. Combines well with most herbs and is especially lovely with silver- and purple-leafed herbs. Performs well in containers and raised beds. Works well in small spaces.

Anethum graveolens
Dill

Family: Umbelliferae.
Varieties:
Anethum graveolens 'Dill Bouquet',
dwarf dill
  2 feet high, compact.
Type: Tender annual.
Origin: Southwest Asia and south-east Europe; naturalized in some areas of North America.
Use: Culinary, cut flower, medicinal.
Texture: Very fine, feathery.
Form: Upright; tall and airy.
Fragrance: Highly aromatic dill-scented leaves, seeds, and flowers.
Foliage: Light green with blue-green stems.
Flower: Yellow; depends on when seed is sown.
Height: 3 feet.
Width: 2 feet.
Spacing: 2 to 3 feet.
Starting size: 1-gallon pot or seed.
Availability: Common.
Soil and moisture: Dill prefers moderately moist and moderately fertile soil. Requires good drainage. Will accept less than ideal conditions. pH range is 5 to 7.
Light and temperature: Prefers full sun, accepts partial shade. Stands up well to heat.
Planting and maintenance: Easy to grow from seed; start seeds when ground is cool in early spring. Use extreme care when transplanting. Dill is a short-lived annual. To keep flowers blooming all summer, make successive plantings every three to four weeks. Plants deteriorate after flowering, especially if the flowers are left on the plant to go to seed. Plants may need to be staked if grown without enough sunlight. Self-seeds readily. Virtually pest and disease free.

Ornamental value: Dill's airy form and soft, feathery texture make it a lovely contrast or accent plant in the herb garden. The light green foliage is set off by pronounced bluish green stems. When in bloom, the large yellow umbels are gracefully ornamental. Sunlight through the lacy flowers and airy foliage creates interesting patterns in the garden. Good mid-to-back-border plant for formal or informal gardens. The sturdy, compact dwarf variety is splendid for roomy raised beds and containers. But remember, dill is short-lived.

Artemisia species
Artemisia

Family: Compositae.
Varieties:

Artemisia abrotanum, southernwood
Aromatic shrub, robust, fast growing; gray-green, finely-cut leaves. Grows 2 feet, up to 4 feet tall, 2 feet wide.

A. absinthium, wormwood
Finely cut silver-gray leaves, pale green when older, grows 1 to 3 feet.

A. absinthium 'Lambrook Silver', wormwood variety
Compact, glistening silver foliage.

A. annua, sweet annual wormwood
Sweet aromatic leaves, small yellow flowers; tall plant, grows 1 to 5 feet.

A. dracunculus var. *sativa*, French tarragon

Artemisia abrotanum
Southernwood

Famous anise flavor. Long, slender, medium green leaves. Tiny white flowers. Must be propagated asexually, since seeds never set. Grows to 2 feet.

A. ludoviciana var. *albula*, 'Silver Queen' and 'Silver King' artemisia
Both have dissected shimmering silver leaves and grow 2 to 3 feet.

Artemisia species, continued

A. pontica, Roman wormwood
Fine gray-green aromatic foliage,
10 inches high.

A. schmidtiana 'Nana', silver mound
artemisia
Bunlike, perfectly rounded form,
1 foot high. Soft, silver, intricately
textured foliage, irresistible to
touch.

A. stellerana, beach wormwood
Lovely plant, silver foliage.

Type: Perennial (subshrub).

Origin: Dry areas of northern hemisphere.

Use: Fragrance, medicinal, dried
flower, moth deterrent.

Texture: Very fine to medium fine.
Many varieties have deeply cut, lacy,
or feathery foliage.

Form: Upright or sprawling; most
are shrublike.

Fragrance: Highly aromatic leaves;
pungent.

Foliage: Silver, white, gray, blue-
green, green.

Flower: Yellow, white, lavender
(flowers of most artemisia varieties
are ornamentally insignificant);
flowering time varies, depending on
variety or cultivar.

Height: 6 inches to 4 feet, depending
on variety.

Width: 1 to 3 feet.

Spacing: 1 to 3 inches.

Starting size: 4-inch to 1-gallon
containers.

Availability: Common; some
varieties: specialty nurseries.

Zone: 4.

Soil and moisture: Accepts dry, infertile soil but must be well-drained. Benefits
from loose, deeply worked soil, which enables the roots to penetrate and expand
to obtain water during dry periods. Optimum pH is 6.7, accepts wider range.

Light and temperature: Artemisias prefer full sun but accept light or partial
shade. Taller varieties may flop if grown in too little light. Very tolerant of hot
temperatures, performs well in areas with high humidity.

Planting and maintenance: The artemisias are tough, robust growers. Usually
trouble free. Taller varieties require regular pruning to maintain neat appearance
and often need staking. Protect from strong winds. Cut back woody stems
in early spring to encourage lush, full, new growth. Selectively prune during the
growing season if plants sprawl or flop unattractively. Plants grown in full
sun are stockier. Silver King and Silver Queen can be invasive. New growth of
southernwood may get aphids. Propagation is by division, cuttings in early
spring, or layering in late summer. French tarragon must have a well-worked,
well-drained soil and requires more frequent watering than other artemisias.

Ornamental value: Artemisias are exceptionally valuable herbs in planting design. They are very ornamental, prized for their silver, gray, or blue-green foliage. They can grow in the difficult combination of intense light, heat, and dry soil. Most artemisias are aromatic. Great candidates for borders, knots, containers, raised beds, and hot, dry, pavement-level plantings. A variety of heights, foliage colors, and textures are available. Silver mound resembles a silver fur muff, making it a fun curiosity plant. Southernwood's finely cut, gray-green leaves create a soft, lacy appearance that is compelling to touch. Artemisias blend well with almost any plant, and are especially lovely when contrasted with dark green and purple-leafed plants. New growth of southernwood is yellow-green, which is complemented by other yellow-green foliaged herbs, such as basil. The many silver-foliaged varieties tend to be eye-catchers as they glisten in the sunlight. A classic color composition in herb gardens includes silver artemisias with blue-green herbs, such as rue and chives, with purple-leafed herbs, such as purple basil, or with purple sage. Also handsome when combined with rose, pink, purple, and blue flowers.

Chamaemelum nobile
Roman chamomile

(Formerly known as *Anthemis nobilis*; also called German chamomile).
Family: Compositae.
Varieties:
Chamaemelum nobile 'Treanague', flowerless chamomile
   Flowerless cultivar, few if any flowers, scented leaves, perennial, grows 2 to 8 inches.

Matricaria recutita, German chamomile
   Annual chamomile, sweet, apple-scented leaves, daisy-yellow and white flowers. Used for commercial teas. Blooms all summer. Grows 1 to 2 feet tall.

Chamaemelum nobile, continued

Type: Perennial.
Origin: Europe.
Use: Beverage, medicinal.
Texture: Very fine.
Form: Low sprawling or matting.
Fragrance: Fragrant leaves and flowers.
Foliage: Bright green.
Flower: Yellow and white, small daisylike rays; June to August.

Height: 2 to 6 inches, up to 12 inches when flowering.
Width: 12 inches or more.
Spacing: 6 to 12 inches.
Starting size: 4-inch to 1-gallon containers.
Availability: Moderately common; varieties at specialty nurseries.
Zone: 3.

Soil and moisture: Prefers dry, well-drained, light soil. Accepts pH range from slightly acid to 7. Tolerant of low fertility.

Light and temperature: Chamomile prefers full sun but will accept light to partial shade. May not bloom well in shade.

Planting and maintenance: Rich soils create lush vegetative growth but few flowers. Mulch in winter in cold climates. If used as a ground cover, extensive weeding is required the first year or two. Does not compete well with weeds. Spreads easily once established. Propagate by seed, root division, or cuttings. German type self-sows readily and can get weedy. Virtually pest and disease free. Requires little maintenance after it becomes established.

Ornamental value: Roman chamomile makes a delicate ground cover with bright green foliage and dainty yellow and white daisylike flowers. Useful in sunny, dry spots. Traditionally used in historical pleasure gardens to cover earth mounds for an extra seat and as a fragrant lawn. The sweet apple-scented German chamomile grows taller than Roman and spreads rapidly, making it useful in hard-to-cover areas. Could get weedy. Both types can be used as a ground cover or rock or wall garden plant. Works well in pavement crevices in lightly trafficked areas. Attractive when allowed to spread out from an informal border.

Chrysanthemum parthenium
Feverfew

Family: Compositae.
Varieties:
Chrysanthemum parthenium 'Aureum', golden-feather feverfew
   Golden yellow foliage, pungent leaves.
Type: Perennial.
Origin: Southeastern Europe; naturalized sporadically in North America.
Use: Cut flower, dried flower, medicinal.
Texture: Medium fine, soft.
Form: Upright. Erect, dense, bushlike.
Fragrance: Very aromatic leaves.
Foliage: Dark green.
Flower: Yellow and white; July to October.
Height: 1½ to 2 feet, up to 3.

Width: 1 to 2 feet.
Spacing: 1½ to 2 feet.
Starting size: 4-inch to 1-gallon containers.
Availability: Common.
Zone: 5.

Soil and moisture: Feverfew prefers average fertility and well-drained soils. Resents wet soil. Prefers pH 6.3.
Light and temperature: Prefers full sun but will accept partial shade.
Planting and maintenance: Fast grower. Plants self-seed. To prevent rampant self-seeding, remove flowers before seed is set and ripe. Prune foliage as needed. Few pests and diseases. Propagate by seed or cuttings in early spring.
Ornamental value: This attractive plant has soft-textured, scallop-edged, dark green leaves with an abundance of cheerful yellow and white flowers. Feverfew is a versatile plant; it works well in formal and informal borders, drifts and masses, raised beds, and containers of all sizes.

Foeniculum vulgare
Fennel

Family: Umbelliferae.

Varieties:

Foeniculum vulgare var. *azoricum*, Florence fennel or finocchio
  Edible, thickened base, anise-flavored. Grows 3 to 4 feet high. Requires more water and fertilizer than *F. vulgare*.

F. vulgare var. *rubrum*, bronze fennel
  Highly ornamental, dark copper-bronze foliage. Great contrast plant.

Type: Perennial, often grown as an annual in the North.

Origin: Southwestern Europe; naturalized in southern United States and coastal areas of California.

Use: Culinary, medicinal, beverage.

Texture: Very fine, feathery.

Form: Upright, tall and columnar.

Fragrance: Licorice-scented leaves, seeds, and roots.

Foliage: Medium green; new growth is a lighter green.

Flower: Yellow; July to September.

Height: 3 feet, up to 5.

Width: 1 to 2 feet.

Spacing: 2 to 3 feet.

Starting size: 4-inch to 2-gallon containers.

Availability: Common.

Zone: 6.

Soil and moisture: Prefers average fertility and moderate moisture. Requires well-drained soil. pH range is 6.5 to 7.5. Accepts drier, less fertile soils but will not tolerate wet, compacted soils.

Light and temperature: Fennel prefers full sun but accepts light and partial shade. Prefers moderate heat, will accept high heat. Finocchio needs more moisture than *F. vulgare*.

Planting and maintenance: Fast, vigorous grower. Prune to maintain neat appearance. Staking may be needed, especially in windy sites. Resents root disturbance. Few pest or disease problems, but can get aphids on new growth. Self-seeds readily. Propagate by seed or division.

Ornamental value: Graceful yet sturdy, fennel has fine, plumelike foliage. The textural quality of the foliage alone can be eloquent in a container or garden. The copper foliage of bronze fennel is exceptionally ornamental, making this variety an excellent contrast or accent plant. The dark foliage combines well with the many shades of green herbs, and is striking with pink-, rose-, and purple-flowering herbs. The tall form and airy texture of both green and bronze fennel contrast well with many smaller shrublike herbs. The flowers are decorative yellow umbels.

Galium odoratum

Sweet woodruff (formerly known as *Asperula odorata*)

Family: Rubiaceae.

Varieties:

Galium verum, yellow bedstraw
Perennial, widely naturalized in the United States. Very fine texture, mossy green whorled leaves, tiny yellow flowers in June–July, sun or shade. Moderately moist to moist soil. Ground cover, can be invasive. Bristle tips of leaves stick to clothing. Roots yield red dye; stems yield a yellow dye. Grows 1 to 3 feet.

Type: Perennial.

Origin: Europe, Asia, Africa.

Use: Culinary, flavoring for May wine, medicinal.

Texture: Fine, delicate whorled leaves.

Form: Spreading to semiupright.

Fragrance: Dried leaves have a strong, sweet scent.

Foliage: Rich dark green.

Flower: White; April to May.

Galium odoratum, continued

Height: 6 to 8 inches, up to 12.
Width: 12 to 24 inches or greater.
Spreading plant.
Spacing: 12 to 24 inches.
Starting size: 4-inch to 1-gallon containers.

Availability: Moderately common; varieties at specialty nurseries.
Zone: 4 to 8.

Soil and moisture: Sweet woodruff prefers moist, fertile soil and accepts moderately moist soil. Requires good drainage. Prefers an acid soil reaction, yet performs well in 4.5 to 5.5 range with an optimum pH of 5. (Woodruff is an exception to the generally preferred slightly alkaline soil reaction for most herbs.) Yellow bedstraw accepts a wider range of soil conditions.

Light and temperature: Sweet woodruff prefers shade to partial shade and cool temperatures. Yellow bedstraw grows well in full sun.

Planting and maintenance: Sweet woodruff can develop fungus problems in late summer, particularly in humid areas and poorly drained soils. Propagate by division in spring or by cuttings. Be careful not to plant too deeply. Strong light and heat may cause scorching and browning of foliage. When planted as a ground cover, weeding is required until established and filled in, then quite maintenance-free.

Ornamental value: Sweet woodruff is a beautiful ground cover for shade. Appropriate in wooded areas, in a park setting, or a cool, shady, north-facing area of a courtyard. The delicate leaves are smooth, shiny, and stiff. Leaves are arranged in whorls around erect stems on six-inch plants. Delicate, white, starlike flower clusters bloom in May. A small, pretty plant for container combinations, raised beds, and wall plantings.

Hyssopus officinalis
Hyssop

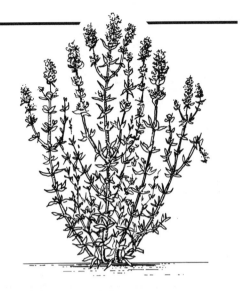

Family: Labiatae.

Varieties:

Hyssopus officinalis 'Alba', white-flowering hyssop

H. officinalis 'Rubra', rose-flowering hyssop

Type: Perennial (subshrub).

Origin: Mediterranean regions and Europe.

Use: Fragrance.

Texture: Fine.

Form: Upright, shrubby.

Foliage: Blue-gray-green.

Fragrance: Fragrant flowers.

Flower: Blue-purple, white, rose-red; June to August.

Height: 2 to 2½ feet.

Width: 1½ to 2 feet.

Spacing: 1½ to 2½ feet.

Starting size: 4-inch to 1-gallon containers.

Availability: Specialty.

Zone: 4 to 7.

Soil and moisture: Hyssop requires well-drained soil. Prefers a light, well-worked, moderately moist soil. Accepts drier soil. Not fussy about fertility. Optimum pH is 6.7, but it tolerates a wider range.

Light and temperature: Prefers full sun, will accept partial shade. Accepts hot temperatures but prefers light afternoon shade in intensely hot regions.

Planting and maintenance: Hyssop is a hardy plant that needs winter protection only in extremely cold areas. Cut back its stems in late fall or early spring to encourage bushy new growth. Plants tend to get woody and produce fewer flowers with age. Can develop fungal problems in humid regions. May require renewal by division every three to five years. Propagate by cuttings, division, or seed in spring or fall.

Ornamental value: Hyssop is an excellent medium edging, hedging, or knot-garden plant. It responds well to clipping for formal situations. This aromatic, shrubby plant can also be used in containers, window boxes, or raised beds. It is a good plant for the hot, dry conditions of pavement level plantings, such as along streetscapes. It cannot tolerate humidity and heat. The flowers are pretty and plentiful, and they attract bees and butterflies.

Iris × germanica
var. *florentina*
Orris or Florentina iris

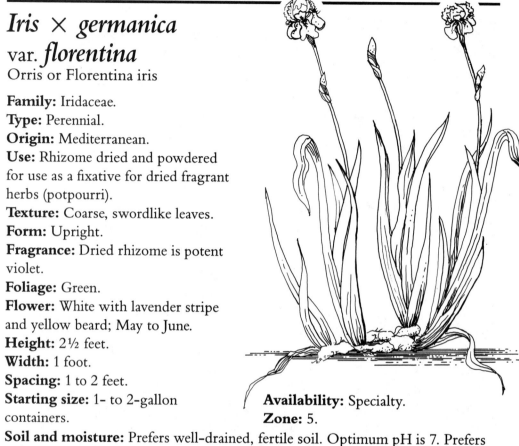

Family: Iridaceae.
Type: Perennial.
Origin: Mediterranean.
Use: Rhizome dried and powdered for use as a fixative for dried fragrant herbs (potpourri).
Texture: Coarse, swordlike leaves.
Form: Upright.
Fragrance: Dried rhizome is potent violet.
Foliage: Green.
Flower: White with lavender stripe and yellow beard; May to June.
Height: 2½ feet.
Width: 1 foot.
Spacing: 1 to 2 feet.
Starting size: 1- to 2-gallon containers.

Availability: Specialty.
Zone: 5.

Soil and moisture: Prefers well-drained, fertile soil. Optimum pH is 7. Prefers moderately moist to drier soil. Intolerant of compacted, waterlogged soils.
Light and temperature: Requires full sun but will accept light to partial shade.
Planting and maintenance: Prone to bacterial rots. If good drainage is provided, however, rotting problems are less likely to arise. Meticulous foliage cleanup in late fall helps prevent iris borer insects from infecting the plant. May need to be divided every three to five years; if so, do in the summer or autumn, after flowering.
Ornamental value: The bladelike iris foliage is a strong contrast to the many shrubby, rounded herb forms in the garden. It is an excellent structural element in an herb bed. Leaves remain erect and attractive following the blooming period. The flowers are interesting but not as showy as hybrid iris. It is also a useful plant for all types of containers as long as the soil is not kept too wet.

Laurus nobilis
Sweet bay

Family: Lauraceae.
Varieties:
Laurus nobilis 'Aurea', golden sweet bay
   Leaves have a golden tint.
L. nobilis 'Undulata'
   Wavy leaf margins.
Type: An evergreen (woody) tree in warm climates, and a tender perennial in colder regions.
Origin: Mediterranean.
Use: Culinary, perfumery, medicinal, wreaths.
Texture: Medium.
Form: Upright, shrublike, but actually a tree in Zones 9 and 10.
Fragrance: Very aromatic leaves.
Foliage: Dark glossy green when young, dulls with age.
Flower: Yellow, small, not showy; spring.
Height: 4 to 5 feet in containers; up to 40 feet or more in extremely warm climates.
Width: 3 feet or more in containers or beds.
Spacing: 1 plant per container.
Starting size: 1- to 2-gallon containers.

Availability: Specialty.
Zone: 7 to 10.

Soil and moisture: Prefers well-drained, moist to moderately moist, fertile soil. Accepts less than ideal conditions. Do not overwater in containers, but allow the soil to approach dryness between thorough drenchings. Keep container-grown plant barely moist during the winter. Optimum pH is 6.2.

Laurus nobilis, continued

Light and temperature: Bay prefers partial shade, especially in hot climates. Accepts sun very well. Golden form prefers more sunlight to maintain leaf color. Protect all the bays from scorching sun, especially in the South. Requires light feedings throughout the growing season. Indoors, grow in cool, sunny location over winter; ideally, 45 to 50 degrees F. Bay is tender in cold northern climates; it should be wintered in a greenhouse or other sunny holding house. Withstands a few light frosts. Do not leave this hard-to-find, slow-growing plant outside to freeze.

Planting and maintenance: Sweet bay is very slow growing when young. Fertilize regularly to encourage maximum growth. Large plants are very hard to locate in the nursery industry, so treasure the ones you have. Smaller plants are relatively expensive because cuttings are not easy to root. Usually best grown in a container so that it can be wintered in a greenhouse. Indoors, sweet bay may get scale insects, otherwise few problems. Prune off suckers that appear at base of plant. Pruning for attractive structure creates a specimen container plant. Propagate by stem cutting in late summer when wood is firm yet bendable; bay can take a few months to root even in the best greenhouse conditions.

Ornamental value: Sweet bay is an excellent container plant. Choose a container design worthy of housing this revered herbal tree. In the garden, makes a focus or entrance plant. Adds height to a grouping of smaller container-grown herbs. Its tiny yellow flowers are followed by more noticeable purple-black berries, which contain one seed each.

Lavandula species
Lavender

Family: Labiatae.
Varieties:

Lavandula angustifolia subsp. *angustifolia*, English lavender
   The most cold-hardy lavender, gray-green to silvery leaves. Lavender-blue flower spikes form above compact plants. Grows 18 to 24 inches.

L. angustifolia 'Alba'
   White flowers.

L. angustifolia 'Hidcote'
   Deep, dark purple flowers, slow compact grower, grows 15 inches.

L. angustifolia 'Munstead'
   Deep lavender-blue flowers, early bloomer, dwarf, grows to 12 inches.

L. angustifolia 'Rosea'
   Pale pink flowers.

L. dentata, fringed or French lavender
   Fringed, toothed leaf margins. Gray-green scented foliage. Profuse, plump, purple flowers. Tender in North, hardy in Zones 8 and 9. Grows 1 to 3 feet.

L. × *intermedia* 'Dutch'
   Dark aster-violet flowers, buds green with violet. Grows 15 to 18 inches, up to 3 feet when in bloom.

L. × *intermedia* 'Grosso'
   Violet flower. Grows 8 to 12 inches, up to 30 inches when in bloom.

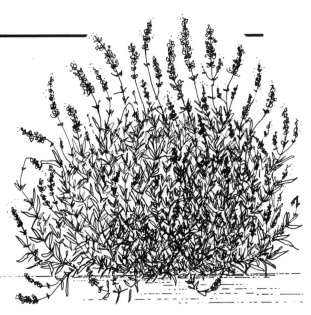

Lavandula angustifolia subsp. *angustifolia*
English lavender

L. multifida, fern-leaf lavender
   Lacy gray-green leaves, dark blue-violet flowers, tender, grows 1½ feet tall, 2 feet wide.

L. stoechas, Spanish lavender
   Tender perennial, Zones 8 to 9. Minty gray leaves, distinctive lavender-blue flowers, grows to 2 feet.

Type: Perennial (subshrub).
Origin: Mediterranean regions to India, Atlantic Islands.
Use: Perfumery, medicinal, dried flower, cut flower, wreaths.
Texture: Fine to medium. Needlelike to lacy, depending on varieties and species.

Lavandula species, continued

Form: Upright, rounded or mounded. Shrubby.

Fragrance: Exceptionally pleasant fragrance, highly aromatic.

Foliage: Silvery gray-green, gray-green, or light to medium green, depending on variety or cultivar.

Flower: Purple, blue, lavender-blue, violet, rose, or white. Richness and intensity of color varies with species and cultivars; June to July, sometimes repeated blooming in autumn.

Height: 1 to 3 feet, 1 to 2 feet in containers.

Width: 2 to 2½ feet.

Spacing: 2 to 4 feet.

Starting size: 4-inch to 1-gallon containers.

Availability: Common. Varieties at specialty nurseries.

Zone: 5.

Soil and moisture: Lavender is intolerant of wet soils but accepts moderately moist soil. This herb prefers alkaline soils, although it accepts pH 6.5 to 8.3. Requires well-drained, light soil. Lavender will dry out and die in prolonged droughts. Needs good air circulation.

Light and temperature: Requires full sun. If grown in partial shade, the plants become leggy and blooms are sparse. Accepts high temperatures. May be grown indoors in cool, sunny locations.

Planting and maintenance: Lavender requires an alkaline soil, so add lime to ground or potting soil. Start with a one-gallon container, since lavender grows slowly when young. A small plant would get lost in a planting bed or larger container planting. To prevent soil-borne and foliar fungus problems, provide good drainage and air circulation, keep water off the foliage, and space plants well. In humid areas leaf spot may occur. Pests rarely bother lavender. Provide winter protection in colder regions. The angustifolias are the hardiest lavenders. Pruning is minimal throughout the growing season, although some of the tender lavender varieties may need light pruning to maintain a tidy appearance. Remove spent blooms after flowering. In spring, wait until you see where the new growth breaks on the branches before cutting back. Propagate by stem cuttings in spring or summer. Grows slowly from seed.

Ornamental value: Lavender has beautiful silvery gray-green foliage and the most prized fragrance of the herb world. Its vibrant flowers are eye catching, forming above neat, rounded plants. The dwarf, compact forms are nice as edging plants. The silver foliage is beautiful when combined with blue-green herbs and exceptionally striking with purple-foliaged plants. Knot gardens, raised beds, borders, and rock gardens are a few of the many situations that set off the beautiful lavender plants. Plant lavenders where people can smell and touch them. Essential in fragrant theme gardens and gardens for the blind.

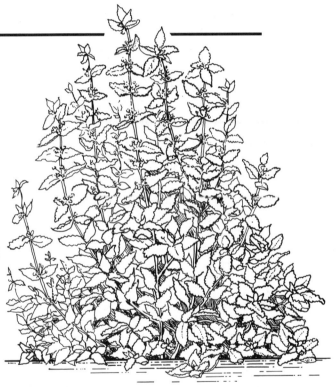

Melissa officinalis
Lemon balm

Family: Labiatae.

Varieties:

Melissa officinalis 'Variegata', golden lemon balm

Gold foliage is pronounced when grown in shade. May revert to green.

Type: Perennial.

Origin: Southern Europe, naturalized in many areas of United States, England, and France.

Use: Fragrance, culinary, medicinal, beverage.

Texture: Medium.

Form: Upright, spreading.

Fragrance: Very fragrant lemon-scented leaves.

Foliage: Deep green.

Flower: Yellow buds, light blue to cream-white blooms; June to September.

Height: 2 to 3 feet.

Width: 2 feet or taller.

Spacing: 2 to 3 feet.

Starting size: 4-inch to 1-gallon containers.

Availability: Common.

Zone: 4 to 8.

Melissa officinalis, **continued**

Soil and moisture: Prefers well-drained, moderately fertile, moist soil. Accepts less than ideal very well. Prefers alkaline pH with optimum of 7; range is 5 to 7.8.

Light and temperature: Lemon balm prefers partial shade but accepts full sun and tolerates shade. Prefers a cool habitat. May wilt in hot temperatures, especially in dry conditions. If grown in full sun, provide afternoon shade to protect against intense heat. Water more frequently if grown in hot, bright locations.

Planting and maintenance: Lemon balm is a tough plant and fast grower, but it may wilt in conditions that are too hot or dry. Its leaves may become yellowish and chlorotic if it doesn't receive sufficient moisture. Susceptible to powdery mildew if grown in stagnant, humid, shady places. Self-seeds rapidly. Propagate in spring or summer by stem cuttings, layering, division, or seed. Mature clumps may be difficult to divide. Performs well in containers, raised beds, or borders.

Ornamental value: Lemon balm is a robust, fast grower of easy culture. The distinctive lemon scent of the foliage makes it a wonderful addition to herb gardens. Its rich, dark-green foliage looks lush and healthy, and it is versatile in many design situations. The leaves are heart or arrowhead shaped, scalloped on the edges, and have pronounced veins. Lemon balm can be used to prevent soil erosion on steep banks.

Mentha species
Mint

Family: Labiatae.
Varieties:

Mentha × *gentilis* 'Variegata', ginger mint
  Ornamental green and yellow leaves. Grows to 15 inches.

M. × *piperita*, peppermint
  Strong scent, smooth dark green leaves; lilac-pink flowers. Grows 2 to 3 feet.

M. × *piperita* var. *citrata*, lemon or bergamot mint
  Smooth leaves, citrus scent.

M. pulegium, pennyroyal
  Very sharp mint-scented leaves. Bluish pink flowers. Tender. Low spreader. Grows to 3 inches.

M. requienii, creme-de-menthe or Corsican mint
  Wonderful flavor and scent of the popular liquor. Tender in northern regions. Requires partial shade. Extremely small leaves, mossy, grows less than 1 inch.

M. spicata, spearmint
  Textured light green leaves; lilac, pink, and white flowers. Grows to 30 inches.

M. spicata 'Crispii' or 'Crispata', curly mint
  Sold under many names. Ruffled leaves, lilac and white flowers. Grows to 2½ feet.

Mentha × *piperita*
Peppermint

M. suaveolens, apple mint
  Apple-scented, round, downy gray-green leaves; tiny white flowers. Grows 2 to 3 feet.

M. suaveolens 'Variegata', pineapple mint
  Bright green-and-white variegated leaves. Strong fruity scent. Grows to 2 feet.

Type: Perennial.
Origin: Europe, widely distributed, naturalized in some areas of United States.
Use: Culinary, fragrance, beverage, medicinal.

Mentha species, continued

Texture: Fine to medium, depending on variety.

Form: Upright, semiupright, or creeping.

Fragrance: Spearmint, peppermint, creme-de-menthe, apple, citrus, pineapple.

Foliage: Medium to dark green. Varieties include gray-green, bright green, variegated green and white, variegated green and gold.

Flower: White, light blue, lilac, lavender, pink; July to August.

Height: 1 to 3 feet.

Width: 2 feet or more.

Spacing: 2 to 3 feet, small varieties 1 foot.

Starting size: 4-inch to 1-gallon containers.

Availability: Common; some varieties at specialty nurseries.

Zone: 5.

Soil and moisture: Mint prefers moist, fertile, well-drained soil but accepts drier soils. Benefits from ample amounts of organic matter in soil. Accepts a neutral to slightly alkaline soil; 6.5 is optimum pH.

Light and temperature: Although mint prefers partial shade, it accepts shade and full sun. It prefers cool temperatures. If grown in full sun, provide afternoon shade to protect against intense heat, and water more often.

Planting and maintenance: Mint can become invasive. Before planting, install underground barriers to keep roots in bounds. This herb can get mint rust, mint anthracnose, and verticillium wilt. To prevent spread of diseases, cut off infected parts and discard them away from the site. Spider mites may appear in hot, dry weather. Mint species readily hybridize among themselves. Hybrids are usually sterile and rarely reproduce true from seed. Propagate by division, cuttings, or layering. Pruning maintenance involves regular deadheading and trimming plant clumps during the growing season. Fall cleanup is needed after a hard freeze.

Ornamental value: Mint varieties offer a vast array of leaf textures, leaf colors, and fragrances. Their spiky flowers bloom prolifically in shades of pink, violet, or white. Their growth habit softens the hard edges of walls, raised beds, and masonry edges. Spirited growth enlivens a container or window box: some stems will spill over the edge and others will reach for the sun. Mint is good for moist, partially shaded spots. Variegated mints can lighten a sunless spot. Curly mints provide highly decorative leaves. The apple- or pineapple-scented mints, as well as the popular spearmints and peppermints, create curiosity favorites in fragrant and tactile gardens. The tiny but enormously flavorful creme-de-menthe plant is another pleasant addition to an herb garden.

Monarda didyma
Bee balm or Oswego tea

Family: Labiatae.
Varieties:
Monarda citriodora, lemon bergamot or lemon bee balm
   Fragrant.
M. didyma 'Alba', white-flowering bee balm
M. didyma 'Croftway Pink', pink-flowering bee balm
M. didyma 'Violacea', violet-flowering bee balm
M. fistulosa, Wild bergamot
   Naturalized in meadows, drought resistant, lavender flowers, grows to 4 feet.
Type: Perennial.
Origin: Eastern United States.
Use: Beverage, flavoring, medicinal.
Texture: Medium coarse.
Form: Upright or shrublike.
Fragrance: Very aromatic minty leaves; fragrance is released when leaves are rubbed or crushed.
Foliage: Dull green.
Flower: Scarlet-red, white, pink, violet, and other colors; July to August.

Height: 3 feet.
Width: 1½ feet.
Spacing: 2 to 4 feet.
Starting size: 1- to 2-gallon containers.
Availability: Common.
Zone: 4 to 9.

Soil and moisture: Monarda prefers moist to moderately moist, well-drained soil but accepts drier soils. Prefers acidic soil. Optimum pH is 6.5. Benefits from additional organic matter or humus in soil.
Light and temperature: Bee balm prefers light to partial shade. Accepts full sun very well. Needs ample air circulation. Withstands heat but not high humidity.
Planting and maintenance: Bee balm's worst enemy is powdery mildew. Anti-fungal foliar sprays and soil drenches with Benomyl or its equivalent are effective

Monarda didyma, continued

preventives. Do not crowd plants. Remove mildew-infected leaves. Bee balm may also get rust problems. In this case, prune and dispose of infected parts. Divide plants every three to five years in early spring. Bee balm may need staking in windy areas.

Ornamental value: The showy flowers—shaggy, tubular florets, arranged in whorls with deep throats—have made bee balm popular plants for flowering perennial borders. Long lasting, they are dramatic when planted alongside catnip with its deep blue flowers, or next to purple-flowering herbs. All varieties are good mid-to-back-border plants, but they can also be grown in roomy raised beds or containers, where they tend to stay smaller than if grown in open ground. Bee balm is a good plant for naturalized plantings in parks and other large open spaces. The bright red flowers of some varieties attract hummingbirds.

Myrrhis odorata
Sweet cicely

Family: Umbelliferae.
Type: Perennial.
Origin: Europe.
Use: Culinary, salad herb, aromatic.
Texture: Very fine, lacy foliage and flowers.
Form: Upright, airy.
Fragrance: Anise-scented leaves, seeds, and fruits.
Foliage: Bright green.
Flower: White; May.
Height: 2 to 3½ feet when in flower.
Width: 1 to 2 feet.
Spacing: 2 to 2½ feet.
Starting size: 1- to 2-gallon containers.
Availability: Specialty nurseries.
Zone: 3.

Soil and moisture: Sweet cicely prefers well-drained, cool, moist soils that are high in organic matter. Does not tolerate bone-dry soils or heavy, waterlogged clay soils.

Light and temperature: Prefers shade but accepts partial shade. Does not tolerate full sun. Prefers cool temperatures.

Planting and maintenance: Sweet cicely is a good plant for cool, northern climates. Hot, bright sun causes yellowing and deterioration of foliage. May need pruning maintenance during the growing season for a tidy appearance. Staking may be needed. Once a plant is established, its deep root is difficult to transplant. Since seed propagation is a very lengthy process, sweet cicely is a hard plant to locate. It loves cool temperatures, moisture, and shade. The plant reseeds and can be propagated by division.

Ornamental value: Sweet cicely is the fern of the herb family. The finely cut leaves are even more intricate and delicate than most ferns. The lacy, white

Myrrhis odorata, **continued**

flowers form flat, dense, compound umbels on branching stems. Its delicacy is set off dramatically when sweet cicely is planted in front of a dark green box-wood or holly hedge. The fine foliage also nicely contrasts with a dark vegetative background. Sweet cicely can be used as a ground cover.

Nepeta cataria
Catnip

Family: Labiatae.
Varieties:

Nepeta cataria 'Blue Wonder'
  Large, deep blue flowers.
N. cataria 'Citriodora', lemon-scented catnip
N. × *faassenii*, catmint
  Larger blue-violet flowers on taller upright plants. Grows to 2 feet. Sterile hybrid, cannot be grown from seed.
N. mussinii, catmint
  Prolific, deep blue-purple flowers that bloom early and last up to one month. Gray-green leaves. Low perennial, grows to 1 foot. Edging plant.
Type: Perennial.
Origin: Europe, Asia, widely naturalized in United States.
Use: Beverage, medicinal; cats crave it.

Texture: Medium, conspicuous leaf veins, heart-shaped leaves.
Form: Upright, spreading.
Fragrance: Very fragrant. Flavorful minty leaves.
Foliage: Gray-green.
Flower: White and purple; varieties are deep blue, lavender, or purple; June to August.
Height: 1½ to 3 feet when in flower.
Width: 1½ feet.

Spacing: 2 to 3 feet.

Starting size: 4-inch to 1-gallon containers.

Availability: Common.

Zone: 3 to 4.

Soil and moisture: Prefers moderately moist to drier, well-drained soil. Accepts a wide range of pH levels with optimum of 6.6. Not fussy with fertility, accepts low to average fertility well. Grows well in light, sandy soils.

Light and temperature: *Nepeta* prefers sun, accepts partial shade very well, and tolerates shade. Accepts fairly hot temperatures. If grown in full sun in hot climates, provide extra moisture and afternoon shade for best appearance and performance.

Planting and maintenance: Catnip is easy to grow. Maintenance involves regular pruning during the growing season to tidy plants and promote bushy growth. Remove spent flowers. Catnip may flop in the middle of summer if not given enough sunlight. Propagate by dividing the dense roots in spring—a very easy process with a shovel.

Ornamental value: Catmint varieties display beautiful, rich blue flowers. They are long lasting and stunning when massed as an edge or in a border, planted as a specimen in a container, or combined with almost any other flower color. The brilliant blue is especially lovely with silver and blue-green foliage. *Nepeta* is drought resistant and long-lived. The catnip that cats love is not particularly ornamental; choose catmints when ornamental value is imperative.

Ocimum species
Basil

Family: Labiatae.
Varieties:
Ocimum basilicum, sweet basil
   Glossy light green leaves. Grows
   2 feet tall and 8 inches wide.
O. basilicum 'Citriodorum', lemon
basil
   Light green, narrow leaves
   with open growth habit. Grows to
   18 inches.
O. basilicum 'Crispum', lettuce-leaf
basil
   Large crinkled leaves, sturdy bushy
   plant. Grows to 2 feet tall and
   2 feet wide.
O. basilicum 'Minimum', dwarf sweet
basil
   Tiny, round, shiny leaves. Great
   small pot or edging plant, grows to
   1 foot.
O. basilicum 'Purple Ruffles'
   Good newer variety.
O. basilicum 'Purpurascens', purple
basil or 'Dark Opal' basil
   Rich, purple-red foliage, highly
   ornamental, pink and purple
   flowers. Grows to 18 inches.
O. basilicum 'Spicy Globe', 'Spicy
Globe' dwarf basil
   Popular variety. Small dense globe
   form. Grows to 10 inches.
Type: Tender annual.

Ocimum basilicum
Sweet basil

Origin: Europe, Mediterranean,
tropics. Cultivated for centuries.
Use: Culinary, perfumery, cut flower,
medicinal.
Texture: Medium coarse. Some
varieties have fine, rounded, or ruffled
leaves.
Form: Upright, bushlike.
Fragrance: Very spicy leaves and
flowers.

Foliage: Light green, yellow-green, or purple, depending on variety or cultivar.

Flower: White or purple-pink, depending on variety or cultivar; July to August.

Height: 12 to 24 inches.

Width: 8 to 12 inches.

Spacing: 8 to 18 inches.

Starting size: 4-inch to 1-gallon containers.

Availability: Common. Some varieties are in specialty nurseries.

Soil and moisture: Basils require well-drained, moist, fertile soils. Optimum pH is 6. Accepts moderate moisture and fertility.

Light and temperature: Prefers full sun or partial shade. Requires warmth and is very intolerant of cold, wet soils.

Planting and maintenance: Transplant basil into warm soil after the frost-free date. Basil won't budge in cold soil. It can be grown from seed if planted in warm, worked ground. Pinch the terminal leaf tips of small plants to encourage branching and continue pinching throughout the growing season. Removing the terminal flowers prevents the plant from going to seed too early in the summer. At some point let the plant flower, then cut it back hard and allow the new growth to bush out into an attractive plant. Fertilize and water frequently. Plants blacken after the first frost; it is necessary to clean up the bed. Propagate by seed or stem cuttings. Japanese beetles or slugs may cause damage.

Ornamental value: The many varieties of basil offer distinctively different and special ornamentation in the garden. The smooth, silky, shiny leaves of sweet basil and the large, crinkly, puffed leaves of lettuce-leaf basil add a nice contrast to more finely textured herbs. Their light green is a good contrast to darker green plants. The tiny, round leaves arranged densely on the small, compact plants of the miniature basils make them interesting as small edge or windowbox plants. They can also be used as miniature knot-garden plants for annual designs. The purple leaves of 'Dark Opal' basil are exceptionally ornamental and striking when combined with silver and blue-green herbs. Pink and rosy flowers are stunning with purple basil. Basil performs well in many situations, from massing in borders to containers of all sizes.

Origanum vulgare
subspecies *hirtum*
Italian oregano

Family: Labiatae.
Varieties:

Origanum compactum, dwarf oregano
  Low-growing, creeping plant.
O. dictamnus, dittany-of-Crete
  Distinctive small, white, woolly
  leaves with small pink and white
  hoplike flowers. Not culinary.
  Spreading habit, grows to 1 foot.
O. onites, pot marjoram
  Newly introduced variety. Good
  sharp oregano flavor. White
  flowers, hairy leaves. Grows to
  2 feet.
O. vulgare, common oregano or wild
marjoram
  Similar to *hirtum* but bracts are
  shorter. White and purple flowers.
  Round green leaves. Upright
  plant, grows to 2 feet.
O. vulgare 'Aureum', golden oregano
  Striking yellow leaves. Few
  flowers. Rarely self-sows. Orna-
  mental.
Also see *Origanum majorana* for related
species and varieties.
Type: Perennial.
Origin: Mediterranean and Central
Asia.
Use: Culinary, dried flower,
medicinal.
Texture: Medium fine.

Origanum vulgare 'Aureum' Golden
oregano

Form: Upright, spreading, mound-
ing, or creeping.
Fragrance: Fragrant, flavorful leaves.
Foliage: Medium to dark green;
varieties and related species include
golden-yellow and white woolly
foliage.
Flower: Pink, white, purple range;
July to September.
Height: 1 to 2 feet.
Width: 1½ feet.
Spacing: 1½ to 2½ feet.
Starting size: 4-inch to 1-gallon
containers.
Availability: Common; varieties at
specialty nurseries. Variety names are
often confused in the nursery trade.
Zone: 5.

Soil and moisture: Requires well-drained soil. Prefers dry to moderately dry soil with average fertility. Prefers slightly alkaline pH with optimum of 6.8.

Light and temperature: Oregano prefers full sun but accepts light to partial shade. Wild oregano grows well in partial shade. Requires warmth and tolerates hot, humid climates.

Planting and maintenance: Be sure you have the right plant. Specify sexually propagated cuttings, since oregano often is not true from seed; its flavor may be different and it may produce flowerless plants. Oreganos can get root rot, spider mites, and aphids. Greenhouse-grown plants are more susceptible to pests than those grown outdoors. The golden variety self-sows. Aroma is weak in overly rich, light soils. Prune to maintain a neat plant appearance and remove spent blooms regularly. May flop over in summer if grown in low light.

Ornamental value: The fine foliage texture and light pinkish purple flowers of oregano make it a versatile herb in planting designs. Italian oregano is often hard to find. (Note that there are more than a dozen genera of plants that yield the oregano flavoring.) Other *Origanum* species and varieties offer quite different ornamental features than *O. vulgare*. Particularly striking is dittany-of-Crete, an attractive hanging-basket plant. Golden oregano has a unique color among herbs. Most oreganos are tough plants and vigorous growers. They are good for front- or mid-borders, containers, raised beds, and window boxes.

Origanum majorana
Sweet marjoram

Family: Labiatae.
Varieties:
Origanum aureum crispum, golden-puckered marjoram
    Puckered leaves, hardy perennial. Grows to 8 inches.
O. pulchellum, flowering marjoram
    Showy pink flowers, good dried flower. Hardy perennial. Grows to 3 feet.

See also *Origanum vulgare* subsp. *hirtum* for related species and varieties.
Type: Tender annual.
Origin: North Africa, naturalized in southern Europe.
Use: Culinary, medicinal.
Texture: Very fine, round leaves.
Form: Upright, shrublike.
Fragrance: Sweet, mildly fragrant and flavorful leaves and flowers.

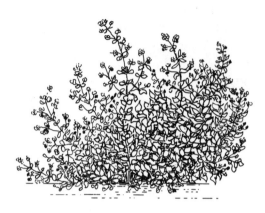

Foliage: Medium green.
Flower: White, pink, purple range; August to September.
Height: 12 to 18 inches.
Width: 6 to 8 inches.
Spacing: 8 to 10 inches.
Starting size: 4-inch to 1-gallon containers.
Availability: Common; varieties at specialty nurseries.
Zone: 9 to 10.

Soil and moisture: Requires well-drained soil and average fertility. Optimum pH is 6.9, prefers slightly alkaline soil.

Light and temperature: Marjoram prefers full sun, but accepts light to partial shade. It tolerates heat. Golden variety is especially colorful in full sun.

Planting and maintenance: Prune often when young to encourage fullness. Best in full sun; shaded plants may get leggy and straggly. Marjoram dies in the cold, but it can be kept in a greenhouse or cold frame throughout the winter. Propagate by cuttings or division; tricky to propagate from seed.

Ornamental value: Marjoram is a pretty plant. It is often called knotted marjoram because small green knots, overlapping buds that contain tiny white flowers, form where the leaves join the stem. This small herb is charming in containers, raised beds, window boxes, and hanging baskets (marjoram can grow in small root areas). It is also a nice rock garden or front-of-the-border plant.

Pelargonium species
Scented geraniums

Family: Labiatae.
Varieties:

Pelargonium crispum, lemon-scented geranium

Small, fine, stiff, serrated leaves. Grows 1 to 3 feet. Slender form with lavender flower clusters on top of plant. Notable cultivars include P. 'French Lace', P. 'Minor', P. 'Prince Rupert', and P. 'Prince Rupert Variegata'.

P. denticulatum 'Filicifolium', fern-leaf scented geranium

Strong pine scent, deeply indented leaves.

P. × *domesticum* 'Clorinda', eucalyptus-scented geranium

Showy; large clusters of bright rose-pink flowers streaked with orange-red markings. Vigorous grower, semitrailing habit, and large-lobed foliage.

P. graveolens, rose-scented geranium

Large heart-shaped, deeply indented, gray-green leaves. Grows 2 to 4 feet upright. Deep rose or lavender flowers that form in umbrellalike clusters at top of plant. Notable cultivars include *P. graveolens* 'Camphor Rose', camphor rose-scented geranium, and *P. graveolens* 'Rober's Lemon Rose', Rober's lemon rose-scented geranium.

P. × *domesticum* 'Clorinda'
Eucalyptus-scented geranium

P. odoratissimum, apple-scented geranium

Dense plant with soft, apple-scented foliage.

P. tomentosum, peppermint-scented geranium

Large heart-shaped, velvet-textured leaves. Dainty white flowers with red centers. Trailing growth habit. Accepts partial shade.

Type: Perennial (hardy to 20 to 35 degrees F). Some are subshrubs having woody portions on older stems.

Pelargonium species, continued

Origin: Tropics and South Africa.
Use: Culinary and fragrances.
Texture: Very fine to coarse. Varieties range from small, finely cut leaves to large, deeply lobed leaves.
Form: Upright, spreading.
Fragrance: Rose, citrus, mint, apple, coconut, cinnamon.
Foliage: Light to dark green, some variegated.
Flower: White, pink, rose, purple, violet, or red (solid or bicolor); blooms when cool, depending on varieties, from 4 to 6 weeks. Some repeated blooming periods.

Height: 1 to 4 feet.
Width: 1 to 3 feet.
Spacing: Varies.
Starting size: 4-inch to 2-gallon containers.
Availability: Common; varieties at specialty nurseries.
Zone: 10.

Soil and moisture: Scented geraniums require well-drained soil. Allow soil to approach dryness between waterings, or maintain moderately moist conditions. Problems arise from overwatering, especially when grown in containers. Not tolerant of prolonged droughts. Fertilize potted plants regularly during the growing season. Best pH range is 6 to 7. "Soilless" potting media, such as the Cornell mix, are fine, but remember that they need more watering and fertilization than a mix containing soil.

Light and temperature: Prefers full sun. The peppermint-scented variety performs well in partial shade. The scented geraniums stand up to heat better than the zonal geraniums. Cool temperatures promote flowering.

Planting and maintenance: Scented geraniums are usually grown in containers, but they also perform very well in beds. Do not overpot. Typically need to be repotted or top dressed with fresh soil annually. Fertilize regularly. Geraniums require frequent tip pinching and occasional cutting back to maintain bushy, attractive form. Allow time for buds to mature and flower, usually several weeks, before pinching the tips. These herbs are grown as annuals, but can be kept indoors throughout the winter in a sunny, cool location, or cut back and kept barely moist in a location that is kept above freezing. In polluted areas, clean the foliage of the varieties that have large, hairy leaves. Propagate scented geraniums by stem cuttings in spring. Plants may get botrytis, stem rot, or whiteflies; employ sanitary horticultural practices for preventive control.

Ornamental value: Scented geraniums are selected for their ornamental leaf shapes, leaf colors, and fragrances. Many of the scented geraniums' flowers are smaller and more delicate than those of the larger, showy zonal geraniums. Scented geraniums are typically planted in a container or raised bed. They are interesting specimens in containers when trained as standards or topiary trees. Peppermint-scented geraniums are novel and successful in hanging baskets. Scented geraniums are appropriate for a tactile or fragrant thematic garden. Their fast growth and range of scents also make them good for children's gardens.

Petroselinum crispum
Parsley

Family: Umbelliferae.

Varieties:

Petroselinum crispum 'Curly Parsley', curly parsley
> Pronouncedly crinkled and curled foliage, sold under many names in the trade.

P. crispum var. *neapolitanum*, Italian parsley
> Smooth, flat, celerylike leaves. Grows to 20 inches.

Type: Biennial, but typically grown as an annual.

Origin: Mediterranean, Europe.

Use: Culinary, beverage, medicinal, dye.

Texture: Fine; intricate and crinkled leaves.

Form: Mounding.

Fragrance: None, but flavorful.

Foliage: Bright, rich green.

Flower: White; early summer.

Height: 8 to 15 inches.

Width: 10 inches.

Spacing: 8 to 12 inches.

Starting size: 4-inch to 1-gallon containers, or seed.

Availability: Common.

Zone: 9.

Petroselinum crispum, continued

Soil and moisture: Parsley prefers moderately rich, moist, well-drained soils. Work soil deeply to allow roots to penetrate. Optimum pH is 6. Fertilize several times during the growing season, and regularly if grown in containers.

Light and temperature: Prefers partial shade, but accepts full sun very well. Not fond of high temperatures. In full sun, provide extra moisture or afternoon shade to prevent exhausting the plant from high heat.

Planting and maintenance: Reputed to be difficult to transplant. As long as the root is not bent or broken in the transplanting process, however, and the growing center is not buried too deeply, parsley will transplant fine. Curly parsley is the hardiest; Italian variety is tender. Grow parsley as an annual since it performs poorly the second year, usually going to seed by early summer. May get parsley worm or spider mites. A lengthy bath with a forceful spray from a hose is an effective preventive practice for discouraging mite infestation. Fertilize container-grown plants regularly. Seeds take up to a month to germinate. To speed the process, soak them overnight before planting. Parsley is sensitive to gaseous pollutants.

Ornamental value: The rich, green, intricately textured leaves of parsley make it a plant with a wide range of planting design possibilities. It blends well with most herbs and other plants. Parsley has a neat, compact growth habit, and can be used effectively as an edging plant for formal or informal gardens. It also makes a good plant for small knot gardens. Its evergreen foliage continues into winter, thus defining the garden edge longer. Performs well in containers, hanging baskets, and strawberry jars.

Poterium sanguisorba
Burnet

Family: Rosaceae.
Type: Perennial.
Origin: Europe.
Use: Culinary, salads.
Texture: Medium fine.
Form: Rosettelike, mounding.
Fragrance: Cucumber scent and flavor.
Foliage: Blue-green.
Flower: Green and purple; May to June.
Height: 1 foot, reaches 2 to 3 feet in flower.
Width: 1 to 1½ feet.

Spacing: 1½ to 2½ feet.
Starting size: 4-inch to 1-gallon containers.
Availability: Moderately common.
Zone: 3.

Soil and moisture: Burnet requires well-drained soil. It prefers drier to moderately moist soils; plants are reported to live longer in drier soil. Will not tolerate wet, compacted soils, especially in winter. Prefers average to moderate fertility.

Light and temperature: Prefers light to partial shade. Accepts full sun. Withstands hot temperatures, but resents high humidity. Grows better in afternoon shade.

Planting and maintenance: Prune the older leaves and spent flower heads regularly to promote fresh growth from the crown. Do not plant too deeply or base stems may rot. Excessively rich, moist soils can also cause rot, especially in winter. Foliage stays green into the winter months, even in northern climates.

Ornamental value: Burnet's intricately detailed, blue-green foliage is lovely with silver- or purple-foliaged herbs. The pastel lavender, violet, blue, and rose flowers of many other herbs combine richly with burnet.

Rosmarinus officinalis
Rosemary

Family: Labiatae.
Varieties:
Upright forms:
Rosmarinus officinalis 'Albus', white-flowering rosemary
  Grows to 3 feet.
R. officinalis 'Arp', 'Arp' or hardy rosemary
  Large, thick, gray-green leaves, light blue flowers. Hardy to −15 degrees F. Native to southwestern United States.
R. officinalis 'Benedin Blue', 'Benedin Blue' rosemary
  Slender, pine-scented leaves, rich blue-violet flowers. Grows to 3 feet.
R. officinalis 'Collingwood Ingram', graceful or 'Collingwood Ingram' rosemary
  Graceful, curving branches. Prolific bright blue-violet flowers. Grows to 2½ feet tall, 4 feet wide.
R. officinalis 'Tuscan Blue', columnar or 'Tuscan Blue' rosemary
  Tall, columnar form. Dark blue-violet flowers. Grows 3 to 4 feet.
Prostrate forms:
Rosmarinus officinalis 'Lockwood de Forest', 'Lockwood de Forest' prostrate rosemary
  Delicate, lighter green foliage. Profuse vibrant blue flowers. Grows 1 to 2 feet tall, 4 to 8 feet wide.

R. officinalis 'Prostratus', prostrate rosemary
  Grows 1 to 1½ feet tall and to 4½ feet wide.
Type: Perennial (subshrub). Cultivated as a tender perennial in colder climates. Evergreen in warm climates (Zones 9 and 10).
Origin: Mediterranean coasts.
Fragrance: Highly aromatic, somewhat piney.
Use: Culinary, perfumery, medicinal. Symbol for love and remembrance.
Texture: Medium fine, needlelike leaves.
Form: Upright or prostrate, dense shrub.
Foliage: Dark forest green.

Flower: Sky blue, bright blue, deep blue-violet, pink, or white; early summer. In warmer climates, intermittent flowering and longer blooming periods (often from December through February).
Height: Upright varieties grow 3 to 6 feet; prostrate varieties, 1 to 2 feet.
Width: Upright varieties grow to 3 feet; prostrate varieties, 3 to 6 feet.
Spacing: 2 to 6 feet.

Starting size: 4-inch to 2-gallon containers. Large sizes are hard to locate.
Availability: Common; many varieties are at specialty nurseries. Some cultivars and varieties are sold under different names. Check plant descriptions in the catalogues to meet your design needs.
Zone: 8 to 10.

Soil and moisture: Rosemary requires a light, well-drained soil. Add chicken grit or similar soil amendments for sharp drainage. Prefers slightly moist to drier soil. pH range is 5 to 8.5; optimum is 6.8. Tolerates temporary but not prolonged droughts. Provide sharp drainage for rosemary in containers, do not overwater, and be sure to fertilize regularly.

Light and temperature: Prefers full sun. Accepts partial shade but flowers may be skimpy and branches may become leggy. Very tolerant of heat outdoors. To overwinter indoors in cold, northern climates, grow in a cool, sunny location.

Planting and maintenance: Rosemary is an excellent performer in beds or containers. The hardiness variability of rosemaries is the primary planting design concern; therefore, check zone information carefully. To protect from winter injury, plant in areas protected from winds, mulch, use antidesiccants, or dig up and overwinter rosemary in a cold frame, greenhouse, or sunroom. Indoors, mealybugs or mites may appear. Diseases are not common afflictions for rosemary; however, root rot and botrytis can occur. To prevent diseases, provide good drainage and air circulation and keep water off the foliage. Prune branches to maintain good plant form. Wait until the new growth appears on the plant in early spring, then cut back to that point. New growth rarely breaks from woody branches at the base of the plant.

Ornamental value: Both upright and prostrate types of rosemary make attractive specimens for containers, raised beds, or borders. In warmer climates, prostrate rosemaries are year-round evergreens, typically used as ground cover. The prostrate rosemaries are novel in hanging baskets or cascading over a wall. Rosemary's rich, dark green color combines well with almost any herb. If grown indoors in cool, sunny spots, plants often bloom at Christmas and last until February. Rosemary makes an excellent bonsai specimen, topiary, or standard.

Ruta graveolens
Rue

Family: Rutaceae.

Varieties:

Ruta graveolens 'Blue Beauty', 'Blue Beauty' rue
  Nonflowering. Striking steel-blue foliage.

R. graveolens 'Blue Mound', 'Blue Mound' compact rue
  Compact plant, colorful variety.

R. graveolens 'Jackman Blue', 'Jackman Blue' compact rue
  Dense, compact growth, blue foliage.

R. graveolens 'Variegata', variegated rue
  Cream and white mottled leaves. Specialty plant.

Type: Perennial (subshrub).

Origin: Southern Europe to Western Asia, Mediterranean.

Use: Medicinal, dye, dried flower. Oils in leaves can cause skin rash.

Texture: Medium fine, intricately patterned leaves.

Form: Upright, mounding.

Fragrance: Pungent leaves. Offensive to some.

Foliage: Steel-blue or blue-green.

Flower: Yellow, small; June to August.

Height: 1½ to 2 feet, up to 3 feet.

Width: 1 to 2 feet, up to 3 feet.

Spacing: 1 to 2 feet.

Starting size: 4-inch to 1-gallon containers.

Availability: Common; varieties at specialty nurseries.

Zone: 4 to 9.

Soil and moisture: Rue requires sharp drainage. Prefers moderately moist to drier soil and average fertility. Intolerant of wet, highly fertile soils. pH range is from 5.8 to 8; optimum is 7.

Light and temperature: Prefers full sun, but accepts partial shade. Too much shade results in weak growth and straggly appearance; rue is sturdier when grown in sun. Foliage color is best when rue is grown in full sun. Rue is tolerant of clay soils.

Planting and maintenance: Sharp drainage and good air circulation prevent most of rue's problems. If rue is grown in a wet, humid, hot location, fungus will be common. Thin branches to create better air circulation if fungus begins. In early spring, prune back to the point where new growth emerges on the plant. (Stems may flop over by late summer if grown in too little light.) Responds well to clipping, which also encourages branches to maintain upright habit. Rue self-sows. Propagate by stem cuttings or division.

Ornamental value: Rue's graceful, lacy foliage and exquisite color make it a wonderful ornament to any planting. The oils in the leaves can cause dermatitis; therefore, do not use where people can get close enough to touch it; mid-to-back-border locations are best. Rue is an excellent knot-garden plant. The steel-blue foliage blends well with green, blue-green, or silver herbs and is striking with purple-leaved or purple-flowering herbs.

Salvia officinalis
Sage

Family: Labiatae.

Varieties:

Salvia azurea, azure sage
  Beautiful blue flowers, gray-blue leaves. Drought tolerant. Flowers August to September. Grows 3 to 4 feet. Texas native, Zone 4.

S. elegans, pineapple sage
  Tender, fruity scent. Brilliant red flowers in late summer. Requires moist soil. Grows to 4 feet.

S. farinacea 'Victoria'
  Tender perennial, grown as an annual for dependable summer-long color. Heat tolerant. Beautiful blue flowers. Grows to 18 inches.

Salvia officinalis, continued

S. greggii, autumn sage
   Red to purple flowers. Drought tolerant. Grows to 3 feet. Texas native, Zone 7.

S. leucantha, Mexican bush sage
   Beautiful blue-violet-white flowers in early autumn. Tender. Grows to 4 feet.

S. officinalis 'Albiflora', white-flowering sage

S. officinalis 'Icterina' or 'Aurea', golden sage
   Light green leaves with golden edge, low spreading form.

S. officinalis 'Purpurascens', purple sage
   Highly ornamental purple foliage.

S. officinalis 'Tricolor', tricolor sage
   Variegated green, white, and purple leaves. Tender.

S. sclarea, clary sage
   Gray-green leaves. Lavender-pink flower spikes, distinctive aroma. Short-lived. Grows to 4 feet.

Type: Perennial (subshrub), evergreen in warmer climates.

Origin: Southern Europe, Mediterranean.

Fragrance: Strong spicy, sweet, anise-clove aroma.

Use: Culinary, medicinal, dried flower, wreaths.

Texture: Medium. Pebbly leaf texture.

Form: Upright, shrublike.

Foliage: Soft gray-green.

Flower: Blue, white, violet to red range, depending on variety or related species; May to June, some varieties bloom in the autumn.

Height: 1 to 2½ feet.

Width: 2 feet.

Spacing: 2 to 2½ feet.

Starting size: 4-inch to 2-gallon containers.

Availability: Common; varieties at specialty nurseries.

Zone: 4 to 8.

Soil and moisture: Sage prefers drier to moderately moist soil. Wide pH range, from 5 to 8 with optimum pH 6.4. Prefers well-drained soil but can tolerate clay soils. In very poorly drained winter soils, sages may perish. Tolerates drought. Pineapple sage requires more moisture than the other sages. Most sages respond well to ample fertility, but they also grow well with less than ideal levels.

Light and temperature: Prefers full sun, but accepts partial shade. Very tolerant of heat and humidity.

Planting and maintenance: Sages are sturdy, easy-to-grow plants. Many varieties grow well in Texas and other hot, dry, sandy regions. Salvias are virtually pest and disease free, but have been known to get root rot and spider mites. Plants growing in dry, bright conditions tend to produce a gray-green leaf; those grown in wetter soils tend to have a greener leaf. Regular pruning maintains an attractive plant form throughout the season. Propagate by stem cuttings in the spring or summer. Divide or layer to propagate in early spring.

Ornamental value: The aromatic sages offer a wide variety of decorative foliage colors. The purple-leaf variety is a very useful plant in an herb garden, beautifully contrasting the many silver and blue-green herbs. The striking golden sage is eye-catching in an herb border, particularly with an abundance of green-foliaged plants. Leaf texture is pebbly. The flowers of the tender sages are exceptionally ornamental, and many bloom in autumn. These can be grown as hardy annuals in warm climates or overwintered in cold frames in the North. Sages can be used in containers, raised beds, front- to mid-borders, or in edges. They do not respond well to close clipping and are therefore more appropriate as informal edging plants. They can also be used as accent plants in a border, in large massings, or as specimens. Because many sages can prevent soil erosion when planted on a steep bank or sloping rock garden, they have earned the honor of being conservation herbs.

Santolina species
Santolina

Family: Compositae.
Varieties:

Santolina chamaecyparissus, lavender cotton or gray santolina
    Furry, silver-gray leaves, corallike texture. Buttonlike yellow flowers. Grows to 2 feet.
S. chamaecyparissus 'Plumosus', lacy lavender cotton
    Lacy, silver-gray leaves.
S. chamaecyparissus 'Nana', dwarf lavender cotton
    Dwarf form. Silver-gray foliage.

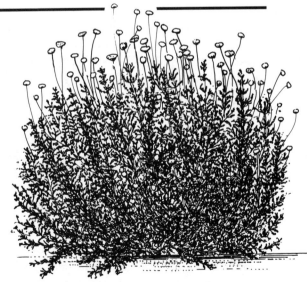

Santolina virens
Green santolina

Santolina species, continued

S. ericoides, compact green santolina
  Rich green leaves. Grows to
  12 inches.
S. neapolitana
  Feathery foliage, silver-gray or
  green. Lemon-yellow flowers.
  Grows to 2 feet.
S. virens, green santolina
  Dark emerald-green leaves. Hardi-
  est santolina. Grows to 2 feet.
Type: Perennial (subshrub), evergreen
in warmer climates.
Origin: Southern Europe, Mediterra-
nean.
Use: Dried flower.
Texture: Fine, intricate, dense, coral-
like foliage.

Form: Upright, shrubby, mounding.
Fragrance: Pungent, musky leaves,
somewhat like lavender.
Foliage: Dark emerald-green or sil-
ver-gray.
Flower: Yellow, buttonlike; June
to July.
Height: 1 to 2½ feet.
Width: 2 to 3 feet, up to 4 feet in hot,
sandy areas.
Spacing: 3 feet.
Starting size: 1- to 2-gallon
containers.
Availability: Common; varieties at
specialty nurseries.
Zone: 6 to 9.

Soil and moisture: Santolina requires sharp drainage. Happy in drier soils.
Prefers sandy, limy soil, pH approximately 6 to 7.5.

Light and temperature: Prefers full sun; accepts partial shade. Plants become
weak and branches separate and flop in shadier situations. Full sun promotes
erect stems. Plants grown in full sun have the richest silver and green colors.

Planting and maintenance: Work the soil deeply before planting so that roots
can penetrate easily and find moisture during a drought. Provide mulch and
other winter protection measures in cold regions. Prune hard in early spring to
encourage stiff, erect branches. May need additional pruning in mid- to late
summer. Branches sometimes separate, leaving gaps in the plant's mound, but
pruning will help restore its appearance. This is not a serious problem unless a
perfect form is a specific design requirement, such as in a more formal planting.
If fungus appears on the foliage, thin plants to increase air circulation. Propagate
by stem cuttings or layering in spring.

Ornamental value: Santolinas are handsome, well-behaved, versatile plants in
the herb garden, prized for their usefulness in planting design. Use them as
front- to mid-border plants, clipped or natural edges and hedges, bank or rock
garden plants. Santolinas are pleasing when planted at the edge of a wall or stair-
way and in containers or raised beds. They are great candidates for contrast,
accent, specimen, or massing plants.

Stachys byzantina
Lamb's-ears

Family: Labiatae.
Varieties:
Stachys byzantina 'Alba', white-flowering lamb's-ears
S. byzantina 'Silver Carpet', 'Silver Carpet' lamb's-ears
   Few flowers, if any. Grows to 6 inches.
S. officinalis, betony
   Ornamental rosy-purple flowers. Green leaves. Grows 1 to 3 feet.
Type: Perennial.
Origin: Southwestern Asia, Turkey, widely cultivated as an ornamental.
Use: Medicinal.
Texture: Coarse; large, very woolly leaves.
Form: Spreading, sprawling; flowers are upright.
Fragrance: Scented leaves and flowers.

Foliage: White, silver, gray.
Flower: Rose to lavender; June.
Height: 8 to 12 inches; flowers up to 18 inches.
Width: 24 to 36 inches.
Spacing: 24 to 36 inches.
Starting size: 4-inch to 2-gallon containers.
Availability: Common; varieties at specialty nurseries.
Zone: 3 to 10.

Soil and moisture: Requires well-drained soils. Prefers a moderately moist (not wet) soil. Ample fertility preferred but not essential. Accepts drier soils well.
Light and temperature: Lamb's-ears prefers full sun but accepts partial shade. Avoid hot and humid spots. Plants detest wet, hot, humid conditions. Betony prefers more shade than lamb's-ears.
Planting and maintenance: Lamb's-ears is prone to leaf and root fungus problems in damp, hot, and humid conditions. Wet soils aggravate root and foliar fungus problems. Otherwise, it is a fast-growing, vigorous plant. Betony can be invasive, especially in fertile soil. Keep plants in bounds or plant where they are free to spread. Cut back spent blooms in spring to encourage reflowering in autumn. Plants may need to be divided every three to four years. Propagate by root division.
Ornamental value: Lamb's-ears' silver foliage has both ornamental value and

Stachys byzantina, continued

design potential. The thick, furry leaf looks and feels exactly like a baby lamb's ear, which makes it a great addition to a tactile-interest garden or garden for the blind. Children love to touch it. It is a versatile accent plant, demanding the eye's attention. Lamb's-ears makes a striking ground cover and looks wonderful with the many blue-green and purple herbs. Its pink-lavender flowers, which form above the ground-hugging silver leaves, are a pretty complement to the pastel flowering herbs.

Symphytum officinale
Comfrey

Family: Boraginaceae.
Varieties:
Symphytum caucasicum, small blue comfrey

    Showy pink buds open to lovely blue flowers. Grows to 2 feet.

S. grandiflorum, ground cover comfrey
    Yellow or white flowers. Compact plant. Grows 12 to 18 inches.

S. officinale 'Rubrum', rose-flowering comfrey

S. officinale 'Variegatum', variegated comfrey

    White leaf margins.

_S._ × _uplandicum_, Russian comfrey
    Rose flowers change to purple. A taller form of comfrey. Grows to 4 feet.

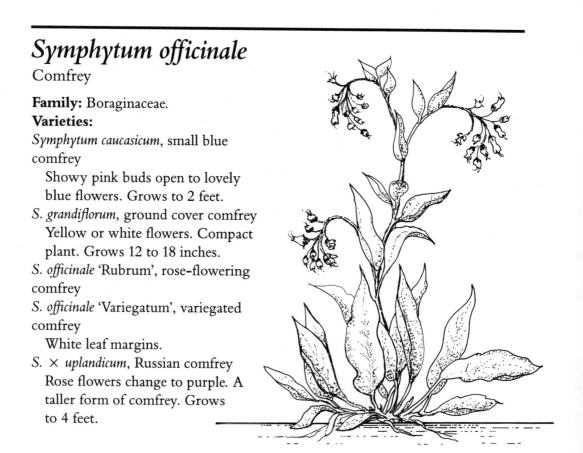

Type: Perennial.
Origin: Europe and western Asia. Naturalized along roadsides of North America.
Use: Culinary, medicinal, beverage; increases nutrients in compost.
Texture: Very coarse, large leaves.
Form: Upright, spreading.
Fragrance: None.
Foliage: Dark green.
Flower: Blue, rose, purple, white, or yellow; May to June, can flower intermittently until frost.

Height: 2 to 3 feet, up to 4 feet.
Width: 2 to 4 feet.
Spacing: 2 to 4 feet.
Starting size: 4-inch to 2-gallon containers.
Availability: Common; varieties at specialty nurseries.
Zone: 3 to 10.

Soil and moisture: Comfrey prefers moderately moist, rich, alkaline soils. Optimum pH is 7.1. Accepts drier soils well. At home in wet areas as long as they are well drained. Tolerates dry spells and less-than-ideal soil conditions.
Light and temperature: Prefers full sun or partial shade. Plants may topple if grown in too much shade.
Planting and maintenance: Comfrey is a vigorous, sturdy plant of easy culture. Pest and disease problems are rare. Choose the planting site carefully because once comfrey is planted, it is there to stay; that is, established roots are virtually indestructible. Propagate by root division or seed in fall or early spring.
Ornamental value: The delicate pink buds and blue flowers of comfrey are a lovely contrast to its large, coarse, dark green leaves. The flowers form on gracefully arched flower stems at the top of the plant. Comfrey's flowers change from pink to blue as they age. Varieties' flowers come in blue, pink, white, yellow, rose, and purple. Plant smaller-growing varieties in front border positions or in containers. Mass comfrey as a ground cover in larger areas.

Tanacetum vulgare
Tansy

Family: Compositae.
Varieties:

Tanacetum vulgare var. *crispum*, curly or fern-leaf tansy

> Very ornamental, luxuriant, rich green foliage. Deeply cut and curling leaves. More compact than *T. vulgare*.

Type: Perennial.
Origin: Europe and Asia. Naturalized in many areas of North America.
Use: Dried flower, wreaths (flowers), medicinal, dye (leaves and roots), insect deterrent.
Texture: Coarse; large, fernlike, coarsely textured leaves. Deeply incised.
Form: Upright, spreading.
Fragrance: Bitter, pungent leaves.
Foliage: Rich emerald green.
Flower: Yellow, flat clusters; July to September.
Height: 3 to 4 feet.
Width: 1 to 3 feet.

Spacing: 1 to 3 feet.
Starting size: 4-inch to 2-gallon containers.
Availability: Common; varieties at specialty nurseries.
Zone: 4.

Soil and moisture: Requires good drainage. Prefers moderately moist soil, accepts drier soil. If grown in rich, moist soils, the foliage becomes very lush. pH range is 5 to 7, 6.3 optimum. Tolerant of a wide range of conditions.
Light and temperature: Tansy prefers light to partial shade. Accepts sun very well. Accepts heat but prefers protection from intensely hot afternoon sun.
Planting and maintenance: Tansy is a fast, vigorous grower with few pest or disease problems. The plants may need pruning to be kept under control and maintain an attractive form. Can be pruned and maintained at 2 or 3 feet.
T. vulgare can be invasive; however, the curly leaf variety has less tendency to

become invasive. Plants may need to be staked, especially if the stem is weak from being grown in too little light. Cut spent flowers, since tansy self-sows rampantly. Propagate by division.

Ornamental value: Tansy's luxuriant, emerald-green, ferny foliage is its prized feature, but the long-lasting button-shaped flowers add to its ornamental value. Curly tansy's deeply cut foliage makes it a better ornamental plant than the common tansy. Curly tansy does not share the roaming habit of the species. Use in massings at middle or back of the border. Tansy also makes a good ground cover or container plant.

Teucrium chamaedrys
Germander

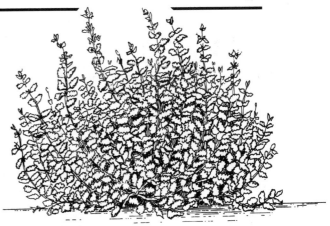

Family: Labiatae.

Varieties:

Teucrium canadense, wood sage or American germander
  Pink to purple flowers. Native to eastern North America. Grows to 3 feet.

T. chamaedrys 'Prostratum', prostrate germander

T. chamaedrys 'Variegatum', variegated germander
  Cream and green leaves that may revert to green.

T. fruticans, tree germander
  Larger leaf with blue to lilac flowers, grows to 4 feet.

Type: Perennial (subshrub).

Origin: Europe, Mediterranean.

Use: Medicinal.

Texture: Fine.

Form: Upright mound, dense.

Fragrance: None.

Foliage: Glossy dark green.

Flower: Rosy lavender; July to September.

Height: 1 to 1½ feet, up to 2 feet.

Width: 2 feet.

Teucrium chamaedrys, **continued**

Spacing: 1½ to 2½ feet.

Starting size: 1- to 2-gallon containers.

Availability: Common; varieties at specialty nurseries.

Zone: 5 to 9.

Soil and moisture: *Teucrium* prefers a moderately moist, moderately fertile, light, well-drained soil. Optimum pH is 6.3. Accepts lower fertility and drier soil.

Light and temperature: Prefers full sun, accepts partial shade. Plants will decline in shade. Tolerates high heat.

Planting and maintenance: Choose at least a one-gallon starting size since young plants are slow to reach specimen size. This is particularly important when germander is used to define the edge of a planting bed. Pinch to encourage fullness. Do not plant too deeply; keep soil line at the same level it was in the container. Although usually problem free, germander may get mildew, rust, or mites. Thin plants during hot, humid weather to improve air circulation within the dense branching and prevent fungus attacks. Mulch in winter to safeguard against cold injury. Propagate by cuttings, layering, or division in spring.

Ornamental value: Germander is a classic edging plant in herb gardens. Its natural form creates a low, shrubby, neat mound for an informal edge. The plant responds very well to close clipping for formal situations. Clipped or natural, the effect is a tidy, orderly edge. Lovely rosy lavender blossoms form on terminal stems. The leaves are a pretty, glossy green with scalloped edges. Performs well in many planting situations: massed in borders, raised beds, containers, streetscape plantings, and knot gardens. Combines easily with most herbs.

Thymus species
Thyme

Family: Labiatae.
Varieties:

Upright and semiupright forms:

Thymus × *citriodorus*, lemon thyme
   Lemon-scented leaves. Pink flowers.

T. × *citriodorus* 'Aureus', golden lemon
thyme
   Variegated leaves have golden edges.

T. nitidus, tiny-leaf thyme
   Grows to 5 inches.

T. pulegioides, oregano-scented thyme
   Spreading, grows 4 to 10 inches.

T. vulgaris, common upright thyme
   Erect. Gray-green leaves. Lavender
   flowers. Grows 8 to 15 inches.

T. vulgaris 'Argenteus', silver thyme
   Silver-edged leaves. Spreading,
   grows to 12 inches.

T. vulgaris 'Broad-leaf', English thyme
   Upright, grows to 12 inches.

T. vulgaris 'Narrow-leaf', French thyme
   Grows to 15 inches.

Creeping forms:

T. herba-barona, caraway thyme
   Caraway scent. Rose-purple
   flowers. Grows 2 to 5 inches.

T. praecox arcticus, mother-of-thyme or
creeping thyme
   Dark green leaves. Rose flowers.
   Strong scent. Grows 6 to 8 inches.

T. praecox arcticus 'Albus', white-
flowering creeping thyme
   Bright green leaves. White flowers.
   Grows to 2 inches.

Thymus vulgaris
Common upright
thyme

Thymus pseudolanuginosus
Woolly thyme

Thymus species, continued

T. praecox arcticus 'Coccineus', red-
flowering creeping thyme
  Prolific red flowers. Dark green
  mat-forming plants.
T. pseudolanuginosus, woolly thyme
  Gray leaves. Rose flowers. Ground-
  matting form.
Type: Perennial.
Origin: Europe, Asia, Mediterranean.
Use: Culinary, medicinal, fragrance.
Texture: Very fine.
Form: Upright, semiupright, creep-
ing, or matting.
Fragrance: Very aromatic leaves.

Foliage: Green, gray-green; varie-
gated varieties are gold and green or
silver and green.
Flower: Red, lavender, rose, pink, or
white; June to July.
Height: Uprights grow 6 to 18
inches; creepers, 2 to 8 inches.
Width: 24 inches or more.
Spacing: 8 to 18 inches.
Starting size: 4-inch to 1-gallon
containers.
Availability: Common; varieties at
specialty nurseries.
Zone: 5 to 9.

Soil and moisture: Thyme requires a moderately moist to drier, light, well-
drained soil. Accepts low fertility but prefers moderate fertility. Optimum pH is
6.3, but tolerates wider range. Intolerant of wet, heavy, compacted soils. Tolerates short-term droughts.

Light and temperature: Prefers full sun, accepts partial shade quite well. Plants
rapidly decline in shade, but do tolerate shade for short periods. Heat tolerant.

Planting and maintenance: Thymes thrive in dry, rocky areas. Prevent tightly
matted clumps of the creepers from getting woody or rotting by removing plugs
from the center of the plant each spring. Common upright thyme may need
some pinching and clipping to maintain fullness. Clipped formal edges of thyme
require pruning every seven to ten days. Protect upright varieties against winter
injury by using antidesiccant spray on the woody stems. Plants get root rot if
grown in wet soil. Propagate by layering, cuttings, or division.

Ornamental value: Upright thymes are excellent edging plants, clipped tightly
for formal gardens or lightly for informal plantings. They are appropriate plants
for a small knot garden. Creeping thymes are very decorative ground covers and
excellent plants for pavement or wall-crevice plantings. When used to spill
over a hard edge, they soften the effect of a retaining wall, raised bed, masonry
edge, container, or window box. They tolerate light pedestrian traffic. Traditionally, thyme has been used along garden walkways where its fragrance would
be released from the leaves when stepped on.

A POTPOURRI OF OTHER HERBS

The herbs in this list are also good possibilities for your plant palette. Each has at least one outstanding characteristic that makes it worthy of consideration in herb gardens.

Acanthus mollis • *artist's acanthus*

Medicinal plant of ancient Greece. The large leaf is used in the classical architectural decoration of the Corinthian column. Grows 2 to 3 feet. Tender perennial in the North; Zone 8. Prefers sun. Showy white flower spike with lilac and rose colorings. Interesting container plant.

Aloe vera (barbadensis) • *aloe*

Medicinal, first aid for burns; cosmetic. Grows 2 to 3 feet. Tender plant in the North; Zone 10. Sun to partial shade. Good small container plant.

Aloysia triphylla • *lemon verbena*

Intensely lemon-scented leaves. Grows to 2 feet. Tender perennial in the North; Zone 8. Prefers sun. Container plant. Becomes woody with age.

Amomum cardamomum • *false cardamom*

Aromatic, fragrance of true cardamom. Grows 2 to 3 feet or more. Zone 10, tender in the North. Sun to partial shade. Long, narrow, lance-shaped leaves. Ginger family; native to East Indies. Good container plant. (The culinary cardamom is *Elettaria cardamomum*. It is a tender plant, requiring a greenhouse environment in northern areas of the country during winter months. Prefers partial shade; if grown in too much shade, it will not flower or set seed.)

Angelica archangelica • *angelica*

Fragrance. Medicinal; stems may be candied. Grows to 5 feet when in flower. Zone 4. Tender biennial in North. Needs moderate moisture and partial shade. Stately white flower spike becomes focus of garden when in bloom.

Anthriscus cerefolium • *sweet chervil*

Culinary, a favorite in French cooking. Grows 1 to 2 feet. Tender annual in North. Requires moist soil, cool temperature, and partial shade. Delicate, finely cut leaves with white umbel flowers. Will reseed often. Intolerant of heat and poor soils.

Borago officinalis • *borage*

Confectionery: flowers can be candied. Culinary: cucumber-flavored leaves can be used in salads, cool drinks, or for pickling. Medicinal: laxative. Grows 1 to 2 feet. Annual. Requires slightly moist soil, sun to partial shade, and cool temperatures. Hairy leaves collect dust. Pretty star-shaped ¾-inch flowers in blue, purple, and white.

Calamintha nepeta • *calamint*

Aromatic, leaves used in sachets; medicinal. Grows 1 to 2 feet. Evergreen in warm climates; Zone 6. Requires sun to partial shade and moderate moisture. Attractive low-growing perennial mint; lavender flowers.

Calendula officinalis • *pot marigold*

Edible flowers and tender leaves; can be used in salads; subject in Shakespearean literature; medicinal; dye plant yielding yellow color. Grows to 2 feet. Tender annual in North. Cheerful yellow, gold, and orange flowers bloom in early spring. Prefers sun to partial shade, and cool temperatures; will not tolerate intense heat.

Capsicum annuum • *cayenne or chili pepper*

Edible fruits, hot peppers; medicinal. Grows 4 to 6 feet. Annual in North. Requires sun. Colorful red and orange fruits, highly ornamental. Container or bedding plant. Many varieties and cultivars available. Native to tropical America.

Capsicum frutescens • *Tabasco pepper*

Edible fruits, hot peppers. Grows 3 to 5 feet. Annual in North. Requires sun. Very colorful fruits. Novelty for container or beds. Native to tropical America.

Carum carvi • caraway

Culinary, seeds used for flavoring; oils used in perfumes; medicinal. Grows to 2 feet. Zones 3 to 9. Hardy perennial or biennial. Requires sun and dry soil. Small white flowers. Foliage often becomes unsightly after blooming.

Chrysanthemum balsamita • costmary or alecost

Culinary, aromatic, medicinal as an astringent or antiseptic. Minty, balsam fragrance. Leaf adds refreshing taste to iced drinks. Grows 1 to 1½ feet. Zone 4. Perennial. If grown in full sun, plants produce buttonlike yellow flowers in loose clusters at top of stem. Gray-green leaves. Propagate by division; produces few seeds.

Coriandrum sativum • coriander
(also called cilantro and Chinese parsley)

Culinary, entire plant used for flavoring extensively in Chinese and Indian cooking; strongly aromatic. Grows to 3 feet. Annual. Easy to grow. Requires sun to partial shade. Flowers are small, white or mauve umbels. Fast to set seed. Native to Eurasia.

Crocus sativus • saffron crocus

The source of true saffron. The yellow spice is made from the plant's stigmas; at only three per plant, 100,000 plants may be required to produce one pound— hence the high price. Grows 3 to 6 inches. Zone 6. Corm. Fall bloomer; fragrant lilac or white varieties. Requires sun or part shade.

Cymbopogon citratus • lemon grass

Perfumes, flavoring, medicinal. Strongly lemon-scented foliage. Long, lance-shaped leaves grow to 3 feet long, ½-inch wide. Plant forms dense clump and grows to 6 feet. Prefers sun. Tender perennial. Performs well in containers. Propagate by division. Native to southern India and Ceylon; widely cultivated in tropics.

Dianthus caryophyllus • *clove carnation*

Fragrance plant; clove-scented leaves used in sachets, potpourris, and cosmetics. Beverage flavoring. Grows 1 to 3 feet. Zones 8 or 9. Many colors. Accepts sun or partial shade. Gray-blue foliage. Varieties include *Dianthus plumarius* 'Garden Pinks', which makes an excellent small, scented, edge plant for herb gardens. Varieties of *D. plumarius* are grown frequently in northern gardens. Blue-green foliage. Flowers are red, pink, white, or salmon.

Fragaria alpina • *alpine strawberry*

Edible, sweet fruits. Grows 8 to 10 inches. Zones 5 to 6. Accepts sun to partial shade. Everbearing, runnerless. Lovely small plant for edges, containers, window boxes, or strawberry jars.

Glycyrrhiza glabra • *licorice*

Medicinal, used as cough syrup. Flavoring for confections. Used to scent soap. Grows 2 to 3 feet. Tender perennial in North; Zone 7. Accepts sun to partial shade and requires rich, moist soil.

Helianthus annuus • *sunflower*

Dye plant, yellow flowers. Attracts wildlife. Introduced to the United States in the seventeenth century from its native Mexico. Grows 3 to 12 feet. Tender annual. Requires sun. A surprise in a city garden. Varieties available.

Helichrysum angustifolium • *curry plant*

Aromatic, curry-scented leaves. (This is not the familiar curry spice; curry is actually a blend of spices.) Grows 1 to 3 feet. Tender perennial in North; Zone 8 or 9. Accepts sun or partial shade and moderately moist to dry soil. Excellent edging plant with small yellow flowers, ornamental gray foliage, and dense, mounding form—looks very herby. Base of plant becomes woody and loses foliage as it becomes older.

Heliotropium arborescens • heliotrope

Aromatic plant; oil used in perfumes. Grows 3 to 5 feet. Tender perennial in North; Zone 10. Accepts sun to partial shade. Intensely sweet, vanilla-scented flowers in blue, purple, or white. Native to tropics.

Levisticum officinale • lovage

Culinary: celery-flavored leaves used to flavor leek or potato cream soups. Grows 3 to 6 feet. Long-lived perennial; Zone 6. Prefers partial shade, cool temperatures, and moderate moisture. Accepts sun but dislikes intensely hot sun. Handsome back-border plant. Light green foliage provides contrast to darker green herbs. White flowers.

Marrubium vulgare • horehound

Aromatic, medicinal, used as cough medicine. Leaves and stems used to flavor candy. Grows 2 to 3 feet. Perennial. Zone 3. Accepts partial shade or sun and dry soil. Downy, gray leaves and white flowers. Contrast plant.

Myrtus communis • sweet myrtle

Fragrance. Grows 3 to 5 feet in containers. Tender subshrub in North; evergreen in Zones 8 and 9, where it can grow to 10 feet. Prefers sun. Must be overwintered in greenhouse or holding house with temperatures kept above freezing. Excellent in containers; a classic topiary herb. Traditional herb garden plant, grown by ancient Romans and Greeks.

Perilla frutescens • 'Atropurpurea', purple perilla

Flavoring plant used in Orient, leaves used to flavor tofu and to garnish tempura. Tender sprouts used as a spice for fish dishes. Grows 1½ to 3 feet. Tender annual, related to common coleus. Accepts sun or part shade and moist or dry soil. Very ornamental dark, reddish purple foliage with a bronze patina. Great contrast plant, looks beautiful with blue-green or silver-gray herbs. Native to southern China, Taiwan, and Japan. Varieties include *P. crispum* 'Atropurpurea', curled purple perilla, which has distinctive ruffled leaves.

Pimpinella anisum • *anise*

Medicinal, used in ancient Greece and Egypt. Flowers used to flavor some vermouths. Seeds and leaves used in medicines, foods, and soaps. Essential oils valuable to perfumes. Grows to 2 feet. Tender annual. Requires sun. Sprawling plant with deeply notched aromatic leaves and whitish yellow flowers. Not ornamental.

Rumex scutatus • *French sorrel*

Culinary, important in French cuisine. Sorrel soup uses its sour-lemon leaves. Not ornamental. Grows 1 to 2 feet. Zone 3. Low-growing perennial weed. Accepts sun to partial shade. Leaves become bitter with age.

Satureja hortensis • *summer savory*

Culinary, typically used to flavor beans and aid digestion. Aromatic foliage. Mint family. Grows to 18 inches. Tender annual. Prefers sun to partial shade. Plants topple over and look attractive spilling from a container. Prone to fungal problems in humid, wet climates. Small flowers are pinkish purple. Works well in window boxes, containers, and front borders.

Satureja montana • *winter savory*

Medicinal and culinary. Tender tips used to flavor crab dishes. Grows 8 to 15 inches. Hardy perennial; Zones 5 to 10. Accepts sun to partial shade. Shrubby plant, similar to *S. hortensis* in appearance. Susceptible to fungal problems. Requires frequent pruning to maintain neat appearance. Varieties include *S. montana pygmaea*, a dwarf form (grows 3 to 4 inches) that makes a nice edging plant.

Valeriana officinalis • *valerian*

Medicinal. Fragrance. Grows 3 to 4 feet. Zone 3. Perennial. Requires moderately moist soil and partial shade. Aroma is similar to heliotrope; often called garden heliotrope. Weedy habit, untidy. Fragrant white, pink, and lavender flowers form a flat head.

FLOWER GARDEN HERBALS

These plants are popular perennial and annual flowers that also have herbal uses.

Achillea millefolium — Yarrow or milfoil

Ajuga reptans and varieties — Carpet bugle

Anchusa officinalis — Alkanet

Anemone pulsatilla — Pasque flower

Anthemis tinctoria — Golden marguerite

Baptisia australis — Blue false indigo

Belamcanda chinensis — Blackberry lily

Calonyction aculeatum — Moonflower

Catharanthus roseus — Madagascar periwinkle

Centaurea cyanus — Bachelor's button

Centaurea montana — Montana cornflower

Centranthus ruber — Red valerian

Cheiranthus cheiri — Wallflower

Colchicum autumnale — Autumn crocus

Colchicum autumnale 'Album' — White-flowering autumn crocus

Chrysanthemum coccineum — Pyrethrum daisy

Dianthus plumarius — Garden pinks

Digitalis purpurea — Foxglove

Echinacea purpurea — Purple coneflower

Epimedium grandiflorum — Bishop's hat

Gypsophila paniculata — Baby's breath

Helleborus spp. — Christmas and Lenten rose hellebores

Hemerocallis minor — Dwarf yellow daylily

Iris kaempferi — Japanese iris

Lilium auratum — Goldband lily

Lilium candidum — Madonna lily

Linum perenne — Perennial flax

Lunaria annua — Dollar plant

Nicotiana 'Sweet-scent' — Flowering tobacco

Nigella damascena — Love-in-a-mist

Papaver orientale — Oriental poppy

Perovskia atriplicifolia — Russian sage

Platycodon grandiflorus — Balloon flower

Platycodon grandiflorus 'Album' — White-flowering balloon flower

Polianthes tuberosa — Tuberose

Pulmonaria officinalis — Lungwort

Pulmonaria officinalis 'Miss Jekyll' — White-flowering lungwort

Rosa spp. — Roses

Tagetes patula — French marigold

Tagetes tenuifolia — Signet marigold

Tropaeolum majus — Nasturtium

HERBAL TREES, SHRUBS, VINES, GROUND COVERS, AND WILDFLOWERS

To maintain the herbal theme of your garden, select trees, shrubs, vines, and ground covers that have herbal uses and aromatic qualities. Since the herbaceous and shrubby annual, biennial, and perennial herbs are relatively small, other plant types are instrumental for design functions that the smaller herbs cannot always achieve. Refer to Design for ideas on using trees, shrubs, vines, and ground covers.

Many popular trees and shrubs may be considered herbs if we define an herb as any plant with fragrance, culinary, household, medicinal, or economic use. Parts of little-leaf linden (*Tilia cordata*), for example, have medicinal use as a tonic to reduce fevers. Serviceberry or shadblow (*Amelanchier arborea*) can be considered an herbal tree, since it has edible fruit. Star magnolia (*Magnolia stellata*) may be deemed an herb because of its fragrance. Parts of the evergreen shrub inkberry (*Ilex glabra*) can be used as a tea or an ink substitute.

Even plants that have no herbal properties may be appropriate for the herbal theme if they are associated with herb gardens by tradition. Especially useful are the evergreens, which have long been used as the winter backbones of herbal plantings.

Vines, such as sweet autumn clematis (*Clematis paniculata*) and southern Carolina jessamine (*Gelsemium sempervirens*), and climbing roses are appropriate, too, since they are aromatic and make lovely companions to herb gardens. Traditional herbal ground covers include the commonly used English ivy (*Hedera helix*) and periwinkle (*Vinca minor*).

In this list, some herbs are referred to as native or naturalized. Native plants are indigenous to a particular region, but naturalized plants were at one time introduced. Many naturalized plants are now well established with indigenous plants and their associated biological communities.

What follows is a list of trees, shrubs, vines, ground covers, and wildflowers that have herbal properties.

Trees

Acer platanoides • Norway maple

Medicinal, as a poultice. Grows 40 to 90 feet. Zones 3 to 7. Wide canopy. Many cultivars. Native to Europe.

Acer pseudoplatanus • sycamore maple

Medicinal, as a tonic and for inflammations. Grows to 90 feet. Zones 4 to 7. Varieties available. Native to Europe and western Asia.

Acer rubrum • red maple

Medicinal, for eye ailments and skin sores. Grows 90 to 120 feet. Zone 3. Requires sun to partial shade. Good wetland tree; grows in many different soils. Ornamental; reddish flowers and small fruits in spring, brilliant fall foliage. Fast growing, weak wood. Many fine varieties. Native throughout North America.

Acer saccharum • sugar maple

Medicinal, as a tonic and poultice; maple syrup. Grows to 120 feet. Zone 3. Beautiful yellow, orange, or scarlet fall color. Wood is stronger than red maple, but this maple is less tolerant of city conditions than Norway maple. Widely native to eastern North America.

Alnus glutinosa • European alder

Wood. Grows to 75 feet. Zones 3 to 7. Native to Europe and Siberia.

Amelanchier arborea • serviceberry or shadblow

Edible fruits. Grows 20 to 60 feet. Zones 3 to 7. Prefers partial sun to shade. Good in moist areas, grows in a wide range of conditions. Small, pretty white flowers in early spring. Native to eastern United States.

Betula lenta • *sweet birch*

Aromatic bark; medicinal; wood; oil; tea. Grows 50 to 75 feet. Zone 3. Native to eastern United States.

Betula nigra • *river birch*

Tea from twigs. Grows to 90 feet. Native to eastern United States.

Broussonetia papyrifera • *paper mulberry*

Paper. Grows to 48 feet. Zone 6. Grows in poor soils; not ornamental. Native to China and Japan. Naturalized in United States.

Carpinus betulus • *European hornbeam*

Wood. Grows 35 to 60 feet. Zone 5. Traditional herb garden tree; responds to shearing and pleaching. Native to Europe.

Carpinus caroliniana • *American hornbeam*

Wood. Grows to 36 feet. Zones 2 to 7. Native to eastern United States.

Carya ovata • *shagbark hickory*

Economic; edible nut. Grows 90 to 120 feet. Zone 4. Hard to transplant. Plant in large areas. Native to eastern United States. Prefers dry soil.

Celtis laevigata • *sugar hackberry*

Wood. Grows to 90 feet. Zone 5. Native to south–central and southeastern United States. Prefers moist soil.

Cercis canadensis • *eastern redbud*

Edible flowers have an acidic taste. French-Canadian settlers used plant for pickle making and in salads. Grows 15 to 40 feet. Zone 4. Grows in shade, partial shade, or sun. Pinkish purple flowers in spring. Native to eastern United States. Prefers woodlands.

Chionanthus virginicus • *fringe tree*

Medicinal, for skin inflammations. Grows to 30 feet. Zone 4. Lovely, fragrant, drooping white flower clusters. Very late to leaf out in spring. Sensitive to high heat. Can grow in sun or shade, prefers moist soil. Native from New Jersey to Florida.

Cornus florida • *flowering dogwood*

Medicinal, as a quinine substitute. Grows to 40 feet. Zone 4. Sensitive to very bright light and soil compaction. Serious blight in Northeast in past decade. Susceptible to borers. Prefers partial shade, accepts sun. Prefers moist, accepts drier soil. Varieties include pink, white, and red flowers. Native to eastern United States.

Cotinus obovatus • *American smoketree*

Wood used in dye. Grows to 30 feet. Zone 5. Prefers sun, but grows in partial shade. Native from Tennessee to Alabama.

Crataegus phaenopyrum • *Washington hawthorn*

Medicinal, for kidney and heart disease. Grows to 30 feet. Zones 4 to 8. Not allowed as a street tree in some cities because of its thorns, which grow 1 to 3 inches. Many varieties. Sensitive to salts. Native to southeastern United States.

Cydonia sinensis • *quince tree*

Edible fruit; fragrance. Grows to 24 feet. Zone 6. Native to China.

Diospyros virginiana • *persimmon*

Edible fruit, becomes sweet after frost; pudding flavoring; wood. Grows 50 to 75 feet. Zones 4 to 9. Native to eastern and southeastern United States. Dry soil.

Franklinia alatamaha • *franklinia*

Fragrance. Grows 20 to 30 feet. Zones 5 to 9. Prefers partial shade but accepts sun. Found in the wilds of Georgia in 1790s; not naturalized since that time.

Fraxinus americana • *white ash*

Medicinal, as a tonic for fevers; wood. Grows to 120 feet. Zones 3 to 9. Prefers sun. Grows in a wide range of soil conditions. Beautiful yellow foliage in fall. Native to eastern United States.

Fraxinus excelsior • *European ash*

Medicinal, as a laxative. Wood. Grows to 120 feet. Zones 3 to 7. Prefers sun. Grows in a wide range of soil conditions. Native to Europe and Asia Minor.

Ginkgo biloba • *ginkgo or maidenhair tree*

Medicinal, for stomach disorders and as a sedative; seed is eaten in Japan. Grows 35 to 80 feet. Zones 3 to 9. Prefers sun, accepts partial shade. Tolerates compacted soil and many soil conditions. Fleshy seeds of female trees are malodorous; therefore, choose male plants. Unique branching structure. Native to eastern China.

Gleditsia triacanthos • *common honey locust*

Edible pod; pod is also used as an anesthetic. Grows to 135 feet but usually smaller. Zones 4 to 9. Prefers sun. Grows in a wide range of soil conditions. Choose thornless cultivars for street plantings and other areas where thorns are undesirable. Native to central United States.

Gymnocladus dioica • *Kentucky coffee tree*

Coffee substitute; tea. Grows 60 to 90 feet. Zones 3 to 8. Native to central United States.

Halesia carolina • *Carolina silver bell*

Dye. Grows to 30 feet. Zones 5 to 8. Prefers partial shade or sun. Attractive white flowers in spring. Native from West Virginia to Florida and Texas.

Ilex opaca • *American holly*

Medicinal; coffee substitute, flavoring. Grows to 45 feet. Zones 5 to 9. Evergreen. Accepts sun to shade. Many varieties. Native to eastern United States. Prefers moist soil but grows well in dry or sandy sites.

Juniperus communis • *common juniper*

Medicinal; flavoring. Grows 5 to 15 feet. Zones 2 to 7. Evergreen. Many varieties. Native to Europe and northeastern Asia; naturalized in northern North America.

Juniperus virginiana • *eastern red cedar*

Dye plant; medicinal, as a stimulant. Grows 40 to 90 feet. Zones 2 to 9. Evergreen. Prefers sun and dry soils, especially limestone. Native to eastern half of the United States.

Koelreuteria paniculata • *golden rain tree*

Medicinal flowers. Grows to 30 feet. Zones 4 to 9. Prefers sun. Grows in wide range of soil conditions. Ornamental yellow flowers in summer. Umbrellalike canopy. Native to China, Korea, and Japan.

Liquidambar styraciflua • *American sweetgum*

Furniture; pleasant tasting twigs. Grows 60 to 120 feet. Zones 5 to 9. Prefers sun or partial shade and moist soil. Ornamental shade tree. Rich burgundy-red foliage in fall. Can be invasive in the South. Native to eastern United States.

Liriodendron tulipifera • *tulip tree or yellow poplar*

Stimulant; wood. Grows 90 to 150 feet. Zones 4 to 9. Prefers sun or partial shade and rich soil. Green and yellow flowers with orange marks form at top of canopy. Native to eastern United States.

Maclura pomifera • *osage orange*

Dye from roots; medicinal, as an eyewash. Native Americans used wood for bows. Grows 20 to 60 feet. Zones 4 to 9. Large fruits litter the ground. Native to south-central United States.

Magnolia grandiflora • *southern magnolia*

Medicinal, as a laxative; fragrance. Grows 60 to 80 feet. Zones 6 to 9. Evergreen. Prefers sun to partial shade. Not suitable for polluted areas; sensitive to sulfur dioxide and smoke. Native to southeastern United States.

Magnolia stellata • *star magnolia*

Fragrance. Grows 15 to 20 feet. Zones 5 to 8. Prefers sun or partial shade. Not for highly polluted areas. Lovely white flowers in early spring. Native to Japan.

Magnolia virginiana • *sweet bay magnolia*

Aromatic; medicinal, as a stimulant. Grows 20 to 30 feet or higher. Zones 5 to 9. Evergreen to semievergreen in southern areas, deciduous in colder zones. Prefers partial shade and moist soil. Native to coastal eastern United States.

Malus coronaria • *wild sweet crab*

Fragrant. Grows to 20 feet. Zone 4. Prefers sun. Many varieties. Native from Pennsylvania to Illinois, south to Tennessee, North Carolina, and Missouri.

Mespilus germanica • *medlar*

Edible fruit. Grows to 15 feet. Zone 5. Crooked tree, allied to hawthorn. Thorny older branches. Native to Europe.

Nyssa sylvatica • *black tupelo or black gum*

Honey; furniture. Grows 50 to 90 feet. Zones 4 to 9. Prefers sun or partial shade. Prefers moist soil but tolerates a wide range of soil conditions. Taproot makes this tree hard to transplant. Brilliant autumn foliage. Native to eastern United States.

Ostrya virginiana • *American hop hornbeam*

Medicinal, as a tonic for fevers. Grows 25 to 60 feet. Zones 4 to 9. Slow growing. Prefers rich soil. Native from Ontario to Texas and eastern United States.

Oxydendrum arboreum • *sourwood or lily-of-the-valley tree*

Medicinal, as a tonic and poultice for fever. Grows 25 to 60 feet. Zones 4 to 9. Prefers partial shade and moderately moist soil. Ornamental, pendulous cream flowers resemble the wildflower. Excellent red to purple foliage in the fall. Grows in wet or dry soil. Native to eastern and southeastern United States.

Paulownia tomentosa • *empress tree*

Wood. Grows 45 to 55 feet, occasionally to 100. Zone 5. Purple drooping flowers. Native to central China, naturalized in eastern United States.

Prunus serotina • *black cherry*

Beverage; edible fruits; furniture. Grows to 90 feet. Zone 3. Ornamental. Native to eastern and central North America.

Quercus alba • *white oak*

Wood. Grows 90 to 150 feet. Zones 3 to 9. Accepts rich or dry soil. Native to eastern United States.

Quercus borealis • *red oak*

Wood. Grows to 75 feet. Zones 3 to 8. Native to northeastern and central North America.

Quercus coccinea • scarlet oak

Wood. Grows to 75 feet. Zone 4. Native to eastern and central United States.

Quercus palustris • pin oak

Wood, used to make shingles. Grows 75 to 100 feet. Zone 4. Prefers moist sites but grows in a wide range of soil conditions. Drooping lower branches. Native to central United States.

Quercus phellos • willow oak

Wood. Grows to 50 feet. Zones 5 to 9. Native to eastern seaboard and Gulf states.

Sassafras albidum • sassafras

Aromatic stems; medicinal, for bronchitis; tea; dye plant. Grows 30 to 60 feet. Zones 4 to 8. Native to eastern and northeastern United States.

Sophora japonica • Japanese pagoda tree

Medicinal, with astringent properties. Grows 50 to 75 feet. Zones 4 to 8. Prefers sun or partial shade. Cultivars available. Native to the Far East.

Thuja occidentalis • American arborvitae

Medicinal, for fevers and rheumatism. Grows 30 to 80 feet. Zones 2 to 7. Evergreen. Accepts sun or shade. Prefers moist sites. Limited use in urban areas; sensitive to ethylene and salts. Native to eastern North America.

Tilia americana • basswood

Medicinal, as a poultice for fever; tea; rope. Grows 80 to 120 feet. Zones 2 to 8. Prefers rich soil. Plant in large areas. Native to eastern United States.

Tilia cordata • *little-leaf linden*

Wood, bark fiber, tobacco; medicinal, as a tea from flowers for fever. Slowly grows 60 to 90 feet. Zones 3 to 7. Very handsome tree. Native to Europe.

Ulmus rubra • *slippery elm*

Medicinal, for sore throats; wood. Grows to 60 feet. Zone 4. Coarse tree, not ornamental. Native from southeastern Canada to Florida and Texas.

Umbellularia californica • *California laurel*

Industry, wood and insecticide; flavoring for soups; medicinal. Grows to 75 feet. Zone 7. Evergreen. Prefers moist soil. Native from California to Oregon.

Shrubs

Acanthopanax sieboldianus • *five-leaf aralia*

Aromatic foliage. Grows to 9 feet. Zone 4. Semievergreen. Native to Japan.

Aesculus parviflora • *bottlebrush buckeye*

Medicinal. Grows 8 to 12 feet. Zone 4. Interesting white flowers in midsummer. Plant as specimen, massed with woods in background. Mounding habit. Native from South Carolina to Alabama.

Amelanchier stolonifera • *running serviceberry*

Edible fruits. Grows 4 to 6 feet. Zone 4. Accepts sun to shade. Native from Newfoundland to Virginia.

Aralia spinosa • *devil's walking stick*

Medicinal, as a blood purifier. Grows to 24 feet. Zones 5 to 9. Accepts sun or partial shade. Good in rich or wet soil. Native to southeastern United States.

Arctostaphylos uva-ursi • *bearberry or kinnikinnick*

Economic plant; tanning; tobacco; medicinal, as a diuretic. Grows 6 inches to 1 foot tall, 4 to 8 feet wide. Zones 2 to 6. Evergreen ground cover, semievergreen in very cold areas. Prefers sun or partial shade. Very tolerant of poor, dry soils and hot sun. Valued ornamental. Foliage turns bronze in autumn. Scarlet berries. Native to North America and Eurasia; widespread distribution and habitats.

Aronia arbutifolia • *red chokecherry*

Edible fruits. Grows to 9 feet. Zone 4. Accepts sun or shade. Brilliant foliage in fall. Native to eastern United States.

Berberis thunbergii • *Japanese barberry*

Edible fruits. Grows 1 to 7 feet, depending on variety. Zone 4. Prefers sun or partial shade. Native to Japan.

Buxus microphylla • *little leaf boxwood*

Medicinal, for rheumatism. Grows 3 to 4 feet around. Zone 6. Evergreen. Traditional herb garden plant. Many varieties, some hardier. Foliage may turn yellowish bronze if grown in cold, windy spots. Native to Japan.

Buxus sempervirens • *common boxwood*

Medicinal, as a purgative and vermifuge. Wood. Grows 15 to 30 feet. Zones 5 to 9, depending on cultivar. Evergreen. Cultivars include 'Suffruticosa', edging or English boxwood; dense, compact form, with smaller, rounded leaves; less hardy. Many cultivars available in nurseries. Traditional herb garden plant. Common boxwood is native to Eurasia and northern Africa.

Callicarpa americana • *American beautyberry*

Medicinal; attracts birds. Grows to 6 feet. Zone 7. Bright purple berries. Native from Maryland to Texas and Oklahoma; southern plant.

Calycanthus floridus • *Carolina allspice*

Aromatic; sedative. Grows to 9 feet. Zone 4. Prefers partial shade to shade. Native to southeastern United States.

Cassia marilandica • *wild senna*

Dye plant; medicinal, as a poultice, cathartic, purgative, and laxative. Grows to 3 feet. Hardy to Zone 2 or 3. Colorful plant; yellow, pealike flowers. Semiwoody. Native to eastern United States.

Cephalanthus occidentalis • *buttonbush*

Medicinal, used by Native Americans. Grows to 15 feet. Zone 4. Prefers wet or moist soil. Native to eastern and western North America.

Chimonanthus praecox • *wintersweet*

Fragrance. Grows to 9 feet. Zone 7. Winter blooming. Prefers light shade. Native to China.

Clethra alnifolia • *summersweet*

Honey; fragrance. Grows to 9 feet. Zone 3. Prefers sun or partial shade and moist areas. Native to eastern United States.

Comptonia peregrina • *sweet fern*

Aromatic foliage; medicinal, for colic. Grows 1 to 3 feet. Zone 2. Prefers sun or partial shade. Grows in dry open areas and steep rocky slopes. Native from Nova Scotia to North Carolina, Indiana, and Michigan.

Cornus amomum • *silky dogwood*

Medicinal, as a stimulant. Grows to 9 feet. Zone 5. Prefers sun or partial shade. Native to eastern United States.

Cornus mas • cornelian cherry

Edible fruit; dye plant. Grows to 24 feet. Zone 4. Prefers sun or partial shade. Native to central and southern Europe and western Asia.

Cornus sericea (stolonifera) • red osier

Native Americans used roots for baskets and tobacco. Grows to 7 feet. Zone 2. Prefers sun or partial shade and moist soil. Good for controlling erosion by water edges. Native to eastern United States.

Cytisus scoparius • Scotch broom

Dye plant. Grows 3 to 7 feet. Zone 5. Prefers sun. Yellow flowers. Introduced from Europe; naturalized sporadically in North America.

Elaeagnus angustifolia • Russian olive

Edible fruit; fragrance. Grows 12 to 20 feet. Zones 2 to 7. Native to southern Europe and western and central Asia.

Euonymus atropurpurea • eastern wahoo

Once medicinal, as liver treatment and a purgative. Grows 6 to 24 feet. Zones 4 to 9. Crimson fruits. Grows in moist to dry soil. Native to eastern United States.

Euonymus europaea • European spindle tree

Medicinal, as a laxative. Grows to 21 feet. Zones 3 to 7. Attracts birds. Native to Europe and western Asia; naturalized slightly in United States.

Fothergilla gardenii • witch alder

Fragrance. Grows to 3 feet. Zones 5 to 8. Excellent autumn foliage, ranging from orange to yellow to scarlet. Native from Virginia to Georgia.

Hamamelis virginiana • *witch hazel*

Medicinal, as an astringent and sedative. Grows 15 to 25 feet. Zones 3 to 8. Prefers sun or shade. Native to eastern and central United States.

Ilex crenata • *Japanese holly*

Traditional edging or hedging for herb growers. Varieties grow 9 inches to 18 feet. Zones 5 to 8. Evergreen. Numerous varieties available. Native to Japan.

Ilex glabra • *inkberry*

Ink substitute; tea. Grows 6 to 9 feet; can be maintained at 3 feet. Zones 3 or 4. Evergreen. Supple foliage. Native to eastern United States and Canada.

Ilex verticillata • *winterberry*

Medicinal, as an astringent and tonic. Grows 6 to 10 feet. Zones 3 to 9. Evergreen. Native to eastern United States.

Ilex vomitoria • *yaupon holly*

Medicinal, as an emetic and laxative. Grows 15 to 25 feet or more. Zones 7 to 10. Southern evergreen; large shrub or small tree. Native to southeastern United States.

Itea virginica • *Virginia sweetspire*

Fragrance. Grows 3 to 9 feet. Zone 5. Requires moist soil. Native to southeastern United States.

Juniperus communis • *common juniper*

Medicinal, as a diuretic and stimulant; oil. Varieties grow 5 to 15 feet. Zones 2 to 7. Evergreen. Many varieties. Native to northern America and throughout the world.

Kalmia latifolia • *mountain laurel*

Medicinal, for infections and rheumatism. Grows 3 to 10 feet. Zones 4 to 9. Prefers shade and well-drained, rocky or sandy soil. Beautiful flowers, evergreen foliage. Native to eastern United States.

Ledum groenlandicum • *Labrador tea*

Leaves used as tea during the Revolutionary War; medicinal, for dysentery. Grows to 3 feet. Zones 2 to 5. Grows in moist soil. Native to northeastern North America.

Ligustrum vulgare • *common privet*

Medicinal, as an astringent. Grows 5 to 15 feet; can be maintained at 3 feet. Zones 4 to 7; evergreen primarily in cold areas. Native to Europe and northern Africa, naturalized in some areas of United States.

Lindera benzoin • *spicebush*

Aromatic (all plant parts are fragrant); medicinal, for circulation and fevers. Grows 6 to 15 feet. Zones 4 to 9. Prefers partial shade and rich, moist soil. Native to eastern United States.

Mahonia aquifolium • *Oregon holly grape*

Edible fruit; dye plant. Grows 1 to 4 feet. Zones 4 to 8. Evergreen. Leaves discolor in cold wind. Native to northwestern United States and Canada.

Myrica cerifera • *southern wax myrtle*

Medicinal, as an astringent and jaundice treatment. Wax for candles. Grows 10 feet, up to 35 feet. Zones 6 to 9. Evergreen. Native from New Jersey to Florida and Texas.

Myrica pensylvanica • *bayberry*

Wax for fragrant candles. Grows 5 to 12 feet. Zones 2 to 6. Evergreen. Prefers sandy soils and marshes. Native from Nova Scotia to western New York and Maryland.

Nandina domestica • *heavenly bamboo*

Tonic. Grows 4 to 8 feet. Zones 6 to 9. Evergreen. Ornamental orange berries. Native to central China and Japan.

Osmanthus fragrans • *fragrant tea olive*

Fragrance. Grows 15 to 20 feet, up to 30 feet. Zones 8 to 9. Evergreen. Large shrub or small tree. Native to Japan.

Osmanthus heterophyllus • *holly osmanthus*

Fragrance, intensely sweet flowers. Grows 10 to 18 feet. Zones 6 to 9. Attractive ornamental evergreen. Opposite leaf arrangement distinguishes *Osmanthus* from *Ilex opaca*. Native to Japan.

Philadelphus coronarius • *sweet mock orange*

Fragrance. Grows 10 to 12 feet. Zones 4 to 8. Prefers sun and dry soil. Native to Eurasia.

Poncirus trifoliata • *hardy orange*

Fruits used in marmalades and beverages. Grows 8 to 25 feet. Zones 5 to 10. Native to China.

Rhamnus frangula • *alder buckthorn*

Medicinal, as a laxative. Attracts wildlife. Grows to 18 feet. Zones 2 to 7. Prefers sun. Native to Eurasia and northern Africa.

Rhamnus purshiana • *cascara sagrada*

Medicinal, as a purgative and laxative. Grows to 45 feet. Zone 6. A West Coast plant, native from Utah to California.

Rhus aromatica • *fragrant sumac*

Medicinal, as an astringent and tonic. Grows 2 to 6 feet. Zones 3 to 9. Prefers sun. Forms handsome colonies. Native to eastern North America.

Rhus copallina • *winged sumac*

Medicinal, as an astringent and antiseptic. Grows 20 to 30 feet. Zones 4 to 9. Prefers sun. Native to eastern United States.

Rhus glabra • *smooth sumac*

Medicinal, as an astringent and for burns; tea, tobacco. Grows 10 to 25 feet. Zones 3 to 10. Prefers sun. Makes handsome colonies for large natural areas. Native to eastern United States.

Rhus typhina • *staghorn sumac*

Edible red berries (the poisonous sumac has white berries); dye plant. Grows to 30 feet. Prefers sun. Will accept poor, dry soil. Excellent red foliage in fall. Striking when massed or used as a specimen. Native to temperate eastern United States.

Rosa multiflora • *Japanese rose*

Fragrance. Grows to 10 feet. Zone 5. Prefers sun. Attracts wildlife. Appropriate for natural plantings. Can be invasive. Native to Japan.

Rosa rugosa • *rugosa rose*

Tea, from the hips. Fragrance. Grows 4 to 6 feet. Zones 2 to 7. Accepts sun to partial shade. Vigorous hedge rose. Native to China, Korea, and Japan; naturalized in northern coastal areas in United States.

Rosa virginiana • *Virginia rose*

Fragrance. Grows 3 to 6 feet. Zone 3. Glossy foliage, pink flowers, and red fruits. Prefers sun and open areas, tolerates sandy soils. Native to northeastern North America.

Rosa wichuraiana • *memorial rose*

Fragrance. Grows 10 to 12 inches. Hardy to Zone 5; semievergreen in many areas. Excellent ground cover, trailer, and climber on slopes and banks. Carefree and attractive. Native to Japan, Korea, Formosa, and eastern China.

Rubus odoratus • *purple-flowering raspberry*

Medicinal; fragrance. Grows 3 to 9 feet. Zone 3. Ornamental flowers, wildlife plant. Good for shade. Native from Nova Scotia to Georgia.

Sambucus canadensis • *American elderberry*

Dye plant. Grows 6 to 12 feet. Zone 3. Purple and black berry clusters. Wildlife plant. Prefers moist open areas. Native to eastern North America.

Sarcococca hookerana • *sarcococca*

Fragrance. Grows to 6 feet. Zones 5 to 8, with protection. Semievergreen in most areas. Attractive when massed. Native to western China.

Simmondsia chinensis • *jojoba*

Industrial plant; wax; lubricant; similar to whale oil. Grows to 7 feet. Zone 10. Dioecious (female plant produces fruits only if a male is planted nearby). Prefers dry soil. Native to southwestern United States and northern Mexico.

Symphoricarpos orbiculatus • *Indian currant or coralberry*

Medicinal, as an infusion for weak or inflamed eyes. Grows 3 to 6 feet. Zones 2 to 7. Prefers moist to dry soil. Native to southeastern and south-central United States.

Taxus baccata • *English yew*

Wood; poison. Grows 30 to 60 feet high and at least 10 feet wide. Zones 5 to 7. Dark evergreen. Large shrub or small tree. Variety 'Repandens' grows 2 to 3 feet, has a spreading form, and is hardy to Zone 5. Native to western Asia, Europe, and northern Africa.

Vaccinium corymbosum • highbush blueberry

Food. Grows 6 to 12 feet. Zone 3. Prefers sun to partial shade and acid soil. Ornamental. Native throughout eastern United States.

Viburnum opulus • European cranberry bush

Medicinal, for infections; good source of vitamin C. Grows 8 to 12 feet. Zones 3 to 8. Prefers sun to partial shade. Maplelike leaves. Varieties available. Native to Europe, northern Africa, and northern Asia.

Viburnum prunifolium • blackhaw viburnum

Medicinal, as a tonic and relaxant for uterine problems and pain; flavoring; beverage. Grows 9 to 15 feet. Zones 3 to 9. Prefers dry soil. Native to eastern United States.

Yucca filamentosa • Adam's needle yucca

Medicinal, as a stimulant. Grows to 3 feet. Zones 5 to 10. Evergreen. Long, sharp, stiff bladelike leaves. Native to southeastern United States.

Vines

Actinidia arguta • bower actinidia

Edible fruit. Grows to 30 feet. Zone 4. Fast growing. Rank in highly fertile soil. Native to Japan, Manchuria, and Korea.

Actinidia chinensis • Chinese actinidia

Edible fruit. Grows to 25 feet. Hardy to Zone 7. Twining. Handsome, velvety, vigorous.

Aristolochia macrophylla (durior) • *Dutchman's pipe*

Medicinal. Grows to 30 feet. Zones 4 to 8. Twining. Large round leaves; small flowers resemble a meerschaum pipe. Vigorous. Old-time favorite. Native to eastern and central North America.

Campsis radicans • *trumpet creeper*

Dye plant. Grows to 30 feet. Zone 4. Shrubby, clinging. Requires regular pruning during growing season. Orange flowers; 'Flava' has pure yellow flowers. Native to southeastern and south-central United States.

Celastrus scandens • *American bittersweet*

Medicinal, as a purgative. Grows to 20 feet. Zone 2. Twining. Suitable for large banks; can choke other plants. Native to eastern North America.

Clematis paniculata • *sweet autumn clematis*

Fragrance. Grows to 25 feet. Hardy to Zone 5. Late summer or fall bloomer; white flowers. Dependable. Native to Japan.

Clematis vitalba • *traveler's joy*

Edible sprouts. Grows to 30 feet. Hardy to Zone 4. Dense foliage for pergola or arbor. Native to Europe and northern Africa.

Gelsemium sempervirens • *Carolina jessamine*

Homeopathic; fragrance. Zones 7 to 9. Semievergreen in the South. Yellow flowers. Native to southeastern United States.

Hedera helix • *English ivy*

Medicinal, for dysentery. Grows to 50 feet or more. Zones 4 to 9. Clinging evergreen. Native to Europe; naturalized sporadically in United States.

Humulus lupulus • hops

Female flowers used for beer; medicinal, as a sedative. Zone 3. Perennial. Native to Europe; naturalized in United States.

Hydrangea anomala subsp. petiolaris • climbing hydrangea

Fragrance. Grows 20 to 30 feet. Zone 4. Ornamental white flowers, good for shade. Slow growing when young. Native to Japan.

Lonicera sempervirens • trumpet honeysuckle

Medicinal, as a tonic for headaches; fragrance (perfume). Grows 10 to 20 feet. Zones 3 to 9. Many varieties and species available. Naturalized in eastern and central United States.

Passiflora incarnata • maypop passionflower

Perfume base; medicinal, for inflammations. Zone 7. Native from Virginia to Florida and Texas.

Wisteria floribunda • Japanese wisteria

Fragrance. Grows to 30 feet. Zones 4 to 9. Hardiest wisteria. Many varieties and colors available. Native to Asia.

Wisteria sinensis • Chinese wisteria

Fragrance. Grows 25 to 30 feet. Zone 5. 'Alba' and 'Jako' are highly fragrant. Blue, purple, or white flowers. Specify plant that is propagated from a blooming parent to assure blooms. Native to Asia; naturalized in United States.

Ground Covers

Ajuga reptans • *carpet bugle*

Dye; medicinal. Grows 4 to 8 inches. Zones 4 to 10. Low matting plant. White or bronze flowers. Purple or variegated leaf varieties available. Accepts sun or shade. Native to Europe.

Hedera helix • *English ivy*

Medicinal, for dysentery. Grows 6 to 8 inches high, spreads 25 feet or more. Zones 4 to 9. 'Baltica' hardier. Also grown as a vine. Native to Europe; naturalized in many areas of United States.

Liriope spicata • *lily-turf*

Medicinal (rhizomes). Grows 8 to 12 inches. Zone 4. Varieties available. Native to China and Japan.

Sarcococca hookerana var. *humilis* • *fragrant sarcococca*

Fragrance. Grows 1 to 2 feet. Zone 5; with protection, to 8. Native to western China.

Vinca minor • *periwinkle*

Medicinal, as an astringent and tonic. Grows 4 to 8 inches high. Zone 4. Blue flowers; white-blooming varieties available. Accepts sun or shade. Native to Eurasia; naturalized in many areas of eastern United States.

Wildflowers

Acorus calamus • *sweet flag or calamus*

Dye; medicinal; fragrance; flavoring. Grows 2 to 4 feet. Zones 3 to 10. Hardy perennial. Yellow flowers. Needs sun and moist soil. Native to northern hemisphere.

Althaea officinalis • *marsh mallow*

Medicinal, used for cough medicines; confectionery, root used in making marshmallow paste. Grows 3 to 6 feet. Zone 5. Prefers moist soil and sun or partial shade. Pink flowers. Native to Europe; naturalized from Connecticut to Florida.

Arisaema triphyllum • *Jack-in-the-pulpit*

Subject in folklore; can be toxic if ingested. Grows 12 to 20 inches. Zone 4. Greenish white flowers. Prefers shade and moist, neutral soil. Native to eastern North America.

Asarum canadense • *wild ginger*

Medicinal; meat preservative. Grows 6 to 8 inches. Zone 2 or 3. Requires partial shade or shade. Brownish flower; attractive foliage. Native from New Brunswick to North Carolina and Missouri.

Asclepias tuberosa • *butterfly weed*

Host plant for monarch butterfly. Grows 1 to 3 feet. Zone 3. Hardy perennial. Orange flowers. Needs sun. Widespread in United States.

Aster novae-angliae • *New England aster*

Used by Native Americans for charms and smoking. Grows 2 to 5 feet. Zones 2 or 3. Hardy perennial. Prefers moist soil. Showy blue flowers. Native from Vermont to Alabama, North Dakota, Wyoming, and New Mexico.

Baptisia tinctoria • *wild indigo*

Dye plant, blue; medicinal. Grows 3 to 4 feet. Zone 6. Yellow flower. Native to eastern and central United States.

Chelidonium majus • *celandine poppy*

Dye plant, yellow; folk medicine; Native Americans used it as ceremonial paint. Grows to 30 inches. Zone 4. Prefers shade or partial shade. Long-blooming yellow flowers. Native to Europe; naturalized in eastern North America.

Chimaphila umbellata • *pipsissewa*

Culinary; medicinal; root beer. Grows 5 to 10 inches. Zone 4. Pink flowers. Prefers shade to partial shade and moist to moderately moist acidic soil. Native to northern Eurasia and America.

Convallaria majalis • *lily-of-the-valley*

Dye plant, green; essential oils used in perfumes. Grows 6 to 8 inches. Zones 2 or 3. Hardy. Prefers shade or partial shade. Small, white blooms in spring. Grows in very acidic soils. Stoloniferous; can become invasive. Naturalized in eastern United States.

Coreopsis tinctoria • *coreopsis or calliopsis*

Dye plant; cut and dried flower. Grows to 2 feet. Annual. Prefers sun. Yellow flowers; crimson-bronze varieties. Cultivar 'Nana' is often cultivated as a perennial. Widespread in United States.

Dipsacus sylvestris • *teasel*

Dried flower; attracts birds in winter; medicinal. Grows to 9 feet. Zone 3. Biennial. Prefers sun. Native European weed; naturalized in Canada and northeastern United States.

Echinacea purpurea • *purple coneflower*

Medicinal, as a stimulant. Grows 2 to 4 feet. Zones 2 or 3. Prefers sun. Grows in dry soil; heat tolerant. Hardy perennial. Rose to rose-purple flowers in summer. Popular garden plant. Native to southeastern United States.

Eupatorium perfoliatum • *boneset*

Medicinal, as a tonic, emetic, and laxative; tea. Grows 2 to 5 feet. Zone 3. Terminal clusters of white flowers. Grows in low, moist areas. Native to eastern North America.

Filipendula ulmaria • *queen-of-the-meadow*

Dye plant, greenish yellow from top part; fragrance. Grows to 6 feet. Zones 2 or 3. Perennial. Yellow flowers. Needs sun. Prefers moderately moist soil. Native to eastern North America.

Fragaria virginiana • *wild strawberry*

Fruit; flavoring. Grows 5 to 8 inches. Zone 3. Prefers sun to partial shade. Native to eastern United States.

Galium verum • *yellow bedstraw*

Dye plant; medicinal; food coloring. Grows 1 to 3 feet. Zone 3. Hardy perennial. Vigorous, can be weedy. Yellow flowers. Sun or partial shade. Widespread in North America.

Gaultheria procumbens • *wintergreen or teaberry*

Medicinal, as a tonic; flavoring. Grows 2 to 5 inches. Zone 3. Prefers shade, accepts partial shade. Prefers dry, moderately acidic soil. Native from Manitoba and Minnesota to northern Florida.

Geranium maculatum • *wild geranium*

Medicinal, used by Native Americans. Grows 1 to 2 feet. Hardy perennial. Zone 4. Prefers sun to partial shade. Pink-purple flowers. Grows in moist soil. Widespread distribution in North America.

Hemerocallis fulva • *tawny daylily*

Medicinal; edible flower buds; delicacy in the Orient. Grows to 2 feet (taller when blooming). Zones 2 or 3. Orange flower. Accepts sun or light shade and dry or moderately moist soil. Native to Eurasia; naturalized in eastern United States.

Hepatica americana • *liverleaf*

Medicinal. Grows 1 to 6 inches. Prefers shade to partial shade and rich, neutral soil. Attractive ground cover; white flowers. Many related species and varieties available, including *H. acutiloba*, which grows to 9 inches.

Heuchera americana • *alum root*

Medicinal, as an astringent. Grows 1 to 2 feet. Zone 4. Hardy perennial. Whitish green flowers. Indifferent to acidity. Prefers moist, open areas. Native to northeastern North America.

Hydrastis canadensis • *goldenseal*

Dye; medicinal, as an antiseptic, sedative, and astringent. Grows 10 to 15 inches. Zone 5. Accepts shade to partial shade and rich, moist soil. Could be toxic if used improperly. Difficult to cultivate. Native to eastern North America.

Hypericum perforatum • *St. John's wort*

Dye plant; legend. Grows 1 to 3 feet. Zone 3. Perennial. Yellow flowers are attractive when massed. Prefers sun or light shade and moderately moist to dry soil. Naturalized in North America.

Inula helenium • *elecampane*

Medicinal; dye plant, blue. Grows to 6 feet. Zone 6. Perennial. Common weed. Large leaves, pubescent underneath; yellow daisylike flowers. Widely naturalized in eastern North America.

Iris pseudacorus • *yellow flag*

Dye plant; medicinal, as an astringent. Grows 2 to 3 feet. Zone 5. Requires wet habitats. Beardless, bright yellow flowers with brown veins. Naturalized in North America.

Iris versicolor • *blue flag*

Medicinal, as a poultice. Grows 2 to 3 feet. Hardy to Zone 3. Beardless blue flowers with yellow markings. Requires wet soils. Native to northeastern North America.

Lobelia siphilitica • *great blue lobelia*

Medicinal. Grows 1 to 3 feet. Zone 5. Prefers partial shade. Requires moist or swampy areas. Erect perennial. Terminal blue flowers. Native from Connecticut to North Carolina to Kansas.

Matteuccia pensylvanica • *ostrich fern*

Edible young fronds, fiddleheads. Grows 4 to 10 feet with an equal spread. Zone 2. Prefers shade to partial shade. Requires cool, marshy habitats. Attractive large fern. Native to north and central North America.

Mitchella repens • *partridgeberry*

Medicinal, as an astringent and diuretic; flavoring. Grows 2 to 3 inches. Zones 3 to 9. Pink-white tubular flowers, red berries in fall. Christmas decoration. Grows in moist, acid soils. Naturalized in eastern United States.

Narcissus jonquilla • *jonquil*

Ancient medicinal plant; narcotic properties; oil used in perfumes. Grows 12 to 20 inches. Zone 4. Accepts sun or shade. Yellow flowers. Many varieties available. Native to Europe and Africa; naturalized widely in United States.

Narcissus poeticus • *pheasant's eye*

Fragrance; perfume; medicinal. Grows 12 to 18 inches. Zone 4. Accepts sun or shade. Solitary white flower with wavy cup edges, often rimmed in red. Many varieties available. Native to southern Europe; naturalized in United States.

Nasturtium officinale • *watercress*

Edible leaves and stems often used as salad green and flavoring. Zone 4. Perennial aquatic plant of the mustard family. Small white flowers. Prefers cold water. Native to Europe, widely naturalized in streams of North America.

Oenothera biennis • *evening primrose*

Medicinal; roots eaten as vegetable by Native Americans. Grows 3 to 4 feet. Zone 4. Biennial. Prefers shade. Yellow flowers. Weedy characteristics. Wide distribution throughout United States.

Osmunda cinnamomea • *cinnamon fern*

Edible young fronds. Grows 3 to 4 feet. Zone 3. Attractive fern. Prefers moist, partly shaded sites. Widespread throughout its native eastern United States.

Panax quinquefolius • *ginseng*

Medicinal; economic herb; root and rhizome. Grows 6 to 18 inches. Zone 3. Genus name comes from Greek *pan-*, "all," and *akos*, "remedy." In ancient times, reputed to be a cure-all for body, mind, and spirit. Popular in eastern cultures, which attributed miraculous healing qualities to its man-shaped root. Red berries.

Requires rich, well-drained soils, with pH 5 to 6.5, and shade to partial shade. On the North American continent, native from Quebec and Minnesota to Georgia and Oklahoma.

Pycnanthemum pilosum • mountain mint

Aromatic; pungent mintlike odor; used by Native Americans. Grows 1 to 3 feet. Perennial. Accepts moderately moist or drier soil, and shade or sun. Variety *P. tenuifolium* is also aromatic. Native to eastern United States.

Sanguinaria canadensis • bloodroot

Dye plant, red; Native Americans used it to make ceremonial face and body paint. Grows 3 to 6 inches. Zone 3. Poppy family; lovely white flowers in spring. Prefers moist, shaded areas and rich acidic soils. Native from southern Canada and eastern United States to Kansas.

Solidago canadensis • Canada goldenrod

Dye plant; used in rubber production. Grows 1 to 4 feet. Zone 4. Prefers sun. Mistakenly thought to be the cause of hay fever. Showy yellow flowers. Great potential as an ornamental. Widespread throughout North America.

Solidago odora • fragrant goldenrod

Medicinal; tea from anise-scented leaves. Grows to 4 feet. Zone 3. Prefers sun. Yellow flowers. Ornamental. Widespread throughout North America.

Trillium grandiflorum • snow trillium

Native Americans used this herb as medicine for easing childbirth. Grows 10 to 18 inches. Zone 4. Prefers shade and moist, rich, neutral soil. White flower that fades to pink; blue-black berry. Beautiful woodland wildflower. Widespread throughout southern Canada and eastern United States.

Verbascum thapsus • *mullein or flannel plant*

Dye plant, sunny yellow; medicinal, for asthma and other pulmonary diseases. Grows 4 to 5 feet. Zone 5. Prefers sun. Yellow flowers. Sturdy, erect stalks, rosette of huge, velvety gray leaves at base. Leaves collect dust, must be rinsed in polluted or dusty areas. European biennial weed, widely naturalized in United States.

Vernonia altissima • *tall ironweed*

Industrial uses: seed. Grows to 6 feet. Zone 4. Perennial. Handsome large border or wild garden plant. Purple flowers. Native to warm regions of North and South America.

Viola odorata • *sweet violet*

Perfume; fragrance; flowers are candied for culinary decoration; medicinal. Grows to 8 inches. Zone 6. Pretty ground cover with deep violet flowers, rarely pink or white. Sun or shade and moderately moist, rich soil. Usually propagated by offsets removed in late winter or early spring, rooted in sand. Naturalized in southern and eastern United States.

Herbal Plants That Grow Well in Cities or Suburbs

Deciduous Trees

Acer platanoides	Norway maple
Acer pseudoplatanus	Sycamore maple
Alnus glutinosa	European alder
Broussonetia papyrifera	Paper mulberry
Carpinus betulus	European hornbeam
Celtis laevigata	Sugar hackberry
Chionanthus virginicus	Fringe tree
Cornus florida	Flowering dogwood
Crataegus phaenopyrum	Washington hawthorn
Cydonia sinensis	Quince tree
Fraxinus americana	White ash
Fraxinus excelsior	European ash
Ginkgo biloba	Ginkgo or maidenhair tree
Gleditsia triacanthos	Common honey locust
Koelreuteria paniculata	Golden rain tree
Magnolia stellata	Star magnolia
Malus coronaria	Wild sweet crab
Mespilus germanica	Medlar
Quercus borealis	Red oak
Quercus palustris	Pin oak
Quercus phellos	Willow oak
Sophora japonica	Japanese pagoda tree
Tilia cordata	Little-leaf linden

Evergreen Trees

Ilex opaca	American holly
Juniperus communis	Common juniper
Juniperus virginiana	Eastern red cedar
Magnolia grandiflora	Southern magnolia
Magnolia virginiana	Sweet bay magnolia
Thuja occidentalis	American arborvitae

Deciduous Woody Shrubs

Acanthopanax sieboldianus	Five-leaf aralia
Aronia arbutifolia	Red chokecherry
Berberis thunbergii	Japanese barberry
Chimonanthus praecox	Wintersweet
Cornus amomum	Silky dogwood
Cornus mas	Cornelian cherry
Elaeagnus angustifolia	Russian olive
Euonymus europaea	European spindle tree
Hamamelis virginiana	Witch hazel
Lindera benzoin	Spicebush
Philadelphus coronarius	Sweet mock orange
Poncirus trifoliata	Hardy orange
Rhamnus frangula	Alder buckthorn
Rhamnus purshiana	Cascara sagrada
Rhus glabra	Smooth sumac
Rhus typhina	Staghorn sumac
Rosa multiflora	Japanese rose
Rosa rugosa	Rugosa rose
Rosa wichuraiana	Memorial rose
Sarcococca hookerana	Sarcococca
Symphoricarpos orbiculatus	Indian currant or coralberry
Viburnum opulus	European cranberry bush
Viburnum prunifolium	Blackhaw viburnum

Evergreen Shrubs

Buxus microphylla	Little leaf boxwood
Buxus sempervirens	Common boxwood
Ilex crenata	Japanese holly
Ilex glabra	Inkberry
Ilex verticillata	Winterberry
Ilex vomitoria	Yaupon holly

Herbal Plants That Grow Well in Cities or Suburbs, continued

Juniperus communis	Common juniper
Ligustrum vulgare	Common privet
Mahonia aquifolium	Oregon grape holly
Myrica cerifera	Southern wax myrtle
Myrica pensylvanica	Bayberry
Nandina domestica	Heavenly bamboo
Osmanthus fragrans	Fragrant tea olive
Osmanthus heterophyllus	Holly osmanthus
Taxus baccata	English yew
Yucca filamentosa	Adam's needle yucca

Ground Covers

Ajuga reptans	Carpet bugle
Hedera helix	English ivy
Liriope spicata	Lily-turf
Sarcococca hookerana var. *humilis*	Fragrant sarcococca
Vinca minor	Periwinkle

Vines

Actinidia arguta	Bower actinidia
Actinidia chinensis	Chinese actinidia
Aristolochia macrophylla (*durior*)	Dutchman's pipe
Campsis radicans	Trumpet creeper
Celastrus scandens	American bittersweet
Clematis paniculata	Sweet autumn clematis
Clematis vitalba	Traveler's joy
Gelsemium sempervirens	Carolina jessamine
Hedera helix	English ivy
Humulus lupulus	Hops
Hydrangea anomala petiolaris	Climbing hydrangea
Lonicera sempervirens	Trumpet honeysuckle
Passiflora incarnata	Maypop passionflower
Wisteria floribunda	Japanese wisteria
Wisteria sinensis	Chinese wisteria

HERBAL NATIVE PLANTS

Native plants are becoming increasingly popular as modern gardeners explore their uses in cultivated gardens. Herb gardens are among the possibilities, and indeed, many North American wildflowers that have herbal uses are excellent choices for residential properties and public parks. Native plants can be beautifully and appropriately incorporated into a variety of planting designs, including sunny meadow gardens and shaded woodland plantings in natural landscapes and other bedding areas.

A delightful benefit of planting herbal natives is that the garden, if planted in harmony with the larger biological community, will attract birds and wildlife as the naturalized planting matures.

The following is a list of native trees, shrubs, vines, and wildflowers with herbal uses. Consult this reference if you're designing a garden with a wild herbal theme.

Native North American Plants

Trees

Acer rubrum	Red maple
Acer saccharum	Sugar maple
Amelanchier arborea	
	Serviceberry or shadblow
Betula lenta	Sweet birch
Betula nigra	River birch
Carpinus caroliniana	American hornbeam
Carya ovata	Shagbark hickory
Celtis laevigata	Sugar hackberry
Cercis canadensis	Eastern redbud
Chionanthus virginicus	Fringe tree
Cornus florida	Flowering dogwood
Cotinus obovatus	American smoketree
Crataegus phaenopyrum	
	Washington hawthorn
Diospyros virginiana	Persimmon
Franklinia alatamaha	Franklinia
Fraxinus americana	White ash
Gleditsia triacanthos	Common honey locust
Gymnocladus dioica	Kentucky coffee tree
Halesia carolina	Carolina silverbell
Ilex opaca	American holly
Juniperus virginiana	Eastern red cedar
Liquidambar styraciflua	
	American sweetgum
Liriodendron tulipifera	
	Tulip tree or yellow poplar
Maclura pomifera	Osage orange
Magnolia grandiflora	Southern magnolia
Magnolia virginiana	Sweet bay magnolia
Malus coronaria	Wild sweet crab
Nyssa sylvatica	Black tupelo or black gum
Ostrya virginiana	American hop hornbeam

Oxydendrum arboreum	
	Sourwood or lily-of-the-valley tree
Prunus serotina	Black cherry
Quercus alba	White oak
Quercus borealis	Red oak
Quercus coccinea	Scarlet oak
Quercus palustris	Pin oak
Quercus phellos	Willow oak
Sassafras albidum	Sassafras
Thuja occidentalis	American arborvitae
Tilia americana	Basswood
Ulmus rubra	Slippery elm
Umbellularia californica	California laurel

Shrubs

Aesculus parviflora	Bottlebrush buckeye
Amelanchier stolonifera	
	Running serviceberry
Aralia spinosa	Devil's walking stick
Arctostaphylos uva-ursi	
	Bearberry or kinnikinnick
Callicarpa americana	American beautyberry
Calycanthus floridus	Carolina allspice
Cassia marilandica	Wild senna
Cephalanthus occidentalis	Buttonbush
Clethra alnifolia	Summersweet
Comptonia peregrina	Sweet fern
Cornus sericea (stolonifera)	Red osier
Euonymus atropurpurea	Eastern wahoo
Fothergilla gardenii	Witch alder
Hamamelis virginiana	Witch hazel
Ilex glabra	Inkberry
Ilex verticillata	Winterberry
Ilex vomitoria	Yaupon holly

Native North American Plants, continued

Itea virginica	Virginia sweetspire
Juniperus communis	Common juniper
Kalmia latifolia	Mountain laurel
Ledum groenlandicum	Labrador tea
Mahonia aquifolium	Oregon grape holly
Myrica cerifera	Southern wax-myrtle
Myrica pensylvanica	Bayberry
Rhus aromatica	Fragrant sumac
Rhus copallina	Winged sumac
Rosa virginiana	Virginia rose
Rubus odoratus	Purple-flowering raspberry
Sambucus canadensis	American elderberry
Simmondsia chinensis	Jojoba
Vaccinium corymbosum	Highbush blueberry
Viburnum prunifolium	Blackhaw viburnum
Yucca filamentosa	Adam's needle yucca

Vines

Aristolochia macrophylla (durior)	Dutchman's pipe
Campsis radicans	Trumpet creeper
Celastrus scandens	American bittersweet
Gelsemium sempervirens	Carolina jessamine
Passiflora incarnata	Maypop passionflower

Wildflowers

Acorus calamus	Sweet flag or calamus
Arisaema triphyllum	Jack-in-the-pulpit
Asarum canadense	Wild ginger
Asclepias tuberosa	Butterfly weed
Aster novae-angliae	New England aster
Baptisia tinctoria	Wild indigo
Chimaphila umbellata	Pipsissewa
Coreopsis tinctoria	Coreopsis or calliopsis
Echinacea purpurea	Purple coneflower

Eupatorium perfoliatum	Boneset
Filipendula ulmaria	Queen-of-the-meadow
Fragaria virginiana	Wild strawberry
Galium verum	Yellow bedstraw
Gaultheria procumbens	Wintergreen or teaberry
Geranium maculatum	Wild geranium
Hepatica americana	Liverleaf
Heuchera americana	Alum root
Hydrastis canadensis	Goldenseal
Iris versicolor	Blue flag
Lobelia siphilitica	Great blue lobelia
Matteuccia pensylvanica	Ostrich fern
Oenothera biennis	Evening primrose
Osmunda cinnamomea	Cinnamon fern
Panax quinquefolius	Ginseng
Pycnanthemum pilosum	Mountain mint
Sanguinaria canadensis	Bloodroot
Solidago canadensis	Canada goldenrod
Solidago odora	Fragrant goldenrod
Trillium grandiflorum	Snow trillium
Vernonia altissima	Tall ironweed

Design

*H*erbs bring beauty and fragrance to your garden. Their unique virtues set them apart from other garden plants. Many herbs have special characteristics that can help you create inviting garden spaces and even solve design problems. But to use herbs most effectively, you must first get to know the plant attributes that make herbs so valuable to the designer.

Foliage color

Color is one of the most outstanding ornamental assets of herbal foliage. Herbs are famous for their many shades of green, bronze, purple, gray, silver, and in the variegated plants, any number of combinations. One colorful sage even has a green leaf with purple, pink, and white variegation. Plants with contrasting foliage colors can be combined in many ways to create almost any result the designer desires.

A calm, gentle beauty is achieved by using herbs with restful blue and blue-green foliage. An especially lovely and rich composition blends silver-gray herbs with blue and blue-green herbs. Purple-leaved herbs are a pleasing addition to this color palette. These color combinations can also be used to create a cooling effect, desirable in hot climates and in hot pockets in the city. An abundance of cool blues and blue-greens, perhaps in combination with pale silvers or light grays, will suggest a cooler atmosphere.

Create an illusion of distance appropriate in small gardens by arranging blue herbs behind yellow-green or yellow herbs. Cool blues and greens recede in space; hot yellows jump forward. Planting large-foliaged plants in front and those with smaller leaves in the middle and back border also creates the illusion of depth.

The many variegated herbs can be used to good effect. The white, cream, silver, or yellow markings in green leaves can brighten a shady spot in the garden. Variegated plants, however, command the eye's attention and should be used sparingly. They are best used in combination with a variety of green plants. This prevents them from creating a cluttered, disharmonious effect, especially jarring in a bed of herbs. Single container plantings using glitzy combinations of variegated herbs might nevertheless be an appropriate bold stroke in certain situations.

There are many other possibilities for using foliage color in your designs. A stunning combination results from placing bronze fennel (*Foeniculum vulgare* var. *rubrum*) as the accent plant among green herbs. Create tension by combining yellow-foliaged herbs with silver herbs. Or experiment with rich contrasts, such as the gray-green foliage of garden sage (*Salvia officinalis*) with dark-leaved herbs.

In your use of foliage color, remember to consider the color of the background. A dark hedge or otherwise shaded background material is helpful in setting off the light foliage of gray and silver herbs. The background should not be so striking that it fights for attention and detracts from the forward plantings. Light-foliaged herbs may become lost against the horizon of open air or up against a light-colored building. The darker herbs are also more effective when set off with a contrasting background. The following pages list herbs by foliage color for easy reference.

Silver or Gray Foliage

Artemisia absinthium	Wormwood
Artemisia absinthium 'Lambrook Silver'	'Lambrook Silver' artemisia
Artemisia ludoviciana var. *albula*	'Silver Queen' or 'Silver King'
Artemisia schmidtiana 'Nana'	'Silver Mound' artemisia
Artemisia stellerana	Beach wormwood
Helichrysum angustifolium	Curry plant
Lavandula angustifolia subsp. *angustifolia*	English lavender
Lavandula angustifolia 'Alba'	White-flowering lavender
Lavandula angustifolia 'Hidcote'	'Hidcote' lavender
Lavandula angustifolia 'Munstead'	'Munstead' lavender
Lavandula angustifolia 'Rosea'	Pink-flowering lavender
Lavandula × *intermedia* 'Dutch'	'Dutch' lavender
Lavandula × *intermedia* 'Grosso'	'Grosso' lavender
Lavandula stoechas	Spanish lavender
Marrubium vulgare	Horehound
Origanum dictamnus	Dittany-of-Crete
Santolina chamaecyparissus	Lavender cotton or gray santolina
Santolina chamaecyparissus 'Nana'	Dwarf lavender cotton
Santolina chamaecyparissus 'Plumosus'	Lacy lavender cotton
Stachys byzantina	Lamb's-ears
Stachys byzantina 'Silver Carpet'	'Silver Carpet' lamb's-ears
Thymus pseudolanuginosus	Woolly thyme

Gray-Green Foliage

Alchemilla alpina	Alpine lady's mantle
Alchemilla mollis	Lady's mantle
Artemisia abrotanum	Southernwood
Artemisia annua	Sweet annual wormwood
Artemisia pontica	Roman wormwood
Borago officinalis	Borage
Calamintha nepeta	Calamint
Chrysanthemum balsamita	Costmary or alecost
Glycyrrhiza glabra	Licorice
Lavandula dentata	Fringed or French lavender
Lavandula multifida	Fern-leaf lavender
Mentha suaveolens	Apple mint
Nepeta cataria	Catnip
Nepeta cataria 'Blue Wonder'	'Blue Wonder' catnip
Nepeta × *faassenii*	Catmint
Pelargonium graveolens	Rose-scented geranium
Salvia officinalis	Garden or common sage
Salvia officinalis 'Albiflora'	White-flowering garden sage
Salvia sclarea	Clary sage
Thymus nitidus	Tiny-leaf thyme

Blue-Green Foliage

Allium christophii	Stars-of-Persia
Allium neapolitanum	Flowering onion
Allium pulchellum	Flowering allium
Allium sativum	Garlic
Allium schoenoprasum	Chives
Allium senescens var. *glaucum*	Flowering allium
Allium tuberosum	Oriental chives
Dianthus caryophyllus	Clove carnation
Dianthus plumarius	Garden pinks
Hyssopus officinalis	Hyssop
Hyssopus officinalis 'Alba'	White-flowering hyssop
Hyssopus officinalis 'Rubra'	Rose-flowering hyssop
Papaver orientale and cultivars	Oriental poppy
Perovskia atriplicifolia	Russian sage
Poterium sanguisorba	Burnet
Ruta graveolens	Rue
Ruta graveolens 'Blue Beauty'	'Blue Beauty' rue
Ruta graveolens 'Blue Mound'	Compact rue
Ruta graveolens 'Jackman Blue'	Compact rue

Colored and Variegated Foliage or Fruits

Capsicum annuum
Cayenne or chili pepper (red fruit)

Capsicum frutescens
Tabasco pepper (red fruit)

Chrysanthemum parthenium 'Aureum'
Golden-feather feverfew (yellow)

Foeniculum vulgare var. *rubrum*
Bronze fennel (copper or bronze)

Laurus nobilis 'Aurea'
Golden sweet bay (gold)

Melissa officinalis 'Variegata'
Golden lemon balm (gold)

Mentha × gentilis 'Variegata'
Ginger mint (green and gold)

Mentha suaveolens 'Variegata'
Pineapple mint (green and white)

Myrtus communis 'Variegata'
Variegated sweet myrtle
(green and white)

Ocimum basilicum 'Purple Ruffles'
'Purple Ruffles' basil (purple)

Ocimum basilicum 'Purpurascens'
Purple or 'Dark Opal' basil (purple)

Origanum vulgare 'Aureum'
Golden wild oregano (gold)

Pelargonium crispum 'Variegatum'
Variegated lemon-scented geranium

Pelargonium varieties and cultivars
Many varieties of other
scented geraniums

Perilla crispum 'Atropurpurea'
Curled purple perilla (dark purple)

Perilla frutescens 'Atropurpurea'
Purple perilla (dark purple)

Pulmonaria officinalis
Lungwort (silver spots on green leaves)

Ruta graveolens 'Variegata'   Variegated rue
(cream on blue-green leaves)

Salvia officinalis 'Icterina' or 'Aurea'
Golden sage (green and gold)

Salvia officinalis 'Purpurascens'
Purple sage (green with purple patina)

Salvia officinalis 'Tricolor'
Tricolor sage (white, green, and purple)

Symphytum officinale 'Variegatum'
Variegated comfrey (white margins)

Teucrium chamaedrys 'Variegatum'
Variegated germander

Thymus × citriodorus 'Aureus'
Golden lemon thyme (gold and green)

Thymus vulgaris 'Argenteus'
Silver thyme (silver-edged leaves)

Foliage texture

Foliage texture, another of the prized features of herbs, can range from fine and intricate to coarse and bold. When the colors of the foliage and flowers are combined with the textures, a vast array of exquisite compositions is possible. A design that emphasizes textural interest produces an overall effect that is richer than the separate parts.

Contrasting foliage, such as the combination of the fine-leafed dill (*Anethum graveolens*) with the robust comfrey (*Symphytum officinale*), can produce a desirable effect. But do not overlook the possibilities of combining herbs with only slight differences in leaf textures. The many herbs of moderately fine texture can be juxtaposed for a beautiful effect. There is enough variation in the leaves to create the elegance and textural richness so admired in well-designed herb gardens. The many varieties of rosemary, for example, all have very similar overall textures with only slight differences in form, leaf size, and branching habit. Even with such subtle differences, a grouping of several of these varieties, perhaps placed together in containers, can create an interesting arrangement. This effect relies solely on textural value. The shapes of leaves and their arrangements on the branches provide the visual interest.

The wide variety of textures among herbs has prompted their use in designs for tactile interest, such as gardens for the blind. Some herbs have pointed and leathery foliage (*Rosmarinus officinalis*); others are velvety to the touch (*Pelargonium tomentosum*). The stiff, corallike foliage of the santolinas and the soft, woolly foliage of lamb's-ears or silver mound artemisia are musts in touch-and-feel gardens. Consult the Plant Profiles for more suggestions.

Flower color

The flowers of herbs create a beautiful, often subtle effect in planting design. Herb blossoms are generally smaller and less strident than those of the showy perennials and annuals. The abundance of restful blues, purples, roses, pinks, and pastels creates a more subdued, gentler beauty.

Herb flowers combine easily and beautifully with each other and with their many foliage colors, creating a wide range of possibilities. Many of the design effects accomplished by careful use of foliage color, such as cooling and distancing, can be achieved through the use of flower color as well.

There are many yellow-flowering herbs, including fennel, santolina, and dill. Most are clear, soft yellows that do not present a problem in blending with the blues, purples, and pinks of other herbs. The bright, orange-toned yellows, however, require judicious placement in a planting. The orange and yellow flowers of pot marigold (*Calendula officinalis*) and the red flowers of pineapple sage (*Salvia elegans*) and bee balm (*Monarda didyma*) provide some of the warmest tones in the herbal palette.

The white-flowering herbs can provide a transition between the colors in planting beds. Especially refreshing when planted with blue flowers, white-flowering herbs create a cooling effect. Sweet cicely (*Myrrhis odorata*) and sweet woodruff (*Galium odoratum*) are two good shade-tolerant plants that can light up a sunless spot, perhaps under a densely canopied tree or a vine-covered arbor.

Even though herbs are most often admired for their gently colored blossoms, many are showy and striking. The deep, vibrant blue of the dwarf lavenders (*Lavandula angustifolia* 'Munstead' or 'Hidcote'), the showy red of the creeping thyme (*Thymus praecox arcticus* 'Coccineus'), and the red-purple sage (*Salvia officinalis* 'Purpurascens') can create striking results in your garden. In fact, some popular herbs, such as lavender, thyme, and yarrow, are commonly used in perennial borders because of their lovely flowers and their unique foliage colors.

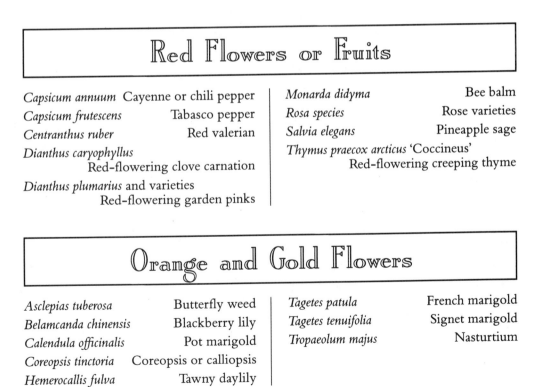

Red Flowers or Fruits

Capsicum annuum Cayenne or chili pepper	*Monarda didyma* Bee balm
Capsicum frutescens Tabasco pepper	*Rosa species* Rose varieties
Centranthus ruber Red valerian	*Salvia elegans* Pineapple sage
Dianthus caryophyllus Red-flowering clove carnation	*Thymus praecox arcticus* 'Coccineus' Red-flowering creeping thyme
Dianthus plumarius and varieties Red-flowering garden pinks	

Orange and Gold Flowers

Asclepias tuberosa Butterfly weed	*Tagetes patula* French marigold
Belamcanda chinensis Blackberry lily	*Tagetes tenuifolia* Signet marigold
Calendula officinalis Pot marigold	*Tropaeolum majus* Nasturtium
Coreopsis tinctoria Coreopsis or calliopsis	
Hemerocallis fulva Tawny daylily	

Yellow Flowers

Acorus calamus	Sweet flag
Alchemilla alpina	Alpine lady's mantle
Alchemilla mollis	Lady's mantle
Allium flavum	Yellow-flowering allium
Allium moly	Yellow-flowering allium
Anethum graveolens	Dill
Anethum graveolens 'Dill Bouquet'	
	Dwarf dill
Anthemis tinctoria	Golden marguerite
Artemisia absinthium	Wormwood
Artemisia annua	Sweet annual wormwood
Baptisia tinctoria	Wild indigo
Calendula officinalis	Pot marigold
Cassia marilandica	Wild senna
Chamaemelum nobile	Roman chamomile
Chelidonium majus	Celandine poppy
Chrysanthemum balsamita	
	Costmary or alecost
Chrysanthemum parthenium	Feverfew
Coreopsis tinctoria 'Nana'	
	Garden coreopsis or calliopsis
Cytisus scoparius	Scotch broom
Filipendula ulmaria	Queen-of-the-meadow
Foeniculum vulgare	Fennel
Foeniculum vulgare var. *rubrum*	
	Bronze fennel
Galium verum	Yellow bedstraw
Hamamelis virginiana	Witch hazel
Helianthus annuus	Sunflower
Helichrysum angustifolium	Curry plant
Hypericum perforatum	St. John's wort
Inula helenium	Elecampane
Iris pseudacorus	Yellow flag
Laurus nobilis	Sweet bay
Levisticum officinale	Lovage

Matricaria recutita	German chamomile
Narcissus jonquilla	Jonquil
Narcissus poeticus	Pheasant's eye
Oenothera biennis	Evening primrose
Santolina species and varieties	
	Lavender cotton or santolina
Solidago canadensis	Canada goldenrod
Solidago odora	Fragrant goldenrod
Symphytum variety	
	Yellow-flowering comfrey
Tagetes patula and *tenuifolia*	Marigolds
Tanacetum vulgare	Tansy
Tanacetum vulgare var. *crispum*	
	Curly or fern-leaf tansy
Tropaeolum majus	Nasturtium
Verbascum thapsus	Mullein

White or Cream Flowers

Acanthus mollis	Artist's acanthus	*Matricaria recutita*	German chamomile
Achillea millefolium	Yarrow or milfoil	*Melissa officinalis* and varieties	Lemon balm
Ajuga reptans 'Alba'	Carpet bugle	*Mentha suaveolens*	Apple mint
Allium neapolitanum	Flowering onion	*Monarda didyma* 'Alba'	

Acanthus mollis   Artist's acanthus

Achillea millefolium   Yarrow or milfoil

Ajuga reptans 'Alba'   Carpet bugle

Allium neapolitanum   Flowering onion

Allium neapolitanum 'Grandiflorum'
    Flowering onion

Allium sativum   Garlic

Allium tuberosum   Oriental chives

Angelica archangelica   Angelica

Anthriscus cerefolium   Sweet chervil

Artemisia abrotanum   Southernwood

Artemisia dracunculus   French tarragon

Artemisia pontica   Roman wormwood

Carum carvi   Caraway

Colchicum autumnale 'Alba'
    White-flowering autumn crocus

Convallaria majalis   Lily-of-the-valley

Coriandrum sativum
    Coriander, cilantro, Chinese parsley

Dianthus plumarius 'Alba'
    White-flowering garden pinks

Digitalis purpurea   Foxglove

Fragaria alpina   Alpine strawberry

Fragaria virginiana   Wild strawberry

Galium odoratum   Sweet woodruff

Gaultheria procumbens   Wintergreen

Hepatica americana   Liverleaf

Hyssopus officinalis 'Alba'
    White-flowering hyssop

Iris × *germanica* var. *florentina* Florentina iris

Lavandula angustifolia 'Alba'
    White-flowering lavender

Levisticum officinale   Lovage

Lilium candidum   Madonna lily

Marrubium vulgare   Horehound

Matricaria recutita   German chamomile

Melissa officinalis and varieties Lemon balm

Mentha suaveolens   Apple mint

Monarda didyma 'Alba'
    White-flowering bee balm

Myrrhis odorata   Sweet cicely

Myrtus communis   Sweet myrtle

Ocimum basilicum   Sweet basil

Ocimum basilicum 'Citriodorum'
    Lemon basil

Ocimum basilicum 'Crispum'
    Lettuce-leaf basil

Ocimum basilicum 'Minimum'   Dwarf basil

Origanum majorana and varieties
    Marjorams

Origanum vulgare and varieties   Oreganos

Pelargonium tomentosum
    Peppermint-scented geranium

Petroselinum crispum and varieties   Parsley

Pimpinella anisum   Anise

Platycodon grandiflorum 'Alba'
    White-flowering balloon flower

Polianthes tuberosa   Tuberose

Rosa species   Roses

Rosmarinus officinalis 'Albus'
    White-flowering rosemary

Salvia farinacea 'Alba'
    White-flowering salvia

Salvia officinalis 'Albiflora'
    White-flowering garden sage

Sanguinaria canadensis   Bloodroot

Stachys byzantina 'Alba'
    White-flowering lamb's-ears

Symphytum officinale 'Grandiflorum'
    Ground cover comfrey

Thymus praecox arcticus 'Albus'
    White-flowering creeping thyme

Pink, Rose, or Lavender Flowers

Agastache foeniculum   Anise hyssop
Agastache rugosa   Korean anise hyssop
Allium christophii   Stars-of-Persia
Allium neapolitanum 'Roseum'
                    Pink-flowering allium
Allium pulchellum   Flowering allium
Allium schoenoprasum   Chives
Allium senescens var. *glaucum*
                    Flowering allium
Aloysia triphylla   Lemon verbena
Althaea officinalis   Marsh mallow
Calamintha nepeta   Calamint
Centranthus ruber   Red valerian
Colchicum autumnale   Autumn crocus
Crocus sativus   Saffron crocus
Dianthus caryophyllus   Clove carnation
Dianthus plumarius   Garden pinks
Digitalis purpurea   Foxglove
Echinacea purpurea   Purple coneflower
Hyssopus officinalis 'Rubra'   Chamomile
Lavandula angustifolia 'Rosea'
                    Pink-flowering lavender
Mentha × *piperita*   Peppermint
Mentha pulegium   Pennyroyal
Mentha spica 'Crispii' or 'Crispata'
                    Curly mint
Mentha spicata   Spearmint
Monarda didyma 'Croftway Pink'
                    Pink-flowering bee balm
Nepeta cataria   Catnip
Nigella damascena   Love-in-a-mist
Ocimum basilicum 'Purpurascens'
                    Purple or 'Dark Opal' basil
Origanum dictamnus   Dittany-of-Crete

Origanum pulchellum   Flowering marjoram
Origanum vulgare
        Common oregano or wild marjoram
Papaver orientale varieties
                    Pink-flowering poppies
Pelargonium × *domesticum* 'Clorinda'
            Eucalyptus-scented geranium
Pelargonium crispum
            Lemon-scented geranium
Pelargonium graveolens
                    Rose-scented geranium
Perilla frutescens 'Atropurpurea'
                    Purple perilla
Rosa species   Roses
Salvia sclarea   Clary sage
Satureja hortensis   Summer savory
Satureja montana   Winter savory
Stachys byzantina   Lamb's-ears
Stachys officinalis   Betony
Symphytum officinale 'Rubrum'
                    Rose-flowering comfrey
Symphytum × *uplandicum*   Russian comfrey
Teucrium chamaedrys   Germander
Thymus × *citriodorus*   Lemon thyme
Thymus herba-barona   Caraway thyme
Thymus praecox arcticus
        Mother-of-thyme or creeping thyme
Thymus praecox arcticus 'Coccineus'
            Red-flowering creeping thyme
Thymus pseudolanuginosus   Woolly thyme
Thymus vulgaris   Common thyme
Valeriana officinalis   Valerian

Blue or Purple Flowers

Aster novae-angliae	New England aster
Baptisia australis	Blue false indigo
Borago officinalis	Borage
Glycyrrhiza glabra	Licorice
Heliotropium arborescens	Common heliotrope
Hyssopus officinalis	Hyssop
Iris kaempferi	Japanese iris
Iris versicolor	Blue flag
Lavandula angustifolia subsp. *angustifolia*	English lavender
Lavandula angustifolia 'Hidcote'	'Hidcote' lavender
Lavandula angustifolia 'Munstead'	'Munstead' lavender
Lavandula dentata	French lavender
Lavandula × intermedia 'Dutch'	'Dutch' lavender
Lavandula × intermedia 'Grosso'	'Grosso' lavender
Lavandula multifida	Fern-leaf lavender
Lavandula stoechas	Spanish lavender
Linum perenne	Perennial flax
Lobelia siphilitica	Great blue lobelia
Lunaria annua	Dollar plant
Monarda didyma 'Violacea'	Violet-flowering bee balm
Nepeta cataria 'Blue Wonder'	'Blue Wonder' catnip
Nepeta × faassenii	Catmint
Nepeta mussinii	Catmint
Perovskia atriplicifolia	Russian sage
Platycodon grandiflorus	Balloon flower
Pulmonaria officinalis	Lungwort
Rosmarinus officinalis	Rosemary

Rosmarinus officinalis 'Arp'	Hardy rosemary
Rosmarinus officinalis 'Benedin Blue'	'Benedin Blue' rosemary
Rosmarinus officinalis 'Collingwood Ingram'	Graceful rosemary
Rosmarinus officinalis 'Lockwood de Forest'	Prostrate rosemary
Rosmarinus officinalis 'Prostratus'	Prostrate rosemary
Rosmarinus officinalis 'Tuscan Blue'	Columnar rosemary
Salvia azurea	Azure sage
Salvia farinacea 'Victoria'	Blue annual salvia
Salvia greggii	Autumn sage
Salvia officinalis	Garden sage
Salvia species	many varieties
Symphytum caucasicum	Small blue comfrey
Vernonia altissima	Tall ironweed
Viola odorata	Sweet violet

Fragrance

The aromatic qualities of herbs should be used to full advantage in the planting design. The experience of fragrance in a garden leaves a lasting impression. Many herb gardens are memorable because of the evocative scents associated with them.

Herb fragrances can be enjoyed just by being near the plants, but touching or brushing the foliage produces a distinctively stronger aroma. The contact releases essential oils from the leaves. Garden visitors should be able to get close enough to fragrant herbs to touch and smell them. Put them in window boxes, containers, pavement-level plantings along corridors, and wherever else their fragrance will be enjoyed.

Lavenders (especially English lavender), rosemaries, thymes, mints, lemon verbena, lemon balm, and bergamot have lovely fragrances. Scented geranium leaves also produce a wide range of aromas, including rose, lemon, mint, eucalyptus, nutmeg, camphor, clove, pine, and others. The herbs listed with the design for A Fragrant, Tactile Herb Garden and in Herbal Theme Gardens will provide you with many possibilities for your fragrance garden.

FORM AND STRUCTURE IN THE HERBAL DESIGN

A collection of plants is interesting and lovely in its own right, but when incorporated into a well-designed composition, the plants become a living work of art. The designer sculpts an ordered framework that the spontaneity of nature enlivens and enriches to produce a living outdoor sculpture. The beautiful array of colors, textures, and organic forms of the plants, the spirited play of light and shadow, and the ephemeral animation and sounds of the outdoor environment combine to create harmonies and magic, transforming the garden into a work of wonder. Cultivating charm in the garden is also designing to allow for natural garden events to occur as they will.

The *form* of a garden is usually determined by the types of lines and shapes that are used. The use of irregular, free-flowing lines conveys a sense of naturalness and informality. In contrast, highly defined, regular lines create a more formal atmosphere. The shapes and lines used in a garden will be partially determined by the atmosphere you want to create, but they must also be informed by the characteristics of the space as it is. The use of form in design should reflect the topography and the surrounding structures. Axial relationships, symmetry or asymmetry, regularity or irregularity of shape, and repetition of elements are all factors and choices in creating a design.

Design *structure* is a term used to describe an organized arrangement among the many components of a garden, site plan, or planting scheme. The structuring principles prescribe the way in which the components perform design functions. The structuring elements are the plants; the major building materials, such as walls, fences, and paving; and other decorative elements, such as birdbaths, furniture, or sculptures. Together, the design principles and the materials used make up the garden's design structure. The way these components are arranged determines their strength in performing design functions.

The pages that follow present and discuss the principles of form and structure that will help you set up harmonious relationships and create pleasurable spaces in the garden. Because of the multiplicity of factors involved in the total design process, however, don't expect to find a recipe for a design that exactly fits your particular site. Instead, let these design basics help you begin exploring the possibilities for whatever landscape setting you may face.

Form

Private gardens have always been the arena for a wide spectrum of personal expression in the landscape. Thus, the form or shape of the site plan or garden is often an expression of the preferences of the individual designer. The following two sections will help familiarize you with the concepts and devices used to plan the form of your garden, as well as with the particular forms your garden can take.

Elements of Form

The forms of gardens have carried symbolic meanings throughout garden history and through many world cultures. The circle may symbolize the ideal and the spiritual, whereas the square represents rationality and science. Free-flowing, meandering lines may be spontaneous, mirroring the organic forms found in nature.

Given a group of random shapes or forms of varying complexity, our eye naturally reduces the more complex forms to simple, regular ones. These regular forms—circles, squares, triangles—evoke a high degree of sensual satisfaction in the garden visitor. Forms with simple, clear geometry therefore provide a good foundation for the herb garden. The basic shapes need not be obvious: they can be crafted and molded into a myriad of interesting derivative forms.

Whether you prefer regular, classical forms, such as the perfect circle or square, or the more irregular, organic ones, or some combination of both, order

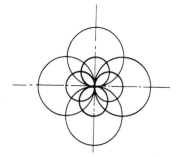

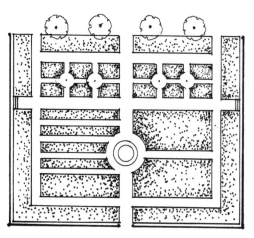

Simple rectangles can be subdivided into beds, as in William Penn's kitchen garden at Pennsbury Manor (right). For designs based on circles, see pages 193 and 221.

and relationship are always of primary importance. Be careful not to confuse formality with order. Highly ordered gardens are not only for spaces closely associated with architecture. Informal does not necessarily mean less ordered or less structured, nor does it preclude coherency between the components and spaces of the garden. However irregular, informal, or free-flowing the forms of a garden may be, the use of regulating lines generated from the surrounding structures will help the spatial forms relate to one another and to the existing site. Even the most informal, casual, or naturalistic gardens will be enhanced by design. Continuity through repetition and coherent relationships among the garden constituents is pleasing to the eye and senses. The way the elements in a design are arranged and the degree to which they reinforce one another greatly influence the ambience and feeling of a garden.

The form of a site plan may appropriately reflect a response to topography or to existing site elements, such as a tree or building structure. The form selected may also refer to the surrounding context of the site. The architectural style of the associated buildings or the cultural or physical history associated with the site may prompt appropriate forms to be expressed in the site plan. The forms used in a garden may echo an architectural detail or adhere to a historically accurate form for a period garden.

Determining the desired function of an outdoor garden space—how it is intended to be used and by whom—is always an important part of the early stages of the design process. Once you know the answers to those questions, you can design it to accommodate and reflect your needs. Another consideration is maintenance. If a garden is easy to care for, then it is a pleasure to work in; if it is cumbersome to maintain, enjoyment in gardening wanes as the gardener loses his or her desire and motivation to tend it.

Form should therefore take into account how the garden is to be maintained and by whom. The plant bed, particularly its dimensions and its relationship to pathways and entrances, should be designed to allow for convenient and easy access. If a bed of herbaceous plants is too wide, then it will be difficult to reach the plants in the middle and back portions for grooming and other maintenance chores.

Stepping stones within the bed or behind the bed may help alleviate that problem. An added benefit of the use of stepping stones is that the areas of soil compaction resulting from foot traffic in the bed are limited. When designing the shape of the bed, allow a comfortable reach to the plants.

Axis. The axis is an effective ordering device for the designer and is especially useful in setting up relationships and organizing the spaces and components of the design form. Interesting garden spaces and their connecting pathways can be ordered around an axis. It can establish the geometry of architectonic designs, or in naturalistic gardens, it can create a linear path through a series of natural habitats.

An axis is a line established by two points in space about which forms and elements can be arranged. A visual axis can occur along a straight line; a physical axis (usually a path) can be a straight line or it can curve and meander both horizontally and vertically. Axial relationships may correspond to the regulating lines of a proportioning grid for a site plan. They may also be superimposed into a totally different ordering system. For example, a free-standing herb garden with a geometric form and an axial ordering system placed into the pastoral setting of a park or large residential property produces an interesting sculptural effect.

Symmetry is the balanced distribution of equivalent forms or spaces about a common line (the axis) or a point (the center). An axial relationship implies, but does not necessarily require, symmetry. It does, however, demand balance. Symmetrical balance comes from equal or like masses or elements balancing on either side of the axis or around the center. Formal designs are often characterized by bilateral symmetry. Asymmetrical balance arises when unequal or unlike elements or masses balance on either side of the axis or around the center. *Asymmetrical occult balance* is the term given to the equilibrium achieved by the mind-eye evaluation of form, mass, value, color, or association around a line or point. This type of balance is prevalent in Japanese viewing garden traditions.

An optical illusion of distance can be created by manipulation of the perspective lines between two points in a planting design. Narrowing the lines of the path or visual frame as it moves away from the viewer creates a sense of greater distance. Conversely, to make an object or space appear closer, gradually widen the axial lines as they approach the distant object or space. This design technique, called *forced perspective manipulation*, uses axial relationships to create a dramatic effect by altering the perception of space between two objects, points, or spaces.

The point of intersection between a primary axis and a cross axis becomes an important position in a geometrical design. In an herb garden this center point is typically held by a sundial, birdbath, fountain, garden sculpture, or special planting. The locations where the axes terminate—physically and visually—are also important in the design. They can be punctuated with ornamental specimen plants, groupings of container plants, vegetative or built structures, garden ornaments, or garden furniture, for example.

Repetition. Repetition and rhythm are valuable design devices. Using the same or similar elements arranged in a regular or repeated fashion sets up a rhythm. This creates a strong sense of order, unity, and visual continuity in the design.

The eye tends to group elements found in a random composition according to similar or common visual characteristics and their proximity to one another. It seeks to make visual relationships, and it wants to be led in a rhythmic manner. But repetition without variation becomes tedious and monotonous, and too much variety without continuity results in a cluttered composition, disturbing rather than pleasing to the eye. A focal element provides a visual resting spot, terminating the rhythmic eye movement. Too many focal elements in a design, however, can cause visual confusion and disharmony.

A strong site structure can withstand a lot of variation of individual parts without losing its overall visual and design integrity. Similarly, a planting bed with a strong unifying edge treatment can support a large variety of plants without becoming cluttered. Keeping these things in mind will help you use repetitive elements to emphasize certain shapes and lines without losing the structure your design needs.

Apply the principle of repetition to all levels of design, from the ordering of the site plan's structure and garden spaces, to the placement of plants in a border or bed, to the design of the edge treatments throughout the garden. The simplest form of repetition is a linear pattern of identical elements. The placement of repetitive elements in the design can reflect the basic form of the garden, whether it is straight lines and rectilinear forms or curvilinear lines and irregular, free-flowing forms. The elements need not be literally identical to achieve a sense of rhythm and continuity. The plant materials may share a common trait, such as foliage color, foliage texture, flower color, plant form, or growing habit. The building materials may reflect order by repetition of material type, color, texture, or patterning. By repeating one or more of these common traits, the plants and building materials provide interest and variety yet belong to a family of shared qualities, which help define the forms and achieve rhythmic continuity in the design.

Garden Forms

Geometric Herb Gardens. The preceding discussion has alluded to two main types of forms: classical forms with highly regular shapes, such as circles and squares, and natural forms with organic, free-flowing shapes. In this section and the next, these two general types of form will be more carefully examined.

The traditional geometric herb garden motif is a highly ordered composition with a harmonious balance of unity and variety. Such designs offer a timeless beauty, as successful in gardens designed today as they have been throughout history. Geometric forms provide an ordered foundation and help develop a clear, coherent design and set up relationships among the components of the garden or site plan.

Geometric gardens are usually highly ordered, stable, unified, and free of tension. Thus, they are an ideal foundation to house the rich variety of herbal plants with their lively array of color, texture, and shape. A unified form with a diversity of plants is a classic combination, offering the essential quiet beauty for which herb gardens are valued. Achieving this balance of order and intricacy is one of the designer's goals. Order without variety can be monotonous or even rigid; variety without unity is merely chaotic and cluttered.

A geometric garden is often ordered by a primary axis and one or more cross axes, which further divide the form into compartments. The axial lines typically become the walkways, with planting beds in the resulting compartments. The beds may be symmetrical or asymmetrical both in shape and in the way they're planted. The use of cross axes increases the variety of geometries and forms. The basic shapes — circles, squares, and triangles — can be crafted and molded to yield their many interesting derivatives.

Natural Herb Gardens. Nature has an exquisite order. Although some people view nature as random, perhaps a more appropriate description would emphasize a degree of order in which spontaneous events—large and small, simple and complex—occur. This description provides a nicely defined goal for designers of various garden and landscape design situations. The degree and balance of order and spontaneity in a design will be your personal choice.

Nature's ordering systems are evident and precise when one considers, for example, the highly ordered arrangement of seed capsules in cross-section. Many have symmetrical compartments of seeds organized around a central point; others attach seeds in a perfect spiral. Another example of nature's order is demonstrated by the line formed by the trees (often a single species that thrives in wet soil) at the edge of a mountain lake. These trees define the meandering form of the lake and move the viewer's eye in a continuous, harmonious line along the water's edge. A different kind of order is the rhythm created by repetition of colors, such as the bright reds and golds of autumn foliage lighting up a mountainside.

These patterns can be repeated in garden design. For example, meandering paths through a garden area could be designed to encourage movement in and out and around and through various landscape spaces. Paths might be enhanced through design manipulation to provide a variety of experiences: light and dark, closed and open, expansive and restricted, transparent and dense.

Experiences of nature can inform design. A dark, densely planted narrow path makes a dramatic entry to a climactic, light-filled open space or a beautiful vista, whether in nature or in the garden. Through design, natural settings create pleasurable access to a variety of interesting landscape events.

Remember, however, that even a natural garden will be much more satisfying if it reflects thoughtful design. Order is not just for formal gardens or gardens influenced by building structures; order must be a part of every design. Natural gardens will be free from many of the restrictions imposed on geometric, classical designs, but they should still have the important combination of unity and diversity. Whether it comes from visual axial relationships or from repetition of color or from complementary curves and angles, order will keep your natural garden from lapsing into random confusion.

Structure

A successful garden design gets its character from the chosen forms, but it must have a clearly defined design structure to support them. Structure ensures the readability of the design by giving definition to its spaces and forms. Coherent relationships among the garden components come from the interplay of form and structure. A strong site structure can withstand a lot of variation without losing its overall integrity. A clearly articulated structure, or lack of one, can make or break a planting design.

The structuring principles suggest ways to translate important design considerations, such as spatial enclosure and edge definition, to the design. The structuring elements of an herbal design are the plants and the building materials. Discovering the ways these work together and reinforce one another presents a great challenge, but at the same time it offers limitless possibilities for expressing your individuality in garden design artistry and craftsmanship.

Structuring Principles

Spatial Enclosure. Space and scale create the atmosphere of a garden. Most people know when they like and feel good in a garden space, but often they don't understand why. Gardens that exhibit a clear, coherent organization of space, usually defined by at least some degree of enclosure, are deemed the most enjoyable.

Outdoor spaces are often leftover spaces, characterized by a disjointed conglomeration of existing elements with weak spatial definition. The work of the garden designer is to explore and discover relationships among those existing elements, knitting them together into a coherent, ordered arrangement. The design should form, mold, and create space, as well as organize the relationships of the garden constituents. The designer is concerned with creating a sense of spatial organization where none previously existed, often by providing a greater degree of enclosure to weakly defined outdoor areas.

A garden with a well-structured series of spaces offers a variety of experiences as one moves through it. The transitions between spaces determine the way a visitor will experience those spaces—visually or physically. Successful transitions flow and blend one type of garden space with another. They reflect changes in form, function, and feeling. There are, however, situations when an abrupt change is appropriate to evoke a certain response.

Outdoor spaces are frequently a consequence of whatever architecture surrounds them. The materials that most often create or define outdoor spaces are the adjacent building walls, the plants, and the garden's built structures, such as a masonry wall or wooden fence. An outdoor space adjacent to a building may be

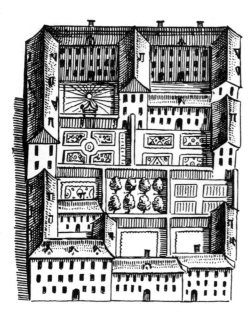

Modern townhouse dwellers will find interesting solutions to garden design in the plans of the Old World. In Turin, courtyard planting beds were integrated with the surrounding architecture.

partially defined by it but may need additional enclosure to complete the desired spatial character.

Regulating the lines of a design. Spaces associated with a building are pleasing when they reflect the proportion, scale, and rhythm of the architecture. By extending the proportions generated by the architecture into the space, an outdoor room that maintains spatial and visual continuity with the associated building is created.

Lines regulating the architecture include those generated from the building corners, windows, doors, posts, or columns. These regulating lines can then be extended into the garden and become guidelines for the design of the forms and spaces of the garden.

A grid reflecting the architectural regulating lines can be a helpful device to organize the design. If no architecture is present at the site, you can create your own grid. The organizing power of the grid results from the regularity and continuity of its pattern. If the grid pattern reflects the regulating lines of the adjacent building, then a harmonious relationship is created between the building and the garden. Outdoor spaces, planting beds, paths, walls, hedges, and other garden elements may vary in form and scale but will share an underlying proportional relationship to each other.

Portions of the grid and the resulting forms, lines, and spaces can be manipulated in response to site topography and other existing elements. A conscious deviation from the grid provides an element of surprise. It may also signal a transition from one type of space to another. Careful attention to the proportions of the grid will allow you to make changes, yet maintain the underlying order.

The trace-overlay technique. An excellent technique for checking the structure and spatial enclosure of your design is the trace-overlay method. You create the trace overlay by placing a piece of tracing paper over the finished design, then outlining or coloring only the structuring components. You may wish to do one overlay for the plants used as structuring components, then another for the built structures. By isolating the two types of structuring elements, the strengths and weaknesses of each become apparent. The overlays show both the relationships among garden components and the success with which the lines and forms define the spaces.

This easy-to-use self-help design tool is effective during the process of constructing the design and as a double check on a completed plan. The technique can also be helpful in checking seasonal color: use at least three overlays, one for each growing season.

Design of Edges. Edging in the herb garden is an age-old tradition that can be functional as well as visually pleasing. The edging plants of a bed or planting area help maintain a neat and orderly appearance, and the continuous edge unifies a garden composition that contains a large variety of plants. The edge is also one of the single most important tools the designer has to provide structure for an herb garden that consists primarily of small plants. Order and continuity result from a well-defined edge of the planting bed or border. Edge treatment gives clear legibility to the form and lines of the garden; that is, the forms created by planting beds and pathways are made more visually prominent by articulation through masonry edges, plants as edges, or a combination of both.

The way the edge is designed tends to strongly influence the overall character or feeling of the garden, particularly its formality or informality. A formal garden may have a single or a limited number of herb species creating the edge of the beds, often making use of those plants that have compact forms or that are closely clipped and manicured. A more informal feeling is created in an herb garden when many species form the edge, especially those that have creeping, flopping, or sprawling growth habits.

The strong edge of a plant bed visually unifies a diverse number of species growing within it. This strong edge may even spare the gardener some maintenance and grooming chores: the clearly legible structure provided by the edge enables the design to hold together even when individual plants inside the edge are not groomed to perfection. As a consequence, the maintenance time and energy required in the garden are reduced.

Structuring Elements

Plants. Plants are, of course, the living, vegetative structuring components of a design. Good use of plants as structural elements of the design will give a garden that desirable but often illusive quality of charm and artistry. Properly chosen plants complement adjacent architecture or garden building components and soften their lines as well. They allow your garden to display a spirited succession of harmonious colors and contrasting textures through the seasons.

Plants perform a number of important design functions, especially giving structure to the design. Since the herbaceous and subshrub annual, biennial, and perennial herbs are relatively small plants, other plant types—trees, shrubs, vines—are instrumental in structural functions, such as providing scale and enclosure, that these smaller plants cannot always achieve. (Refer to the extensive listings of herbal trees, shrubs, and vines in the Plant Profiles.)

Trees, shrubs, and vines. Evergreen trees and shrubs can provide a strong degree of definition in a garden design. They can be used to form living walls that enclose an outdoor space, thus creating an intimate outdoor room. These living walls may also be used as a screen to block undesirable views. Evergreen trees and shrubs, as well as densely branched deciduous plants, make excellent windbreaks to deflect cold winds from the garden. These rich green plants are often used as a background to set off colorful herbs and flowering perennials.

Evergreens are particularly useful for maintaining the visual integrity of the design during the winter months, when most of the herbaceous or shrubby herbs have died back or become dormant. Evergreen ground covers provide a year-round green carpet in areas of the country where snow doesn't accumulate.

Deciduous plants can also perform a number of important and interesting functions in a design. A row of deciduous trees along both sides of a path will create a lovely corridor. Its canopy, when mature, may be dense enough to become a ceiling, further defining a volume of outdoor space. Shady canopies provide a cool refuge from hot summer sun. They can also protect garden visitors from a sudden summer storm. A protected spot where one can watch and listen to a rain shower without becoming drenched is one of the special treats a garden offers. The varying densities of branching habits and the type and size of foliage of deciduous trees may create an interesting interplay of light and shadow, lending movement and an ephemeral quality to the garden space.

Vertical elements in outdoor spaces can make a tremendous visual impact. Trees and tall shrubs placed at the edge of a garden space may create a dramatic frame for a view, leading the eye out into the larger landscape. In the heart of the garden they may be a focal element in the design.

A specimen tree or shrub that displays an interesting overall form, branching habit, foliage or flower color, or foliage texture could be used to mark a point of axial intersection or to terminate a visual line or a physical pathway. An espaliered tree or shrub makes a unique sculptural element in the design scheme.

Vines trained on arbors, pergolas, or pavilions can soften the lines of built structures, provide shade, or offer protection from rainfall. A vine-covered trellis can be an attractive disguise for a bare wall.

Herbaceous and subshrub herbs. The herbaceous and shrubby herbs may also function as structuring elements. They can be used to articulate and reinforce the forms and lines of the garden. Plantings of these herbs often reflect the regulating lines generated by the surrounding architecture or an independent proportioning system, such as a grid. Herbaceous or subshrub herbs used with built structures—raised beds or masonry edges, for example—provide stronger definition than when used alone.

These herbs play a very important role as edging and hedging plants, defining the lines and shapes of the planting beds, borders, and pathways. In large masses, beds, or knot-garden patterns, they generate ground-level interest. Specimen herbs in containers and herbal topiaries can serve as focal points in the garden.

Herbs, because they come in so many sizes, forms, colors, textures, and growth habits, make excellent edging plants. Many respond well to close clipping. Others have looser yet naturally compact growth habits, which are useful for informal designs. Trailing herbs are a good choice for softening a hard masonry edge or for cascading from a raised bed or retaining wall.

A large variety of species in an edge can create visual unity through the repetition of common traits. Common foliage colors, foliage textures, or plant forms, when arranged in a repetitive pattern along an edge, will result in visual order. For instance, the many varieties of creeping and ground-matting thymes share a sprawling form and a spirited, irregular growing habit, though they may vary in foliage color, flower color, and foliage texture and form. They are popular edging plants for a more casual herb garden. Dianthus, dwarf lavender, lamb's-ears, and dwarf sage are also lovely and useful edge plants. Although they differ in their growing habits and form, they share silver or silver-gray foliage.

Edging and hedging herbs, particularly those that respond to clipping, are excellent knot-garden plants. The ornamental and contrasting foliage colors and textures of the dwarf conifers make them attractive knot-garden plants, too. Use them in larger, more substantial knots appropriate for large areas. Their slow growth rates and naturally compact forms require infrequent clipping and shaping—a plus where maintenance is a concern.

Specimen herbs in containers and herbal topiary sculptures can be positioned to complement the design, mark a center or entrance, terminate a sight line, punctuate an intersection, signal a change in elevation, or create a focal feature. Herbs that adapt well to topiary sculpture or a wire form include scented geraniums, prostrate and upright rosemaries, large lavenders, hyssops, and lemon verbena. These same plants are excellent for creating a classic herbal topiary, usually geometric.

A *standard* is a topiary in which an herb's foliage is trimmed to grow in a full globe on top of its straight, single stem; it resembles a lollipop. To create a standard, choose an herb whose mature stem becomes woody. The woody stem is necessary to support the heavy ball of foliage that will result. Select a nursery plant with a straight stem. Clip off all the lateral branches and continue to do so as it grows. Encourage straight, upward growth by staking and tying. When the long, skinny plant reaches the desired height (from six inches to three feet), pinch the terminal tip to encourage lateral branching. Continue to pinch terminal tips to create a full, attractive mound of foliage and flowers on top of the single stem. In one to three years the stem should be woody enough to support the top growth without the stake. Ongoing maintenance will include clipping for shape and health. Remember that herbs in containers may freeze faster than they would in the ground and usually need to be moved indoors for the winter.

Attractive container specimen herbs include bay laurel, rosemaries, myrtle, lavenders, and scented geraniums. Rosemary, lavender, and hyssop make lovely bonsai; they respond well to root pruning and branch wiring.

Built Structures. The built structures of an herbal planting design are instrumental as structuring components and space-defining elements. These, along with the plants, work in unison to create a successful scheme. Paving, edges, steps, raised beds, walls, lattices, trellises, arbors, pergolas, pavilions, amphitheaters, and existing buildings can all be used as structuring elements. Site furnishings and ornaments, such as benches, fountains, containers, lights, and outdoor sculpture, also provide structure in a design. The way these elements are arranged, organized, and related to one another determines the degree to which they function as structuring elements.

Walls and ornamental posts provide a strong structuring element; the paving divides and defines the area within the space. This 1577 garden is enclosed with trellis railings.

Paving. The configuration of the pavement plays an important role in defining the garden's form. The type and style of paving material influence the overall character of the garden design. A change in paving material can differentiate between the path of movement and the places of rest. In cities, where paving surfaces abound, they present an especially important design opportunity.

The current wide selection of colors, textures, and types of paving materials, as well as the design pattern, make possible numerous interesting combinations and patterns. Brick and stone are traditional paving materials in herb gardens. The design pattern for paved surfaces can reflect refined detailing in an herbal design. Consult landscape architectural and landscape construction books for examples of traditional brickwork patterns, such as running bond, basket weave, and herring-bone, and for installation options and procedures.

Masonry edges. These perform both a visual and a practical function in the herbal design. When incorporated into the paving pattern, they can be very effective. A brick walk with a granite edge is an especially nice combination. Hard edges used in combination with herbal edges strengthen the definition of the line. Edging herbs with trailing habits can soften the hard edge while maintaining the line.

The practical benefits of the hard edge are many. It deters people from entering planted areas and injuring plants. Along paved areas, such as sidewalks, streets, or plazas, where drainage water can carry salts and grime into the planting bed, a slightly raised hard edge can prevent the contaminants, as well as the excessive water, from entering. A change in masonry material at the edge of a walk, coupled with a slightly raised masonry edge, becomes a safety signal for wheelchair users or the blind. Finally, a hard edge can be designed to accommodate the tire width and weight of a mower and serve as a low-maintenance measure in areas where grass is adjacent to a planted area, eliminating the need to edge the lawn.

Site structures. These are also effective structuring components. Free-standing or retaining walls, raised beds, fencing, or iron railings provide varying degrees of enclosure, defining spaces in much the same way that evergreen trees and shrubs do. Arbors and pergolas can articulate a path or corridor. Trellises dress a bare wall attractively. Steps make a transition from one elevation to another, often denoting a change of mood or function.

Rooftop gardens, courtyards, terrace areas, and pedestrian malls frequently rely on such site structures as raised beds and free-standing walls to enclose space or articulate pathways. Arbors, pavilions, and pergolas define space as well as provide protection from sun, wind, and rain. These lightweight structures become even more useful on decks and rooftops, where weight limitations prohibit the massive amounts of heavy topsoil needed to grow trees and shrubs.

Furnishings and ornaments. These also are used to perform structuring functions. Attractive containers of herbs can designate an entrance, frame a view, mark a center, or terminate the sight line of an axis. Lampposts set at regular intervals along a corridor or walkway can set up rhythm. Benches can be positioned advantageously to provide panoramic views, as well as to allow the enjoyment of up-close appreciation of intricate plantings or interesting species.

The style and material of garden ornaments contribute greatly to the overall character of the garden and present the opportunity for personal expression. Garden ornaments and outdoor sculpture can also be structural elements in a design. Garden sculpture can be the focus of a design, perhaps occupying the important point where two axes intersect. Sculpture with a botanical or an ecological theme could be used as an evocative garden centerpiece. An ornamental wall fountain can terminate an important sight line. Pools and fountains can be structuring elements when they mark a center of a space, as seen in the traditional geometric four-quartered herb gardens. An armillary sundial or a modern outdoor sculpture are both interesting choices for an herbal design.

Building Materials. The type and style of the building materials selected for the edging, furnishings, ornaments, paving, walls, and other garden structures greatly influence the overall character of the herb garden design. Bricks used as paving or in a pierced brick wall, a wrought iron fence or gate, or an ornamental urn with a classical motif all contribute to a formal feeling in a garden. In contrast, a stone dust pathway, a wooden picket fence, and a rough-cut stone birdbath create a more informal garden character.

Construction materials can be selected to beautifully complement herbs. The texture and color of the materials can blend with or set off the many rich, lovely colors of herb foliage and flowers.

Traditional materials. Weathered brick, stone, wood, and decorative wrought iron harmonize beautifully with herb plants. These materials convey a sense of permanence and are rich with historical overtones. They are very appropriate and easily adaptable to many residential and urban sites.

Teakwood's weathered gray is especially lovely with silver, blue-green, and purple foliage. Garden ornaments made of bronze, copper, stone, wood, and wrought iron are beautiful complements to herb plantings. Armillary sundials are traditional herb garden ornaments available in a number of interesting designs.

Modern materials. Tremendous opportunity exists for creatively combining modern construction materials with herb plantings. Contemporary containers also can be attractively planted with herbs, creating a modern design appeal.

The wide selection of colors used today to tint concrete offers interesting design possibilities. A two- or three-tone paving design creates interesting ground-level patterns, perhaps echoing a knot-garden pattern in a nearby bed. A rose-tinted paving can set off the many pink, rose, violet, purple, and blue flowers of herbs and is especially stunning with silver or purple foliage. A dark-gray concrete container or raised bed would be an effective contrast to a silver-gray artemisia or a gray-green lavender or garden sage.

A dark gray concrete wall would be striking with the bright, rosy lavender flowers and gray, downy foliage of woolly thyme draped over it or even planted in it. The browns and earth tones of granite and tinted concrete blend well with most herbs and are especially pleasing with the yellow-orange flowers of calendula or the chartreuse flowers of lady's mantle.

The newer cut-in-place concrete patterning technique can create highly ornamental paving patterns that provide a refined level of detailing in the herbal design.

Consult the references in the back of this book, as well as landscape architecture and garden design magazines, to find suppliers of garden and site structures, furniture, containers, sculpture, sundials, and other garden accessories and building materials.

DESIGN CUES FROM HISTORICAL PRECEDENTS

Historical herb gardens offer a wealth of design ideas and illustrate excellent design principles. Most of these designs are geometric and are easily restated or modified to harmonize with the architectural fabric of today's urban and suburban areas. They can also be crafted and molded into a variety of landscape settings.

Many herb gardens designed today adhere to the traditional geometric forms that portray classical beauty and balance. Some modern designs are descendants of the ancient Roman and Greek kitchen garden, the medieval cloister and physic garden, or the Colonial American kitchen garden. Knot gardens, popularized in sixteenth- and seventeenth-century England, are often translated to today's herb gardens.

Designers need not feel confined to merely copying traditional herb garden styles. Reinterpreting these traditional motifs in new ways is an exciting possibility. You may want to extract a component of the old and use it in a new way. For example, a terrace design could become an herbal tapestry derived in part from the tradition of formal knot gardens. The creative use of herbs in contemporary landscape design is limited only by the designer's imagination.

This section offers suggestions for ways to adapt ideas from historical garden design precedents. Suggestions for contemporary designs echoing these historically rooted cues follow.

The Quadripartite Motif

The formal quadripartite, or four-quarter, motif is the traditional herb garden design form. Four bilaterally symmetrical compartments are formed by the bisection of a square or rectangle with primary and cross axes.

This form, which traces its origin through centuries and cultures, is rich with religious and literary symbolism based on the number four. In ancient gardens the four beds represented the elements of fire, water, air, and earth. In early and medieval Persian and European gardens the beds symbolized the four rivers of Paradise described in Genesis: "a river went out of Eden to water the Garden; and from thence it was parted, and became four beds." A symbolic fountain or pool of water marked the center of the garden.

During the Europeans' explorations of the sixteenth and seventeenth centuries, the four beds represented the four corners of the earth or the four known continents of the period: Asia, Africa, the Americas, and Europe. Many newly discovered herbs were grown in physic gardens, where their medicinal uses were

The quadripartite, or four-quarter, garden is highly ordered and stable. It has formed the basis of many geometric herb gardens, including the sixteenth-century Botanical Garden of Padua (right).

investigated. Pleasure gardens contained many of the aromatic herbs. In monastic gardens herbs were studied and beautifully illustrated in the early herbals.

The early botanical gardeners, concerned with classification of the newly introduced plants, placed them in an orderly, scientific arrangement, often using the four-quarter form or a variation of it. It was then commonly believed that Paradise had been scattered after the Fall. Newly discovered plants were thought to be pieces of the Lost Paradise, and botanical gardens were the repositories where these pieces could be gathered together in an attempt to recreate Paradise on Earth.

The Botanical Garden of Padua in Italy (1543) used the quadripartite motif in a circular form to represent a spiritual dimension to the earthly four-square symbol. The circle represented the spiritual and ideal; the square represented science, the mind, or rational man.

The quadripartite form has been the most frequently used garden form throughout history worldwide. It is still a very functional, as well as symbolic, garden form for cultivating herbs and other plants traditionally grown for utilitarian purposes. In both function and beauty, the geometric herb garden has maintained a lasting status in the designed landscape. The simple configurations of this basic four-square are highly ordered. As such, they are a visually pleasing and appropriate foundation for the variety of plants in an herb garden collection.

Like other geometric forms, the four-quarter can be easily translated into outdoor spaces that are governed by the regulating lines stemming from the surrounding architecture. They can also be freestanding entities in the landscape. The religious, historical, and even personal symbolism associated with these forms adds to the richness of the design.

The Hortus Conclusus

The *hortus conclusus* ("enclosed garden") is a garden form that has expressed biblical and literary symbolism throughout garden history. The *hortus conclusus* was a sacred garden. In the secular Renaissance pleasure garden, the *hortus conclusus* was a secret place within the larger garden complex. It typically contained a symbolic rose garden, luscious fruits, aromatic herb-lined walks, shady vine-covered arbors, and a cooling, melodic fountain. Perhaps these were the first gardens of the five senses.

The *hortus conclusus* form is also functional. Ancient Egyptian and Persian gardens were enclosed to protect plants from hot, drying winds. In today's gardens, enclosed areas protect the borderline-hardy herbs from damaging winter winds. They also help to retain the aroma of the many fragrant plants within the enclosure. The enclosing structures or plants define the space and create the scale, proportion, and form of the design. Enclosed outdoor spaces offer a private place of intimate charm in which to relax and garden.

There is something inherently enchanting about an enclosed herb garden. Upon entering, one immediately experiences the tranquility and mystique that stem perhaps from such a garden's rich symbolic heritage, orderly geometry, and gentle beauty. In modern designs, the *hortus conclusus* is still a sacred garden, offering a healing and rejuvenating refuge.

Islamic Gardens

The concept of a safe, sacred, paradisiacal garden goes back to the beginning of history and is beautifully expressed in the traditional Islamic garden. Two fundamental tenets of Islam are that universal unity and order pervade all of life, regardless of the diversity of experiences, and that the element of water provides relief to body and spirit and represents timelessness. Thus, Islamic gardens are enclosed, highly ordered (quadripartite in rectangle form), and unified, and contain the important element of water. Islamic gardens and their associated architecture exhibit masterly use of light and shadow to create mystical ambience in garden spaces. The simple, elegant design qualities and techniques used in Islamic garden traditions are worth emulating in modern landscape designs.

Traditional Islamic gardens employed the full spectrum of water in the garden. Pools and fountains were typically placed axially in the simple, ordered designs. There were deep, still reflecting pools, musical fountains and cascades, and channels and rills, often used for irrigation. In modern gardens the cooling effect of water is a wonderful element. Still, deep reflective pools can be calming and therapeutic. Moving water, which has been popular in modern landscape designs, offers a soothing, musical effect in a garden space.

Use Islamic motifs in intriguing and provocative ways. Combine the traditional Islamic garden spatial, light, and hydric characteristics, which create a calm and tranquil atmosphere, with an abundance of herbs, particularly the aromatic ones, to enhance a garden's healing, therapeutic qualities.

Knot Gardens

Knot gardens are made by weaving continuous bands of neatly clipped herbs into knotlike patterns. The knot motif was used in the decorative arts of Rome, Islam, and medieval Europe. An interlocking knot signified infinity because it had no beginning and no end. The knot garden was enormously popular during the sixteenth- and seventeenth-century English Renaissance, particularly the early Tudor and Elizabethan periods. Graphic examples of knot configurations appeared in many garden books of the period. *The Profitable Arte of Gardening* (1568) and the *Gardener's Labyrinth* (1577) by Thomas Hill are two such publications.

Simple geometric shapes — circle, square, semicircles — form the basis of this knot garden from The Gardeners' Labyrinth, *by Thomas Hill (London, 1571). Plants with contrasting foliage enable the eye to follow the pattern.*

A closed knot garden has flowers or herbs occupying the spaces created by the interwoven bands of herbs. An open knot does not have anything planted in the voids. Mulch materials, often colorful, may be used to contrast with or complement the foliage of the knot plants.

Knot garden is sometimes used loosely to describe a garden in the quadripartite motif, that is, a square garden divided into quadrants or beds separated by walkways. The edge of this simple configuration is usually defined by a continuous clipped boxwood, yew, or herbal hedge. The insides of the boxes may be filled with colorful mulch materials or with herbs or flowers. Sometimes topiary is used to punctuate bed corners or walkway intersections. Traditionally, the center of the four-square design is marked with a pool, fountain, sundial, or other garden ornament.

Knot-garden designs add interest to a garden space. Consider the interesting and lovely view from a window out onto a beautiful knot garden planted in a terrace or courtyard. An elevated perspective from a balcony or porch sets the knot garden below at its breathtaking best. Knots are appropriate in small nook-and-cranny areas of the city or as the central focus of a larger design. A small knot garden becomes the jewel of the garden when it is used to occupy the center of a four-square garden or one of the many derivative geometric garden forms.

The knot designs on these pages are but four of literally thousands of knot patterns that were illustrated in garden books of the sixteenth and seventeenth

centuries. These knot designs can be recreated in your garden. Many herbaceous and woody herbs lend themselves well to formal or informal knot patterns. A good knot-garden plant has a naturally tidy, dense-branching growth habit and striking foliage color and texture and will accept light or heavy clipping.

A small knot garden can be as pleasing and effective as a larger one. For a small knot garden, choose plants that stay small, such as common upright thyme (*Thymus vulgaris*), English thyme (*Thymus vulgaris* 'Broad-leaf'), French thyme (*Thymus vulgaris* 'Narrow-leaf'), silver thyme (*Thymus vulgaris* 'Argenteus'), dwarf lavenders (*Lavandula angustifolia* 'Hidcote' and 'Munstead'), germander (*Teucrium chamaedrys*), dwarf santolinas (*Santolina chamaecyparissus* 'Nana' and *Santolina ericoides*), compact rues (*Ruta graveolens* 'Blue Mound' or 'Jackman Blue'), and small artemisias, such as *Artemisia schmidtiana* 'Silver Mound' and Roman wormwood (*Artemisia pontica*). Good choices for one-season knot or edge plants include such annuals as the dwarf basils (*Ocimum basilicum* 'Minimum' and 'Spicy Globe') and biennials like parsley (*Petroselinum crispum*). For a tiny knot garden include tiny-leaf thyme (*Thymus nitidus*) and dwarf winter savory (*Satureja montana pygmaea*).

A good selection of medium-size knot-garden herbs includes English lavender (*Lavandula angustifolia* subsp. *angustifolia* and cultivars *Lavandula* × *intermedia* 'Dutch' and 'Grosso'), hyssop (*Hyssopus officinalis* and varieties), upright rosemary (*Rosmarinus officinalis* and cultivars), gray santolina or lavender cotton (*Santolina chamaecyparissus*), green santolina (*Santolina virens*), and rue (*Ruta graveolens*). These plants have tidy, naturally dense growing habits and respond very well to the close clipping required for a formal garden. The desired width can be achieved either by choosing a plant that matures at that size or by using two or more plants.

For a large knot garden, evergreen shrubs and dwarf conifers create a substantial planting. Boxwood, holly, and yew are traditional knot-garden plants and are also used as border hedges for outlining an enclosed knot garden. Dwarf conifers are excellent knot plants; their dense-branching habits, slow growth rates, and compact forms, as well as their interesting foliage colors and textures, make them ideal. Choose from a wide variety of conifers, including dwarf forms of *Chamaecyparis*, *Picea*, *Pinus*, *Thuja*, *Tsuga*, and others.

Parterres

Seventeenth-century gardeners considered the parterre garden an art form. Parterre gardens are very precise designs that require controlled horticultural and pruning methods. They originated in a period of garden history when the control, even domination, of nature was prevalent in the design of landscapes.

Parterres were usually designed to be viewed from an elevated garden platform or indoor room. Most are quite elaborate and follow an intricate geometric framework. They often look as if they were sculpted out of a solid evergreen base. The outlining border is usually a continuous dense evergreen hedge. The solid tendrils and curls of a scroll or embroidery pattern are formed by clipped boxwood, clipped herbs, or turf panels. The spaces inside the solid pattern are filled with colorful mulches to set off the intricate evergreen design. As its name implies, the *parterre de broderie* borrows its motif from the fancy embroidery of the day.

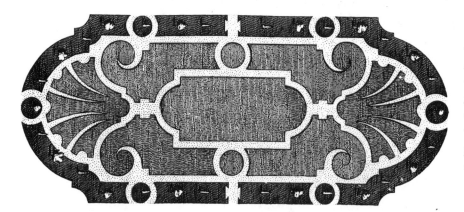

In full scale, a parterre garden requires considerable attention. Today's gardener might want to create a scaled-down version or plant just a portion of a historical design.

The Kitchen Garden

The history of the kitchen garden has been the story of man's endeavors to cultivate plants for food and other purposes. Worldwide and through the centuries, plots of earth ranging from very large to small were used for food production, medicinal ingredients, and horticultural experimentation. Kitchen gardens were cultivated in Egypt, Rome, and Greece, as well as in the Americas, Asia, and Africa. Some of the early gardens in both western and eastern cultures were also devoted to meditation and ritual.

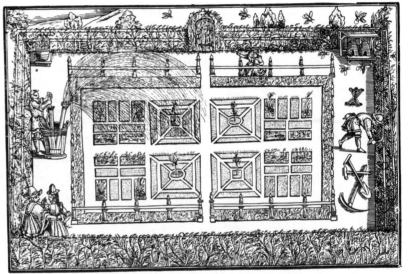

The four parts of a typical kitchen garden were subdivided, and the whole was often enclosed by walls of grapevines, fruit-bearing canes, or espaliered trees. Such gardens are just as practical and attractive today as they were several centuries ago.

The form and function of the European kitchen garden was influenced most strongly by the early medieval monastery garden, the medieval *hortus*, and the Mediterranean gardens they descended from, particularly those of Rome and Greece. The walled kitchen garden of Europe reached its zenith between the seventeenth and nineteenth centuries, when kitchen gardens of various sizes, some as large as several acres, were typical elements on estate landscapes. The kitchen garden's primary purpose was utilitarian: food production, flavoring, and other household uses. Whether massive or modest, the basic form was a simple fourquarter layout for ease and practicality of cultivation. It was divided by pathways of gravel or other earthen materials, with beds further divided in the simplest of geometric shapes. The beds were often slightly raised to improve drainage in the wet climate of northern Europe.

The kitchen garden was always enclosed by a wall to create a microclimate conducive to growing fruits and vegetables. Fruit trees were typically espaliered in beds by the walls to conserve garden space. The walls also created a defensible space and screening from the estate. Sited within the service or stable areas of the estate grounds, the kitchen garden was conveniently located for harvesting, cultivating, and access to stable manure for fertilization. This garden was kept out of sight: the kitchen garden was not intended to be ornamental.

The basic characteristics of the kitchen garden—walled enclosure, simple form, basic function, and second-class location—resisted change for a few hundred years. In 1727, however, Stephen Switzer's *The Practical Kitchen Gardener* introduced the innovative concept of ornamental use of kitchen gardens. This idea enjoyed a short-lived period of experimentation in more refined design treatments before such gardens returned rather quickly to the simpler, strictly utilitarian layouts within high screening walls.

Herbs continued to be grown almost exclusively within enclosed gardens on the expansive English estates, even after the eighteenth-century English landscape movement took down walls elsewhere in the landscape. This was a response to the changing view of nature. The seventeenth-century approach of domination and control was giving way to new concepts of nature as benevolent. The new sentiment was to embrace nature and to integrate its basic beauty and goodness into one's life and landscape. The walls of earlier gardens were intended to keep out not only pilferers and animals, but also the dangers (both physical and metaphorical) believed to be inherent in the wilderness. But even though the greater landscape was changing dramatically, becoming more naturalized and unbound in expression, herbs were still grown in simple, four-quarter beds within the confinement of the walled kitchen garden.

The basic concept and components of the European kitchen garden were transplanted to Colonial America. The prototypical enclosed, four-quarter layout—with dividing paths and a pool, well, cistern, sundial, or other feature to mark the center—is mirrored repeatedly in restored period gardens in this country. Herbs were cultivated for culinary, aromatic, medicinal, and household use and were typically grown with vegetables and flowers. It was later, during the specialty gardening rage, that herbs were lifted from their mixed plantings and put into separate herb gardens, still in the four-square kitchen garden design.

Elaborations of the basic pattern were developed later on grand estates, with decoration as well as function guiding the design. The restored kitchen gardens at Mount Vernon, George Washington's Virginia home, are a good example. Detailed, ornamental brick walls enclose the ample kitchen garden. A series of well-designed beds, simple geometric derivatives of the four-square, divided by pathways of grass or crushed gravel, hold dozens of useful household plants. Herbs are grown separately and in combination with vegetables and flowers. Espaliered fruits and small fruit trees and berries are also found in the kitchen garden. The planting combinations are attentive to decorative effects.

Archaeological investigations of the site of Monticello, Thomas Jefferson's home in Charlottesville, Virginia, indicate that herbs were planted with vegetables and flowers in a series of rectangular plots organized in simple rows and divided by paths. The siting of this garden—like the siting of the home on top of a hill—was innovative for the time. The garden was located on a terraced hilltop that offers majestic panoramas of the greater landscape.

Monticello aside, most herb gardens were restricted to rear or side service areas. The dooryard garden of Colonial America was a fairly common exception. Herbs were blended in an informal arrangement with flowers and vegetables in beds located close to the front door. The idea of using herbs in front entry areas of residences can easily be translated to today's homes. Herb gardens are charming additions to entrance areas. Both informal plantings and the more structured geometric herb garden designs are appropriate, lovely, and welcoming in entry areas. Function and practicality are still important considerations for modern herb gardens, but today, design aesthetics deserve a much higher priority.

Historical garden design projects or restorations may require a considerable amount of research. Garden form, spatial relationships of garden elements, and site location in relation to the house should be determined, as well as plant types and varieties of the period. Recreating an exact replica of a period garden is not always feasible or the only valid approach to historical garden design. You may want to interpret the spirit of the period, and yet show the passing of time. The blending of the old with the new is a popular approach in many public and private historical design projects and restorations.

The use of walls is an appropriate restatement of the traditional kitchen garden. The spatial qualities provided by enclosure are desirable elements in well-designed modern gardens. Garden walls protect plants from the harsher elements and create microclimates conducive to growth. This is especially important, since the cold-hardiness of many of the herbaceous and shrubby herbs is unpredictable, and many typically require winter protection in colder regions of the country. Espaliers and dwarf fruit trees also benefit from the wall's protection.

Enclosed outdoor spaces are quite pleasing to those who use the space. The detailing, style, and choice of materials used for the enclosure afford great opportunity for your artistic and personal expression. You can also use the enclosing walls to reflect the context of the locality.

One good place for an enclosed herb garden is alongside the wall of a residential building, in a front, side, or back yard. By moving foundation shrubs from the base of the home to the property line, you provide spatial distinction between the public and the private. In this location the hedge offers privacy, a sense of intimate enclosure, and a background for herbal plantings. Remember to consider the view of the garden from inside the home.

The currently popular concept of ornamental edible landscaping reflects not only the traditional use of herbs with vegetables and flowers but also a contemporary emphasis on ornamental plant arrangements and combinations within a well-structured design. Today's herb and edible gardens are planted in a variety of garden forms. They often make use of free-flowing, curvilinear, organic forms, rather than the highly ordered, four-quarter kitchen gardens of the past. Yet this newfound freedom in garden design harkens back to the historical kitchen garden.

The advantages of using raised beds were recognized centuries ago, as this 1542 drawing attests. The space-saving techniques help today's gardener make every cubic foot count.

DESIGN CUES FROM WORKS OF RECOGNIZED DESIGNERS

Works of recognized designers, both past and contemporary, are valuable resources. Consult these works to develop ideas that may be adapted for your own projects. Even those that do not specifically use herbs can prompt design ideas. Look for books and magazines under the headings of landscape design, garden design, and landscape architecture at your local library. If literature is limited there, an interlibrary loan service may give you access to books from a library that has a specialized collection in these subject areas. Libraries of botanical gardens and other plant societies, as well as those of universities specializing in botany, horticulture, or landscape architecture, are wonderful places to explore.

Gertrude Jekyll

Translating principles of art to garden design is an intriguing concept illustrated, for example, in the work of the English painter-turned-gardener Gertrude Jekyll (1843–1932). During the past decade, the runaway popularity of perennial flower gardening in America has brought Jekyll's designs and theories to the public eye. Her books have been reprinted and her designs have been published in current gardening literature, thereby making her work very accessible to beginning garden designers.

Jekyll's color theories for the flower garden can be applied to herbal planting designs. She argued, for example, the importance of observing and judging the value of a particular plant's flower or foliage color in relation to the colors of the other plants in proximity to it. She wrote about the way our eye moves through a garden, and this understanding is reflected in her sensitive garden designs, which include carefully sequenced color progressions punctuated by exciting visual peaks and balanced with quieting transitions. She skillfully used silver- and gray-foliaged herbs and other flowering perennials as transitional and accent plants in her planting and garden designs.

Jekyll's garden designs illustrate masterly use of garden structures, ornaments, and furniture to organize the site plan and to perform such design functions as enclosing a volume of outdoor space, establishing relationships in the design, setting up rhythm through repetition, marking a center location or terminating a visual or physical axis, signaling a change in grade, and framing an entrance or a view.

Gertrude Jekyll's plant palette includes many of the herbal plants found in the Plant Profiles, including native woodland and meadow wildflowers, herbal trees and shrubs, flowering perennials, and herbs. Her books include illustrated garden plans with accompanying plant lists and detailed descriptions of the designs. Bear in mind, however, that the climatic conditions in Great Britain—intensity and quality of sunlight, temperature extremes and variations, moisture levels, and humidity—differ from what we experience in most parts of North America. When referring to British garden literature, one must adapt principles and ideas rather than copy designs, plants, or horticultural instructions verbatim.

Jekyll worked extensively with the leading English architect of the arts-and-crafts movement, Edwin Lutyens. Their many country estate projects, including Goddards, Marsh Court, Deanery Gardens, and Jekyll's home, Munstead Wood, show a close integration of house and garden. In much of their collaborative work, Jekyll's designs adhere to the regulating system of the associated architecture. The proportion, scale, and even building materials extend into the adjacent open space to create continuity. Jekyll also used her horticultural expertise and artistic hand to create woodland gardens in appropriate natural areas of these large country estates.

Roberto Burle Marx

Brazilian landscape architect and artist Roberto Burle Marx (b. 1909) is known as the father of modern garden and landscape design. His unique expressions of abstract painting principles were incorporated into his landscape designs. His organization of plants and built materials was original in the 1930s and 1940s. He used indigenous tropical plants with contrasting foliage and flower colors and textures to create living paintings. Since herbal plants also offer many interesting colors and textures, herbal designs could effectively reflect some of the principles illustrated in Burle Marx's work.

Burle Marx drew his inspiration from the natural landscape. He frequently used free-flowing, undulating organic lines and forms abstracted from the South American countryside. Yet certain of his public urban plaza designs made use of classical spatial qualities and regular geometric forms, from large site plans to planting beds. For example, a planting bed that is a perfect circle would be filled with indigenous plants arranged as bright swashes of color. Burle Marx's design vocabulary, unique for his time, made use of underlying concepts and sources of inspiration that are now used extensively. His use of native plants in a variety of design modes, as well as his artistic sensitivity to the landscape, make his work a unique source of interest and ideas.

Beatrix Jones Farrand

American landscape architect Beatrix Jones Farrand practiced from 1890 to 1940. Her breadth and excellence in planting and site design is exemplified in her outstanding gardens at Dumbarton Oaks in Washington, D.C. Here she created a series of strongly structured and interrelated, yet individually unique, outdoor garden rooms. She made excellent use of the Italianate garden design tradition, noted for masterly integration of house to garden and building to site, and adept use of both plants and building materials to structure the garden spaces. Dumbarton Oaks is a model of successful scale, proportion, and spatial hierarchy in designed outdoor space.

Special elements of interest in Farrand's work include her sensitive use of plants. She also designed site structures and garden ornaments whose placement in the site plan structured and organized the overall design. Her use and design of both plant and building materials create a unified, highly ordered composition, enriched and balanced by the beautiful and variable qualities of the plants and the ephemeral nature of the outdoors. Her other works include perennial flower border designs in the tradition of Gertrude Jekyll.

OTHER SOURCES FOR DESIGN IDEAS AND INSPIRATION

The list of works by recognized landscape and garden designers is virtually endless. While consulting garden design literature, you will invariably encounter many fine and inspiring works created by designers unknown to you; don't overlook the possibilities there. Furthermore, landscape designers and landscape architects practicing in your locality, especially those who specialize in gardens and who are knowledgeable in horticulture and plants as well as site planning and design, could be sources for ideas and professional help.

Visiting gardens is a great learning adventure. Pay attention not only to what you see, but also to what you feel. Notice your intuitive responses as you move through a well-designed garden space or series of spaces; nothing can take the place of firsthand experience. Keep a photographic record of gardens you've visited and liked. It will be an excellent source of reference as well as a fun project to document your travels.

Horticulture and design seminars, plant society shows, garden tours, and classes at universities, colleges, nurseries, botanical gardens, arboretums, nature centers, and other botanical institutions are great ways to obtain knowledge and ideas as well as to find friends and colleagues who share a common passion.

Sense of Place

You may want to attempt to reflect your area's natural physical characteristics and its traditions of land use in your designs. Every region, town, even neighborhood has a unique character. Your design should be responsive to the individuality of its location. A sense of place is characterized by many factors, including types of vegetation, topography, even light quality and sky–horizon relationships. It is also established by the cultural and historical heritage of the area, including settlement and development patterns, traditional and current land uses, and architectural fabric and flavor.

Expressing elements of the local context in your own work will allow you to maintain continuity in your neighborhood or region. Reflecting vernacular architectural garden styles and their building materials in your garden or site structures is one way to express a sense of place.

Another is the use of indigenous plants. This is an excellent way to convey an appropriate sense of place in planting design. Native plants lend unity and continuity with the greater landscape, and since they grow well in their native climate, they are quite practical. (Remember, however, that in intensively designed spaces the growing environment may be so altered from the plant's natural habitat that some modifications may be necessary.)

Many other landscape elements, in addition to native plants, contribute to a region's uniqueness and can help maintain continuity between the greater and the designed landscape. For example, in rural, agricultural regions the rectilinear geometry of fields and fencerows is a prominent characteristic of the landscape. This geometry could be reflected or abstracted in residential garden designs in such rural areas.

Decorative Arts

The design motif of a decorative art can be an excellent source of ideas for design details of garden structures or even the site plan form and pattern. The use of decorative art patterns works best when the patterns reflect the heritage of the area. For example, the traditional French *parterre de broderie* garden motif was taken from the popular embroidery patterns of the seventeenth century. In similar fashion today, the design pattern for garden paving materials for a terrace or plaza might borrow from modern or historical textiles. Patterns from ethnic and cultural arts can be reproduced using several colors or textures of brick or concrete pavers. For instance, a beautiful Amish quilt may be the inspiration for a paving design in a rural Pennsylvania garden project. The design motif of a Native American blanket may be reflected in a brick paving or wall pattern, honoring the traditions of a tribe rooted in the region.

Nature

Many indigenous American herbaceous wildflowers and woody shrubs and trees have herbal uses (refer to the list of native plants in the Plant Profiles). Through the use of herbal natives, garden designers can use natural habitats as a source of inspiration. A naturalistic planting using native herbal plants can be a practical as well as lovely design option for woodland or meadow gardens. Drifts of woodland edge shrubs and wildflowers, perhaps accented with small flowering trees, are a beautiful addition to any landscape and, once established, require less maintenance than a mowed lawn.

Current Trends

One relatively new idea for gardeners is the edible landscape, in which fruits, vegetables, and herbs are grown with flowering plants and other ornamentals in a pleasing visual array.

A more recent popular garden movement is environmental gardening. Environmentally conscious gardeners are planting native herbal trees, shrubs, and herbaceous wildflowers. The gardens are designed to simulate the microclimate and macroclimate of native plants in the wild. When plants are put where they thrive, they are healthier, more vigorous, and thus more resistant to disease and insect problems. Healthy plants often do not require the use of environmentally harmful chemical sprays or drenches.

Another facet of environmental gardening is water conservation. When placed in locations that mimic their natural habitats, plants that tolerate cool temperatures and shade require less care, especially in terms of watering, than they would if grown in stronger light or heat. Although many herbs are drought tolerant, and thus excellent plants where water is limited, water conservation is a responsible idea. Refer to the moisture lists under Herb Culture to see which plants will tolerate low moisture levels.

Intuition

Do not underestimate the power of your own intuition as a source of design inspiration. Images may surface as you contemplate a design project or as you study and move through the project site. The ideas that keep returning, intuitively, might be the right ones to follow.

People experience outdoor space in different ways. The same volume of outdoor space may feel uncomfortable and confining to one person, yet pleasurable and intimate to another. One person may prefer a particular color palette while someone else finds those combinations jarring. One person may view the degree of symmetry in design as rigid and too formal, and another may see it as pleasingly ordered. Nostalgia may be the leading force in establishing favorite plants; perhaps they are reminders of a fondly remembered time or a particularly favorite place. Listen to these feelings as you imagine your design, clarify them, and use them to full advantage to make your garden a source of joy and comfort.

In life, as in good garden design, we all need both structure and spontaneity to be successful and happy. The balance of these elements, however, varies from person to person and even within an individual at different times of his or her life. In your design, work to achieve the balance that feels most comfortable to you.

HERBAL THEME GARDENS

Theme gardens present the opportunity to express and display the fascinating qualities of herbs. They can be designed for education or for the pure fun of it. The themes around which herbal theme gardens can be built are innumerable.

A popular theme is the five senses. This garden should contain aromatic herbs for fragrance, flavorful herbs for taste, textured herbs for touch, colorful herbs for beauty, and a fountain to create melodic sounds. If your location is well chosen, you may also have the pleasing sounds of birds and the wind in the trees. These sensory gardens are lovely for unsighted users. They may include plant labels in Braille and barrier-free architecture, such as raised path edges, ramps, or railings.

Another theme garden may feature herbs that are important to a particular ethnic group. Native Americans used herbs for dyes, medicine, flavoring, and religious ceremonies; these would make an interesting theme garden. A Mexican culinary garden would contain several ornamental hot peppers, in addition to the many other herbs found in a culinary garden.

Colonial American gardens used herbs for flavoring, medicine, dyes, fragrance, and other household purposes. These gardens contain many of the most ornamental herbs, thus making them beautiful as well as useful.

A theme garden may also be based on literary sources, such as Shakespeare or the Bible.

Historically important medicinal herbs make interesting themes in hospital gardens. Moreover, herb gardens are life-assuring simply because of their beauty and lovely fragrant qualities, and thus they are especially appropriate for hospitals or rehabilitation centers.

Many native American and Canadian meadow and woodland plants have been used for medicine, dyes, teas, and ceremonial plants. Theme gardens designed to highlight native plants and their uses are often very satisfying. In addition, the use of native plants conveys an important ecological and conservation message. Because public appreciation for native plants is high, and since naturalized plantings can reduce maintenance, wild herbal gardens are an intelligent and interesting design concept. Remember that native plants should not be removed from the wild; most are available from specialized nurseries around the country.

Educate visitors to your herbal theme garden by including labels. These typically include the botanical name, common name, origin, and a phrase or two explaining the herb's use, historical significance, or lore. A plaque or an attractive sign explaining the theme can be placed in the garden to add to people's enjoyment, sparking their curiosity for further herb study. Theme gardens are excellent for parks, and civic-minded volunteers can conduct educational garden tours for school groups or the public.

Colonial American Garden

Achillea millefolium	Yarrow or milfoil
Agastache foeniculum	
	Anise hyssop or giant blue hyssop
Allium schoenoprasum	Chives
Angelica archangelica	Angelica
Borago officinalis	Borage
Calendula officinalis	Pot marigold
Chrysanthemum balsamita	
	Costmary or alecost
Chrysanthemum parthenium	Feverfew
Dianthus caryophyllus	Clove carnation
Dianthus plumarius	Garden pinks
Digitalis purpurea	Foxglove
Foeniculum vulgare	Fennel
Galium verum	Yellow bedstraw
Iris × *germanica* var. *florentina*	
	Orris or florentina iris
Iris pseudacorus	Yellow flag
Lavandula angustifolia subsp. *angustifolia*	
	English lavender
Levisticum officinale	Lovage
Marrubium vulgare	Horehound
Mentha x *piperita*	Peppermint
Mentha pulegium	Pennyroyal
Mentha spicata	Spearmint
Monarda didyma	Bee balm or oswego tea
Myrrhis odorata	Sweet cicely
Nepeta cataria	Catnip
Nigella damascena	Love-in-a-mist
Ocimum basilicum	Sweet basil
Origanum majorana	Sweet marjoram
Origanum vulgare	
	Common oregano or wild marjoram
Petroselinum crispum	Parsley

Colonial American Garden, continued

Pulmonaria officinalis	Lungwort
Rosmarinus officinalis	Rosemary
Ruta graveolens	Rue
Salvia officinalis	Garden sage
Salvia sclarea	Clary sage
Santolina chamaecyparissus	
	Lavender cotton or santolina
Satureja hortensis	Summer savory
Satureja montana	Winter savory
Stachys byzantina	Lamb's-ears
Stachys officinalis	Betony
Tanacetum vulgare	Tansy

Tanacetum vulgare var. *crispum*	
	Curly or fern-leaf tansy
Teucrium chamaedrys	Germander
Thymus praecox arcticus	
	Mother-of-thyme or creeping thyme
Thymus vulgaris	Common upright thyme
Thymus vulgaris 'Broad-leaf'	
	English thyme
Tropaeolum majus	Nasturtium
Valeriana officinalis	Valerian
Verbascum thapsus	Mullein or flannel plant
Viola odorata	Sweet violet

Fragrant Garden

Agastache foeniculum	
	Anise hyssop or giant blue hyssop
Agastache rugosa	Korean hyssop
Aloysia triphylla	Lemon verbena
Angelica archangelica	Angelica
Artemisia abrotanum	Southernwood
Artemisia annua	Sweet annual wormwood
Calamintha nepeta	Calamint
Centranthus ruber	Valerian
Cheiranthus cheiri	Wallflower
Cymbopogon citratus	Lemon grass
Dianthus caryophyllus	Clove carnation
Dianthus plumarius	Garden pinks
Helichrysum angustifolium	Curry plant
Heliotropium arborescens	Heliotrope
Hemerocallis minor	Dwarf yellow daylily
Hydrangea petiolaris	Climbing hydrangea
Hyssopus officinalis and varieties	Hyssop

Iris × *germanica* var. *florentina*	
	Orris root iris
Laurus nobilis	Sweet bay
Lavandula angustifolia 'Alba'	
	White-flowering lavender
Lavandula angustifolia subsp. *angustifolia*	
	English lavender
Lavandula angustifolia 'Hidcote'	
	'Hidcote' lavender
Lavandula angustifolia 'Munstead'	
	'Munstead' lavender
Lavandula dentata	French lavender
Lavandula × *intermedia* 'Dutch'	
	'Dutch' lavender
Lavandula × *intermedia* 'Grosso'	
	'Grosso' lavender
Lavandula multifida	Fern-leaf lavender
Lavandula stoechas	Spanish lavender
Lilium candidum	Madonna lily
Matricaria recutita	German chamomile

Fragrant Garden, continued

Melissa officinalis	Lemon balm
Mentha × *gentilis* 'Variegata'	Ginger mint
Mentha × *piperita*	Peppermint
Mentha piperita var. *citrata*	
	Lemon or bergamot mint
Mentha pulegium	Pennyroyal
Mentha requienii	
	Creme-de-menthe or Corsican mint
Mentha spicata	Spearmint
Mentha suaveolens	Apple mint
Mentha suaveolens 'Variegata'	
	Pineapple mint
Monarda didyma and varieties	Bee balm
Myrtus communis	Sweet myrtle
Narcissus jonquilla	Jonquil
Narcissus poeticus	Pheasant's eye
Nepeta cataria	Catnip
Nepeta cataria 'Citriodora'	
	Lemon catnip
Nicotiana 'Sweet-scent'	Flowering tobacco
Pelargonium crispum	
	Lemon-scented geranium

Pelargonium graveolens	
	Rose-scented geranium
Pelargonium odoratissimum	
	Apple-scented geranium
Pelargonium tomentosum	
	Peppermint-scented geranium
Perovskia atriplicifolia	Russian sage
Polianthes tuberosa	Tuberose
Pycnanthemum pilosum	Mountain mint
Rosmarinus officinalis and cultivars	
	Rosemary
Rosmarinus officinalis 'Prostratus'	
	Prostrate rosemary and cultivars
Ruta graveolens	Rue
Salvia elegans	Pineapple sage
Salvia officinalis	Garden sage and varieties
Santolina chamaecyparissus and varieties	
	Lavender cotton
Santolina virens	Green santolina
Solidago odora	Fragrant goldenrod
Thymus × *citriodorus*	Lemon thyme
Valeriana officinalis	Valerian

Culinary Garden

Allium sativum	Garlic
Allium schoenoprasum	Chives
Allium tuberosum	Oriental chives
Anethum graveolens	Dill
Anethum graveolens 'Dill Bouquet'	
	Dwarf dill
Angelica archangelica	Angelica
Anthriscus cerefolium	Sweet chervil
Artemisia dracunculus	French tarragon
Borago officinalis	Borage

Calendula officinalis	Pot marigold
Capsicum annuum	Cayenne or chili pepper
Capsicum frutescens	Tabasco pepper
Carum carvi	Caraway
Coriandrum sativum	Coriander
Crocus sativus	Saffron crocus
Foeniculum vulgare var. *azoricum*	
	Florence fennel or finocchio
Fragaria alpina	Alpine strawberry
Fragaria virginiana	Wild strawberry

Culinary Garden, continued

Galium odoratum	Sweet woodruff
Glycyrrhiza glabra	Licorice
Hemerocallis fulva	Tawny daylily
Laurus nobilis	Sweet bay
Levisticum officinale	Lovage
Marrubium vulgare	Horehound
Matteuccia pensylvanica	Ostrich fern
Melissa officinalis	Lemon balm
Mentha × *piperita*	Peppermint
Mentha requienii	Creme-de-menthe or Corsican mint
Mentha spicata	Spearmint
Myrrhis odorata	Sweet cicely
Nasturtium officinale	Watercress
Ocimum basilicum	Sweet basil
Ocimum basilicum 'Citriodorum'	Lemon basil
Ocimum basilicum 'Crispum'	Lettuce-leaf basil
Ocimum basilicum 'Minimum'	Dwarf basil
Ocimum basilicum 'Purpurascens'	Purple or 'Dark Opal' basil
Origanum compactum	Dwarf oregano
Origanum majorana	Sweet marjoram
Origanum onites	Pot marjoram
Origanum vulgare subsp. *hirtum*	Italian oregano
Osmunda cinnamomea	Cinnamon fern
Pelargonium graveolens	Rose-scented geranium
Petroselinum crispum and varieties	Parsley
Petroselinum crispum var. *neopolitanum*	Italian parsley
Pimpinella anisum	Anise
Poterium sanguisorba	Burnet
Rosmarinus officinalis and cultivars	Rosemary

Rumex scutatus	French sorrel
Salvia officinalis	Garden sage
Salvia officinalis 'Nana'	Dwarf sage
Satureja hortensis	Summer savory
Satureja montana	Winter savory
Thymus × *citriodorus*	Lemon thyme
Thymus pulegioides	Oregano-scented thyme
Thymus vulgaris	Common upright thyme
Thymus vulgaris 'Broad-leaf'	English thyme
Thymus vulgaris 'Narrow-leaf'	French thyme
Tropaeolum majus	Nasturtium

CONTEMPORARY EXPRESSIONS

The garden designs that follow are accompanied by written explanations and legends for the plants and building materials. This graphic medley is intended to illustrate how the ideas and information presented in this book can be put to work. It includes both contemporary and traditional designs, many with an innovative twist. It offers design suggestions for a variety of site situations and scales. The examples are meant to spark your enthusiasm and boost your confidence, ultimately motivating you to proceed with your own herbal design project.

Adapt these sample designs, and the ideas they generate, to your own specific requirements; don't just copy them without regard to the complexity of the other factors influencing your particular site. Consider the existing conditions of the site, the intended use, and the environment.

Bear in mind that the specific planting designs rendered in this section stand in isolation from both the immediate and the larger context of your site. Thus, your design will have to relate to what is traditionally referred to as the *genius loci*, the pervading spirit of your site. Try to achieve a balance, complementing the local and regional context of your site while still allowing your design to exhibit its own unique qualities. Let your design also reflect your personality and your needs.

Remember to consider the time and energy that will be required for maintenance, as well as the budget for the project and its upkeep. Herb garden maintenance can range from very high to quite low, but a planting is never maintenance free. Design structure and plant selection are the two factors that will determine the level of maintenance your garden requires. You should be thinking about these considerations carefully and realistically from the very start. For example, a clipped, formal knot-garden pattern can require pruning as often as every ten days to two weeks during the growing season to maintain its form. If you don't want to spend that much time on maintenance, you must choose plants with a naturally neat and compact habit or create only a small knot.

Appropriateness is an important consideration when using herbal plants. Because herbs carry a certain mystique—perhaps the result of their rich historical legacy and their reputed abilities to heal and rejuvenate mind, body, and spirit—they deserve to be respectfully and sensitively placed in the landscape. It is inappropriate to plant them in forgotten areas or those that receive little or no maintenance attention. Herbs are used appropriately anywhere people meet, congregate, pause, or pass by. They can animate, stimulate, soothe, and delight. From city to country, herbs grace the landscape with their beauty, fragrance, and utility. They are an uplifting reminder of the mystery and wonder of our world.

An Herbal Tapestry

This design reinterprets the traditional knot-garden motif, creating a contemporary planting design for a plaza or terrace. The garden lines are extensions of the architectural lines, contributing to the unity of this successful design. Plants with contrasting foliage colors and textures are placed in an interwoven pattern to create an herbal tapestry. The view from above is spectacular.

Evergreen trees and shrubs are instrumental in creating this garden's structure. Since many perennial herbs die back in winter, evergreen shrubs and trees, together with the site structures, must maintain the integrity of the garden's form and spatial definition throughout the year. (Refer to the Plant Profiles for lists of evergreen shrubs and trees with herbal uses and those with city adaptability.) During the hot summer months, deciduous trees provide a cool, shady canopy. They also define the property boundary between public and private domains.

The focal knot garden at the main entrance signals arrival and welcome. Dwarf conifers are excellent plants for larger knot gardens. They offer a vast array of foliage colors and textures and create stunning tapestry patterns. Their dense branching habits, slow growth rates, and compact forms reduce the need for pruning and trimming. Choose from a wide variety of dwarf conifers, including *Chamaecyparis*, *Picea*, *Pinus*, *Thuja*, and *Tsuga*.

Heat-loving herbs, such as artemisia, rosemary, lavender, santolina, sage, dianthus, germander, and scented geraniums, create a beautiful woven pattern for sites facing south or southwest.

Continue the color and pattern of the garden tapestry across the sidewalk by using contrasting colors and sizes of concrete, stone, or brick pavers. Grassy paths and stepping stones not only contribute color to the design but also provide access into the planted space for recreation and enjoyment.

This design idea can be modified and used in a residential setting and is especially appropriate for a townhouse or home that overlooks a terrace, courtyard, or rooftop garden. Where weight limitations exist, an herbal planting such as this becomes a practical and beautiful design solution.

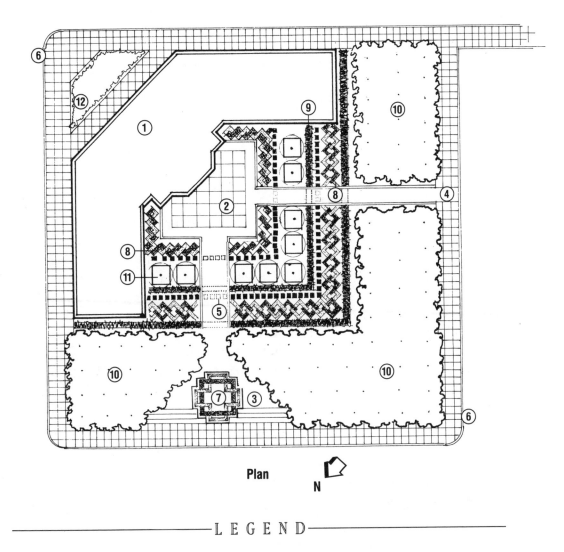

Plan

N

——————————— L E G E N D ———————————

1 Building
2 Paved forecourt
3 Main entrance area, stepping up from public sidewalk
4 Secondary entrance from adjacent parking lot
5 Colored concrete pavers
6 Public sidewalk and curb

PLANTS
7 Focal knot garden
8 Perennial herbs and dwarf conifers
9 Hardy herbal evergreen hedge
10 Herbal trees in terraced plantings
11 Small, flowering herbal trees in raised planters that serve as seating
12 Street-level planter at secondary entrance

An Entrance Court with Herbal Plantings

In this design a common front yard is transformed into an attractive entrance courtyard garden, featuring a center knot garden and border beds of herbs enclosed by a dense privacy hedge. This entrance treatment offers a place for people to interact with one another. It functions much the same way the traditional front porch does to foster a sense of community.

The small knot-garden centerpiece in this design is a good example of the way historical precedents can be adapted to meet the needs of contemporary garden design situations. It is a simplified version of the historical knot garden design.

The evergreen hedge creates a dark backdrop to set off the colorful herbs positioned in beds facing the house. Hedges, often used for foundation plantings, can be put to better use on the property perimeter. This arrangement offers excellent views of the garden courtyard from inside the house, and the hedge creates a barrier between the public sidewalk and street and the private residence. One must pass through a gate to enter into the private garden domain. These vegetative walls enclose the entrance, creating an intimate atmosphere and most enjoyable outdoor room.

Notice that the lines of the hedges, beds, paving edges, and the decorative brick bands laid in the paving correspond to the proportioning system originating from the regulating lines of the architecture. Matching the brick paving colors to the building brick also helps to integrate the house and garden.

The concepts underlying the illustrated entrance court design can be easily translated to a smaller front yard.

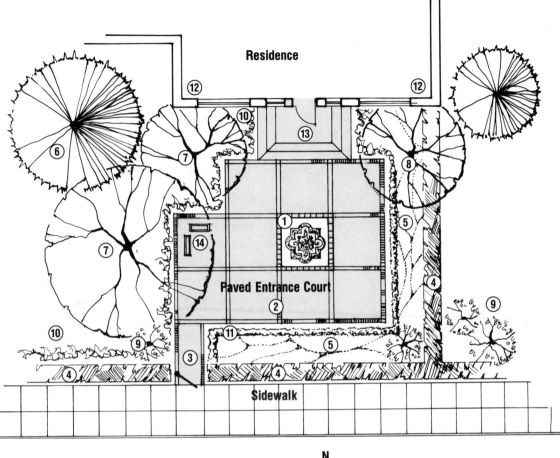

Residence

Paved Entrance Court

Sidewalk

Plan

N

L E G E N D

1 Knot garden with seasonal herbs, perennials, annuals, and bulbs

2 Paved terrace with inlaid decorative brick bands

3 Entrance gate

4 Evergreen hedge

5 Planting beds of herbs mixed with flowering perennials and bulbs

6 Evergreen tree that protects terrace from winter winds

7 Small, flowering herbal trees that protect entrance court from summer sun

8 Small, flowering herbal tree

9 Fragrant flowering shrub

10 Herbal ground cover with drifts of spring-flowering bulbs

11 Herbal evergreen and semievergreen edging plants

12 Windows

13 Brick platform and steps leading from entrance door to paved court

14 Garden bench

An Outdoor Room

This terrace herb garden functions as an outdoor room for the adjacent building. Evergreen hedges relate closely to the architectural lines, extending to form the walls of the garden room. These hedge walls correspond to the regulating lines of the architecture and originate from the building's corners, doors, and windows. Proportion, scale, and rhythm are thus achieved between the indoor and the outdoor spaces.

Plants and built materials work together to provide the structure. In this design, a handsome brick or stone wall or a fence would serve the same design function as the hedges. Matching the brick paving with the brick of the building contributes to the strong integration of garden and building.

Year-round interest is important in this terrace design because of its close visual connection to the indoors. The many perennials that die back to the ground during the winter must be allowed to disappear without jeopardizing the integrity and readability of the garden's design structure. The evergreen shrubs and herbs serve the important purpose of maintaining the lines, form, and spatial definition of the garden room in winter. Furthermore, the evergreens can also provide privacy or screen an undesirable view. Don't forget that deciduous plants fail to perform these functions in winter.

Herbs are planted within the compartments formed by the evergreen walls. You may choose to set up thematic plantings of herbs in the various compartments or simply create aesthetic compositions of herbs with attention to size, texture, and color. Designate places within the planting beds for annual herbs, flowers, and bulbs.

Create an illusion of distance by arranging blue-foliaged and blue-flowering herbs behind yellow-green or yellow-flowering or yellow-foliaged plants. Cool blues and greens recede while the hot yellows jump forward. Similarly, a yellowish orange red moves closer to the eye than a bluish purple red. Planting larger foliage in front and smaller-leaved plants in the back also creates the illusion of distance.

In a hot climate you may want to use an abundance of cooling white- and blue-flowering plants, perhaps in combination with herbs whose foliage is silver, light gray, blue, or blue-green. A strategically located herbal tree shades the terrace and house from the brutally hot south and southwestern afternoon sun.

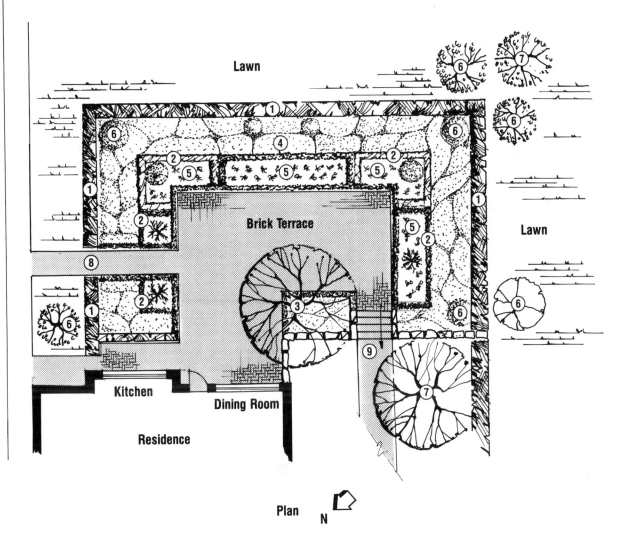

Plan   **N**

LEGEND

1 Evergreen hedge walls defining perimeter of garden

2 Smaller clipped evergreen herbs, and those with foliage that persists long into colder months.

3 Herbal shade tree

4 Medium to tall herbs and flowering perennials

5 Seasonal-color beds of small spring-flowering bulbs followed by flowering and herbal annuals

6 Aromatic flowering shrubs

7 Flowering herbal trees

8 Entrance walk to garden

9 Steps leading down to another outdoor garden area

A Garden for the Five Senses

This garden will stimulate the senses. Lovely aromatic herbs with a variety of fragrances, textured foliages, and palate-pleasing flavors, accompanied by a soothing, melodic fountain, make this garden a stunning composition of textural and color harmonies. The colors, especially the silvers and whites, seem to shimmer and glow in the light of the moon, creating an evocative, mystical ambience. You will spend many pleasant evenings in this sensory garden.

The vine-covered trellis and the reflection pool and fountain provide a focus for the design. The trellis provides a vertical element to the design, making a great visual impact. The simplicity of the stone raised bed and the single tree species used for background and enclosure provide unity. This enables a variety of plants to be used without resulting in a visually confusing composition.

More order and unity come from the repetitive use of identical plants and plants with common characteristics. In this planting, the silvers, grays, blues, and whites of the foliage and flowers strongly unify the overall design.

The illustrated raised bed is approximately 24 feet long and 26 inches high and has an inner planting width of 4 feet. The stone wall cap is 10 inches wide. The underlying concepts and the plant palette of this design could be successfully adapted for smaller or larger spaces.

───── L E G E N D ─────

1   *Mentha requienii*, creme-de-menthe or Corsican mint
2   *Mentha suaveolens* 'Variegata', pineapple mint
3   *Mentha × piperita* var. *citrata*, lemon or bergamot mint
4   *Thymus vulgaris* 'Argenteus', silver thyme
5   *Mentha puleguim*, pennyroyal
6   *Thymus pseudolanuginosus*, woolly thyme
7   *Artemisia schmidtiana* 'Nana', silver mound artemisia
8   *Stachys byzantina*, lamb's-ears
9   *Salvia officinalis* 'Purpurascens', purple sage
10 *Santolina virens*, green santolina
11 *Rosmarinus officinalis* 'Prostratus', prostrate rosemary
12 *Artemisia abrotanum*, southernwood
13 *Heliotropium arborescens*, heliotrope
14 *Lavandula angustifolia* subsp. *angustifolia*, English lavender
15 *Rosmarinus officinalis* 'Benedin Blue', 'Benedin Blue' rosemary
16 *Polianthes tuberosa* 'Double Pearl', tuberose
17 *Hyssopus officinalis* 'Alba', white-flowering hyssop
18 *Artemisia ludoviciana* var. *albula*, 'Silver Queen' and 'Silver King' artemisia
19 *Salvia officinalis* 'Albaflora', white-flowering sage

Elevation

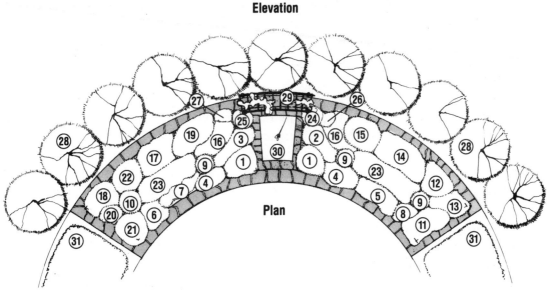

Plan

——————————————— L E G E N D ———————————————

20 *Nigella damascena*, love-in-a-mist
21 *Pelargonium tomentosum*,
        peppermint-scented geranium
22 *Perovskia atriplicifolia*, Russian sage
23 *Salvia farinacea* 'Victoria', blue sage
24 *Clematis* 'Ramona', 'Ramona' clematis
        vine
25 *Clematis paniculata*, sweet autumn
        clematis vine
26 *Ipomoea purpurea* 'Heavenly Blue',
        morning glory vine

27 *Calonyction aculeatum*, moonflower vine
28 *Juniperus chinensis columnaris*, columnar
        Chinese juniper
29 Arched wooden trellis
30 Reflecting pool and fountain
31 *Rosa* 'La Reine Victoria' and 'Louise
        Odier', Bourbon roses, and
        Pelargonium graveolens cultivars,
        rose-scented geraniums

A Fragrant, Tactile Herb Garden

This sensory garden design contains aromatic herbs and those of unusual textures that are interesting and fun to touch. Sensory gardens are evocative and make a lasting impression wherever they are encountered.

Raised beds are appropriate structures for sensory gardens because they enable people to reach, touch, and enjoy the plants. When the leaves of aromatic plants are touched and rubbed, the fragrance of their essential oils is released. A fragrant, tactile garden is a lovely idea for areas used by the unsighted. Be sure to identify plants with labels written in Braille.

For the sighted, the silver- and gray-foliaged herbs make this an eye-catching design. English lavender, one of the loveliest of the scented herbs, is featured in the center of this design. Also included are sweet-scented pineapple sage, apple mint, and the peppermint-scented geranium, with its velvety leaves. The pungent green santolina is selected for its unique leaf texture. Its stiff, intricately branched stem resembles sea coral.

Lamb's-ears is a popular sensory garden plant and is used as the edging plant in the front position of the pictured design. The silver leaf color is ornamentally valuable. Another favorite sensory garden plant is silver mound artemisia, which is placed on the outer edges of this planting because it is also astonishingly soft to the touch. It, too, has silver-gray foliage and a neat, bunlike form. Purple sage has a unique, pebbly leaf texture, and the purple foliage contrasts beautifully with the silver plants in the planting composition.

This planting requires at least four to six hours of unobstructed sunlight daily, and well-drained soil is a necessity. Moderate applications of a high-phosphorus fertilizer (15-30-15) two to three times per growing season will enhance the appearance of the plants and maintain health, vigor, and resistance to insects, disease, and cold injury.

The illustrated design is suitable for most areas of the country. The lavenders and santolinas, however, are susceptible to foliar and root fungal problems in climates with prolonged periods of intense heat coupled with high humidity. In these areas, use varieties of rosemary and artemisia, which are not prone to fungal problems.

The dimensions of the illustrated masonry raised bed are approximately 6 feet wide by 18 feet long by 2 feet high. The wall cap is 10 inches wide. Raised beds are important in the site plan; they can be used to define the garden's forms, lines, and spaces, and provide a sense of enclosure.

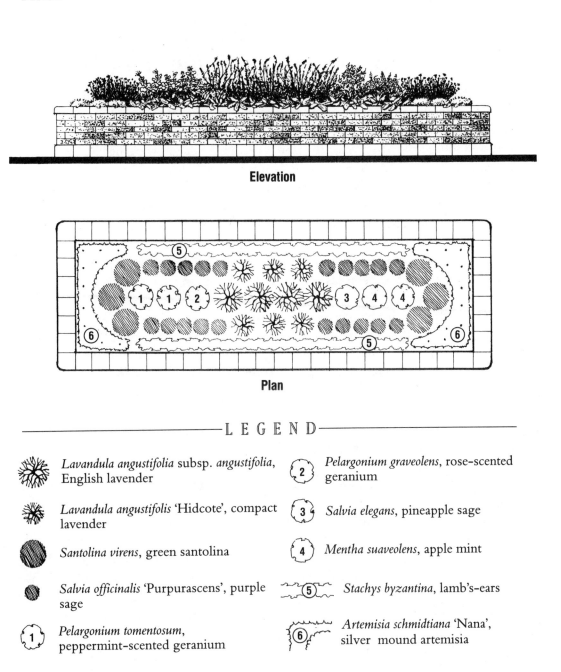

Elevation

Plan

——————— L E G E N D ———————

Lavandula angustifolia subsp. *angustifolia*, English lavender

Lavandula angustifolis 'Hidcote', compact lavender

Santolina virens, green santolina

Salvia officinalis 'Purpurascens', purple sage

(1) *Pelargonium tomentosum*, peppermint-scented geranium

(2) *Pelargonium graveolens*, rose-scented geranium

(3) *Salvia elegans*, pineapple sage

(4) *Mentha suaveolens*, apple mint

(5) *Stachys byzantina*, lamb's-ears

(6) *Artemisia schmidtiana* 'Nana', silver mound artemisia

A Culinary Herb Garden in a Raised Bed

The herbs selected for this thematic design are familiar culinary favorites, including ornamental varieties of parsley, sage, rosemary, and thyme. Foliage textures and colors are the focal points in this raised-bed design. The gray-green, pebbly-textured foliage of garden sage is planted beside the deep green, needlelike leaves of hardy rosemary. The linear, blue-green foliage of chives contrasts with the low, mounding, dark green foliage of lemon thyme. The striking purple foliage of Dark Opal basil enriches this colorful planting. The rosy-pink flowers of chives and thyme and the sky-blue flowers of rosemary complement the rich foliage.

Because parsley is compact and uniform, it is used as a line to frame the herbs in the raised bed. The cascading foliage of lemon thyme softens the stone edges of the planting.

Other culinary herb favorites you may want to grow in a culinary garden include lovage (*Levisticum officinale*), dwarf dill (*Anethum graveolens* 'Dill Bouquet'), sweet basil (*Ocimum basilicum*), lemon basil (*Ocimum basilicum* 'Citriodorum'), burnet (*Poterium sanguisorba*), French tarragon (*Artemisia dracunculus* var. *sativa*), mints (*Mentha* species and varieties), sweet marjoram (*Origanum majorana*), and oregano (*Origanum vulgare* subsp. *hirtum*).

To incorporate these herbs into the design shown, maintain the edge definition by using a limited palette of plants. Keep rosemary as the strong focus. Plant the other culinary herbs in large groups to give them presence. They might balance well in one of the two positions where the garden sage or the purple basil is shown.

This planting is recommended for sites that receive full sun to partial shade. Sharp drainage is necessary, and parsley and basil prefer a little extra moisture. The herbs in this design all have well-behaved growing habits. Maintenance is limited to removing spent blossoms and clipping an occasional wayward branch.

The raised stone planter is approximately 5 feet wide by 15 feet long and 20 inches high. A raised bed with a high, wide wall cap enables you to sit comfortably as you harvest and tend your culinary herb garden.

Stone, a traditional masonry material used in herb gardens, complements the foliage and flower colors of the plants.

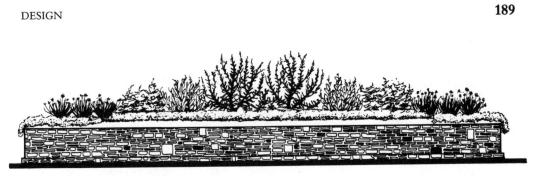

Elevation

Plan

———————————— L E G E N D ————————————

   Rosmarinus officinalis 'Arp', hardy rosemary

   Salvia officinalis, garden sage

   Ocimum basilicum 'Purpurascens', purple
or 'Dark Opal' basil

   Allium schoenoprasum, chives

①   *Thymus × citriodorus*, lemon thyme

②   *Petroselinum crispum*, parsley

A Container Planting of Culinary Herbs

A single container planting of culinary herbs will yield a steady and ample supply of flavors throughout the growing season. This is a surprise and delight to many, particularly apartment and townhouse dwellers.

Most culinary herbs combine well, giving a charming tussie-mussie effect. A pot garden of herbs is an animated composition with spirited herbs spilling out over the edges. Enriched by the diversity of forms, colors, and textures, it is nevertheless unified by the container.

A culinary herb container planting could stand alone as an attractive specimen, or it could be the focal accent within a larger garden or in a grouping with other smaller containers. Position it on a deck, balcony, rooftop garden, terrace, or patio. And of course, a culinary pot garden is perfect for a sunny spot by the kitchen door.

Select a large container that allows sufficient soil area to hold enough moisture and provide enough space for plant root growth. The inside dimensions of the container illustrated are 24 inches in diameter and 18 inches high. Use a soil that drains well and be sure the excess water escapes through the holes in the bottom; placing broken pieces of clay pots over the holes will prevent them from becoming clogged with compacted soil. If you use a pot with a saucer, do not let water stand in it after watering.

Most culinary herbs love sun. They will do well in partial shade as long as they receive approximately six hours or more of direct sun per day. They benefit from monthly applications of a complete liquid fertilizer.

A good variety of herbs can be planted in a culinary pot garden because the plants will be constantly snipped for use. Harvesting will keep them smaller than if they are allowed to grow to mature size. Many of the herbs in this planting will grow for two or three years if the pot is overwintered in a cool, sunny, indoor location. In spring the annual herbs can be added after danger of frost has passed. By the second year, however, the perennial plants may be too large for a single container and may need to be divided into a second planter.

A word of caution: do not plant mints in your pot garden. Mints are refreshing in the summer, but because of their aggressive growing habit, they should be planted in separate containers. They grow well in sun or partial shade and a moderately moist, well-drained soil.

L E G E N D

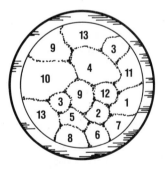

4 *Anethum graveolens* 'Dill Bouquet', dwarf dill

5 *Ocimum basilicum* 'Spicey Globe', dwarf basil

6 *Petroselinum crispum* var. *neopolitanum*, Italian parsley

7 *Origanum majorana*, sweet marjoram

8 *Poterium sanguisorba*, burnet

9 *Salvia officinalis* 'Icterina' or 'Aurea', golden sage

10 *Rosmarinus officinalis* 'Prostratus', prostrate rosemary

11 *Origanum vulgare* subsp. *hirtum*, oregano

12 *Levisticum officinale*, lovage

13 *Thymus* × *citriodorus*, lemon thyme

1 *Thymus vulgaris* 'Narrow-leaf', French thyme

2 *Artemisia dracunculus* var. *sativa*, French tarragon

3 *Allium schoenoprasum*, chives

A *Modern* Hortus Conclusus

There is something innately beautiful about an enclosed herb garden. Entering into the garden, one experiences the symbolism of stepping out of the hurried, harried pace of life and into a beautiful, peaceful haven where evocative fragrances linger. The meditative and introspective quality of an enclosed herb garden is reminiscent of the historical *hortus conclusus*, the "enclosed," "sacred," "protected" garden. Today as in the past, an enclosed garden functions as a place for pleasure, meditation, and healing of the spirit.

The perfect geometry and symmetry make this garden design still, centered, balanced, and free of tension. The form offers a high degree of order, visually unifying the lively diversity of plants and preventing it from becoming a cluttered, chaotic composition. This lovely balance of unity and spontaneity, as well as the play of light and shadow and the other ephemeral qualities of the outdoor environment, creates a remarkable atmosphere.

The illustrated garden is organized around a central planting bed. It is edged with garden pinks (*Dianthus plumarius*) and dwarf lavender (*Lavandula angustifolia* 'Munstead'). This central bed is highly visible and thus is an excellent location for seasonal-interest plants, such as spring-flowering bulbs or summer annuals. A sundial, birdbath, or other garden ornament punctuates the center.

Brick pathways extend from the center bed, defining the elongated planting beds. The masonry edge is both reinforced and softened by small herbs. You may want to repeat the garden pinks and dwarf lavender of the center bed, combining them with a variety of creeping and upright thymes. These can be planted in an irregular but repetitive fashion. The flowering perennials and herbs in the larger beds are visually unified by this edge treatment.

As you arrange the perennials and herbs in the larger beds, try to create a pleasing rhythm through the garden by repeating drifts of the same plants at various intervals. A minimum of three groupings of the same plant is a good rule of thumb. Another way of achieving rhythm is to repeat common characteristics of different plants, such as flower color, foliage color, height, or form.

The entire garden is enclosed by an ornamental wrought iron fence and gate in front, a pierced brick wall in back, and evergreen herbal hedges, such as boxwood, inkberry, or yew.

This free-standing garden would be a stunning sculptural element in a residential landscape or a public park. This is a garden for four seasons, lovely even under a light covering of snow.

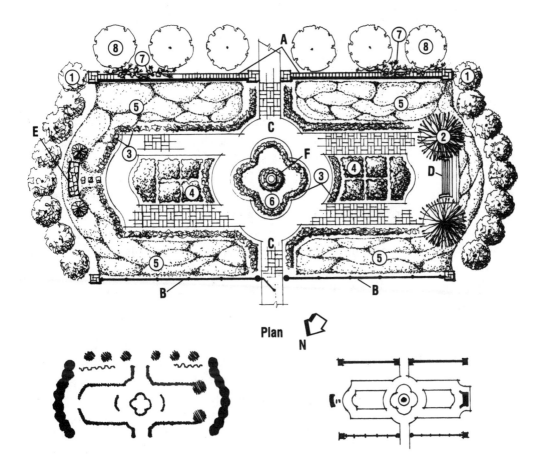

Plan

N

───────────── L E G E N D ─────────────

PLANTS

1 Evergreen herbal hedge
2 Small, fragrant herbal tree
3 Small edging herbs
4 Culinary and aromatic herbs
5 Ornamental herbs and flowering perennials
6 Seasonal-interest flowering herbs, annuals, and bulbs
7 Fragrant herbal vine and climbing Old World roses
8 Dwarf fruit trees

BUILDING MATERIALS

A Free-standing, pierced brick wall with end piers
B Antique wrought iron fence and gate
C Brick paver paths in basketweave pattern
D Teakwood garden bench
E Stone garden seat
F Sundial or birdbath garden ornament on stone paver platform

An Herb and Vegetable Garden Rooted in History

In this garden the simple home vegetable plot is enhanced by historical garden elements. The octagonal, four-quarter culinary herb garden adds spice and flavor and helps transform the simple vegetable plot into a designed garden—and a much more enjoyable place to work and relax. Other additions to the garden include mixed herb and flower beds, small fruit and berry beds, a grape arbor, a shaded sitting area with a garden bench, a sundial, and an enclosing fence and gate, all within a series of interrelated beds and connecting paths.

This design borrows its basic elements—the enclosure, the rectangular and geometric four-square forms, the utilitarian purpose, and the plants themselves—from the early European kitchen gardens. Unlike its historical precedent, however, this garden places value on design aesthetics. Portions of the illustrated design, particularly the geometric herb garden and the well-edged perennial flower and herb beds, would be beautiful additions to any living space.

The type and style of the garden's building materials and the design of the edges of the paths, beds, and garden perimeter influence the character of the garden. The informal feeling of this design comes from the wooden picket-fence and gate, the paths of stone dust, grass, and mulch, the wooden bench, and the abundance of creeping edge plants that spill onto the path areas. If a country-casual feeling is what you want, use a wattle or split-rail fence to enclose the garden. Or dress it up by using a Chinese Chippendale gate and bench. Or, for a still more elegant feeling, consider the building materials in A Modern *Hortus Conclusus* (page 192). There are innumerable ways that you can set the tone for your garden while keeping essentially the same layout.

The components of this garden design can be easily adapted to smaller or larger spaces. This particular garden is approximately 40 feet wide and 100 feet long. The rectangular vegetable and cutting garden beds are 4 feet by 12 feet. They are slightly raised using thin landscape timbers. All perimeter beds are 4½ feet wide. The geometrical culinary herb garden is 16 feet in diameter and has 18-inch inner paths. The garden's primary paths are 3½ feet wide, and the secondary paths are 2 feet wide.

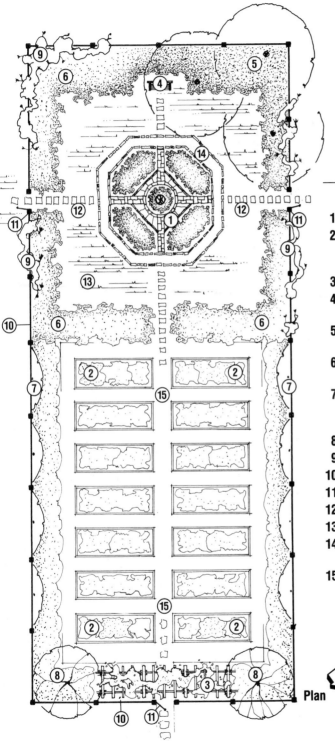

LEGEND

1 Culinary herb garden with sundial
2 Vegetables, cutting flowers, drying herbs and flowers, melons, and roses
3 Grape arbor
4 Wooden bench in shaded sitting area
5 Shade trees with shade-loving herbs beneath
6 Flowering perennials, annuals, bulbs, and ornamental herbs
7 Espaliered dwarf fruit trees along fence with small fruits and berries in beds
8 Dwarf fruit tree
9 Fragrant flowering herbal vine
10 Wooden picket fence
11 Wooden gate
12 Stepping stone pavers
13 Grass
14 Stone dust path edged with stone pavers
15 Wood chip paths

Plan N

A Rosemary Topiary Standard

Topiary is the art of shaping plants into various forms by careful pruning, shaping, and training. A standard is a topiary with a globe trained on a single straight stem. Trained as a topiary standard, *Rosmarinus officinalis* makes a unique container specimen. It is a living sculptural piece, traditionally occupying an important design position, such as the center of a knot garden or the terminus of a garden path.

To be a candidate for topiary standard training, the plant must have a woody mature stem to support the heavy ball of foliage on top. Many of the subshrub herbs—sweet myrtle, sweet bay, hyssop, heliotrope, certain lavenders, and the larger, upright scented geraniums—are excellent standard specimens and can be trained just like the rosemary. It takes approximately two years to create a geranium standard and three or more for the slower-growing herbs.

To create a standard, choose a nursery plant with a straight central stem. Plant it in a heavy pot (to prevent strong winds from toppling the topiary). Carefully remove all side branches. Stake and tie the stem for support and to encourage a straight stem. Water, fertilize, and provide good light as it grows. Continue to trim off lateral branches until it reaches the desired height, then pinch out the tip. This will stimulate lateral branching. Continue to pinch the tips of newly developed branches in the head area to encourage fullness. Remove the stake when woody material forms on the maturing main stem. The stem will then be strong enough to support the lush ball of foliage on top.

Take advantage of rosemary's lovely aromatic qualities by placing it in locations where people sit or gather. This plant sculpture can also be effective on a deck or terrace where it can be seen from indoors. Herbal container standards are attractive specimens used to flank an entrance door, lending a formal atmosphere.

A container standard is practical, as well as attractive, because the containers can be easily transported indoors for the winter. Most herbal topiary plants are not wintered outside, since plants grown in containers are more susceptible to cold injury than those growing in the ground.

An Early Spring Container Planting

Curly parsley (*Petroselinum crispum* 'Curly Parsley') and calendula or pot marigold (*Calendula officinalis*) are excellent choices for an early spring planting; both enjoy cool temperatures. They prefer full sun in early and mid-spring with light to partial shade during the hotter summer months. The cheerful yellow and orange flowers of calendula identify it as a member of the daisy family. Its loose, carefree branching form contrasts with the crisp, uniform border of curly parsley. Parsley is sensitive to airborne pollutants, so avoid planting it where traffic is heavy. The illustration shows a low, wide, rounded container, but smaller plantings would do equally well.

A Container Planting of Contrasts

A dark gray concrete planter sets off the rosy-red flowers and the gray-white foliage patina of woolly thyme (*Thymus pseudolanuginosus*), which drapes gracefully over its edge. Massed in the center is English lavender (*Lavandula angustifolia* subsp. *angustifolia*). With its silvery gray-green foliage and bright blue flowers, lavender creates a striking contrast to the dark planter and complements the rose-flowering thyme. Many of the interesting varieties and cultivars of both lavenders and thymes can be used.

A Scented Hanging Basket

The form and growth habit of the peppermint-scented geranium (*Pelargonium tomentosum*) are well suited for a hanging basket. This scented geranium's soft, velvet-textured leaves release a potent, pepperminty scent when touched or rubbed. The large, dark green, heart-shaped foliage forms a handsome trailing silhouette. When in bloom, this plant's delicate white flowers light up against the rich, dark foliage. The peppermint-scented geranium hanging basket is attractive as a single specimen or grouped with flowering annual baskets.

Peppermint-scented geranium is easy to grow, and unlike most other scented geraniums, it can grow well in partial shade as well as in full sun. Monthly applications of fertilizer during the growing season will keep the plant healthy and lush. My experience has been that moderate fertilization of herbs does not reduce the strength of the fragrance, contrary to some reports, and container-grown herbs need regular feeding to maintain an attractive appearance. Never add fertilizer—even a liquid—to dry soil or the roots may be burned.

Keep up on watering maintenance for hanging baskets. Since they are exposed to the wind and the elements, they dry out twice as fast as other container plantings and perhaps three times as fast as ground plantings. A porous clay pot dries out much faster than a plastic container. It is critical that you empty excess water from the saucer soon after watering; otherwise, air spaces in the soil will fill up with water, suffocating the plant.

Use a sterilized soil medium—a good general practice, since all geraniums tend to be susceptible to soil-borne fungi. This plant is not hardy in northern climates and must be overwintered indoors. You can take stem cuttings of the plant or cut it back before bringing it inside for the winter.

An Elegant Container P

The graceful branching habit and delicate, fernlike (*Foeniculum vulgare* or *rubrum*) make an elegant for iron planter. The rich, unusual bronze-purple fo Common fennel (*Foeniculum vulgare*) is very similar green leaves. Fennel's umbellate yellow flowers are this herb interesting in specimen or combination pl flavor and fragrance.

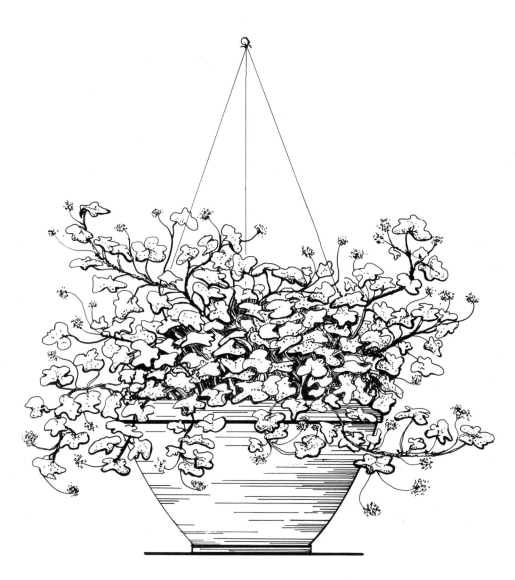

An Elegant Container Planting

The graceful branching habit and delicate, feathery foliage of bronze fennel (*Foeniculum vulgare* var. *rubrum*) make an elegant specimen in a formal cast-iron planter. The rich, unusual bronze-purple foliage is a mark of distinction. Common fennel (*Foeniculum vulgare*) is very similar to bronze fennel, but it has green leaves. Fennel's umbellate yellow flowers are also ornamental, making this herb interesting in specimen or combination plantings. Fennel has an anise flavor and fragrance.

A Planting of Contrasts Beneath an Airy Canopy

Purple perilla (*Perilla frutescens* 'Atropurpurea') is a sturdy plant with ornamental, ruffled, plum-colored foliage. The texture and tiny leaves of closely clipped English thyme (*Thymus vulgare* 'Broad-leaf') make a striking contrast to purple perilla and create a crisp, orderly edge as well. Both prefer a moderately moist soil but will accept drier. Though perilla and thyme perform best in full sun to light shade, they accept the partial shade beneath an airy canopy. The terminal shoots of perilla should be removed regularly during the growing season.

A slightly raised brick edge in the basketweave pattern sets off the planted area from the surrounding pavement. Choose herbal trees from the Plant Profiles to complement your herbal planting. For town or city areas, select trees that are tolerant of urban conditions.

The illustrated planting would be a welcome novelty beneath a street tree in a sidewalk planter. Why not be the first to enliven your neighborhood with herbal plantings?

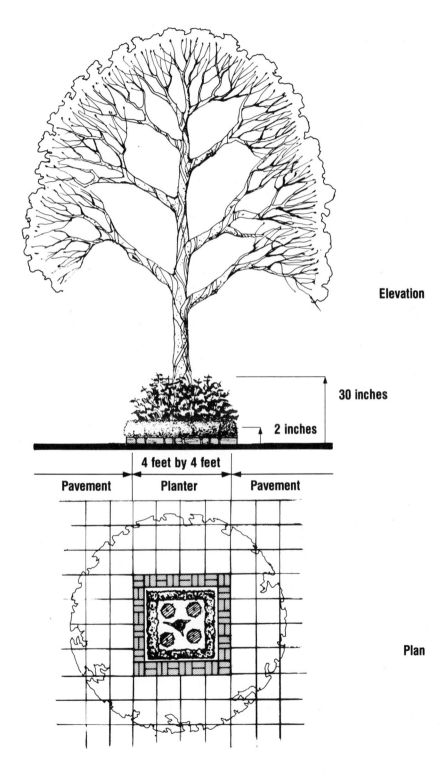

Elevation

30 inches

2 inches

4 feet by 4 feet

Pavement   Planter   Pavement

Plan

A Deep Green Planting Beneath an Airy Canopy

The coarse, fernlike foliage of curly tansy (*Tanacetum vulgare* var. *crispum*) creates a luxuriant ground cover beneath an airy canopy. Tansy's deeply incised, dark, rich emerald–green leaves and yellow buttonlike flowers in flat-topped clusters make it a valuable ornamental. The leaf of the curly form is more deeply divided and its growing habit more compact than common tansy (*Tanacetum vulgare*). Curly tansy offers a handsome planting that has the character of a fern, but it is a tough plant and grows more robustly than the delicate fern. It prefers full sun to light shade and moderately moist to dry soil.

Stone pavers at the edge of the planting area not only add interest and definition to the design, but also keep people from stepping into the plants and injuring them. Choose an herbal tree from the Plant Profiles.

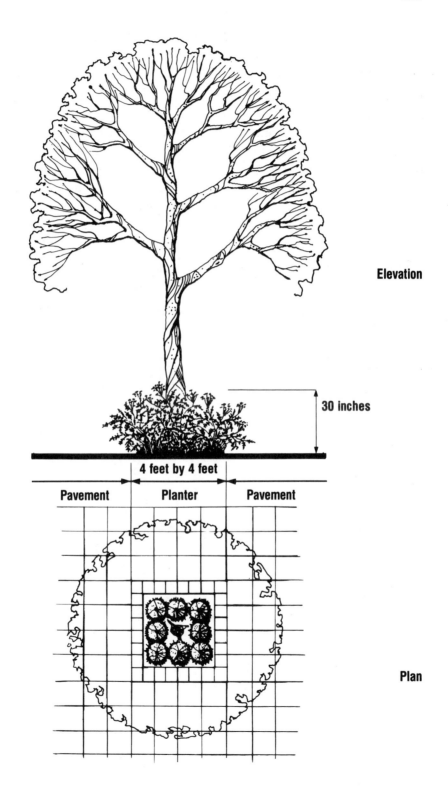

Elevation

30 inches

4 feet by 4 feet

Pavement   **Planter**   **Pavement**

Plan

A Soft Planting Beneath a Dense Canopy

Lady's mantle (*Alchemilla mollis*) is a lovely plant with unusual, coarse-textured leaves contrasted by frothy yellow flowers above the loosely mounded foliage. The blossoms often flop and sprawl in a playful, spirited manner. Lady's mantle and a smaller variety, *Alchemilla alpina*, are excellent plants for softening the edge of a planting bed or for lightening a dark, shady spot under a tree or vine-covered arbor. They perform well in shade or partial shade and moderately moist soil and are tolerant of drier soil conditions. The brick edge sets off the planting area from the surrounding pavement.

Choose an herbal tree from the listing found in the Plant Profiles to complement your herbal planting theme.

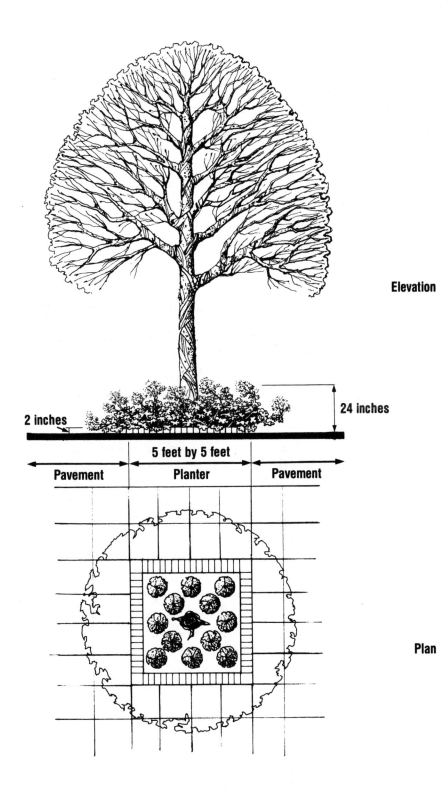

Elevation

2 inches

24 inches

5 feet by 5 feet

Pavement | Planter | Pavement

Plan

A Natural Garden

Many native herbaceous and woody plants have herbal uses; they can be naturalized in woodland areas, along woodland edges, or in open meadows. Naturalized plantings are pleasing and practical, and the use of indigenous plants is an important ecological statement.

Interest in environmental gardening is increasing. Our society is learning to accept and take responsibility for respecting, protecting, and even restoring the environment. A naturalistic planting using native herbal plants conserves water and requires little or no chemical fertilizers or pesticides. If attention is given to planting herbal natives in the context of their larger biological community, associated wildlife will eventually follow, becoming frequent visitors to the naturalized planting.

The essence of environmental gardening is choosing the right plant for the right place and vice versa. Plants thrive when grown in an environment that mimics their natural habitat. By choosing plants that flourish in conditions the same as or similar to your planting site, you will be designing *with* nature, not against it. Consequently, your plantings will be healthy and happy without excessive, wasteful use of natural resources, dangerous chemicals, or artificial growing methods.

Native and naturalized plants can be beautiful, interesting additions and intelligent choices for many landscaping situations. For a partially shaded woodland edge planting, attractive possibilities include great blue lobelia (*Lobelia siphilitica*), mountain mint (*Pycnanthemum pilosum*), bloodroot (*Sanguinaria canadensis*), ostrich fern (*Matteuccia pensylvanica*), sassafras (*Sassafras albidum*), Carolina allspice (*Calycanthus floridus*), fringe tree (*Chionanthus virginicus*), flowering dogwood (*Cornus florida*), and eastern redbud (*Cercis canadensis*).

For a sunny open area, native herbal plants of merit include wild indigo (*Baptisia tinctoria*), butterfly weed (*Asclepias tuberosa*), fragrant goldenrod (*Solidago odora*), purple coneflower (*Echinacea purpurea*), bearberry or kinnikinnik (*Arctostaphyllus uva-ursi*), tawny daylily (*Hemerocallis fulva*), rugosa rose (*Rosa rugosa*), bayberry (*Myrica pensylvanica*), eastern red cedar (*Juniperus virginiana*), and trumpet honeysuckle (*Lonicera sempervirens*). Woody shrubs such as sweet fern (*Comptonia peregrina*) and fragrant sumac (*Rhus aromatica*) make handsome drifts along banks.

For moist planting sites, attractive native and naturalized plant selections may include marsh mallow (*Althaea officinalis*), New England aster (*Aster novae-*

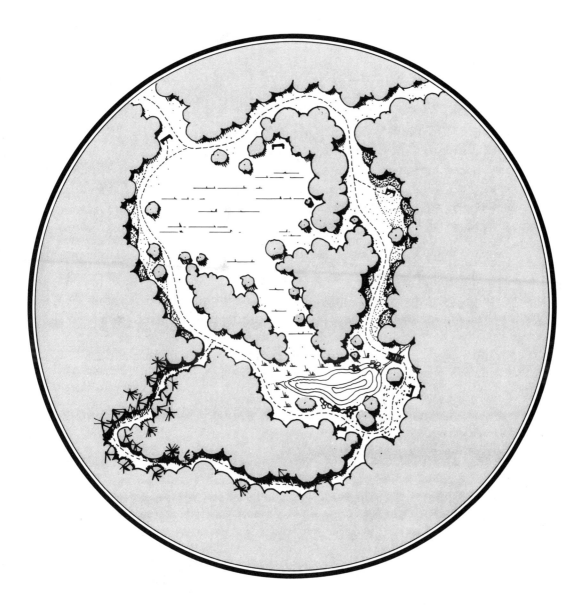

A path through various natural habitats can be an interesting and educational journey. Provide a series of contrasting experiences along the way, such as constriction and expansion, light and dark, dense and open, steep and even, hard and soft, smooth and rough. Position benches to take advantage of a beautiful view or to allow for close-up views of an interesting plant or plant community.

angliae), alum root (*Heuchera americana*), sweet cicely (*Myrrhis odorata*), bee balm (*Monarda didyma*), sweet violet (*Viola odorata*), summersweet (*Clethra alnifolia*), buttonbush (*Cephalanthus occidentalis*), red chokecherry (*Aronia arbutifolia*), spice-bush (*Lindera benzoin*), winterberry (*Ilex verticillata*), red osier dogwood (*Cornus sericea,* or *stolonifera*), serviceberry or shadblow (*Amelanchier arborea*), pin oak (*Quercus palustris*), red maple (*Acer rubrum*), American sweetgum (*Liquidambar styraciflua*), and black tupelo or black gum (*Nyssa sylvatica*).

The illustration shows how a path through various natural habitats can be designed as an interesting and educational journey. Provide a series of contrasting experiences along the way, such as contraction and expansion, light and dark, dense and open, steep and even, hard and soft, smooth and rough. Position benches strategically to take advantage of a beautiful view or to allow for close inspection of an interesting plant or community.

The Plant Profiles contain extensive listings of native and naturalized trees, shrubs, and wildflowers with herbal uses. Your selections should take into consideration the indigenous flora and your regional environmental conditions, as well as the more immediate habitat and microclimate of your planting site. When creating, enhancing, or restoring an indigenous planting, research and attention to both the immediate and the larger biological community of your site are warranted. The best place to look for the answers is nature itself.

A Woodland Meditation Garden

An interesting juxtaposition occurs when the perfectly regular geometrical form of this meditation garden contrasts with the organic forms of the woodland. The dance of light and shadow, the textural harmonies and plant fragrances, the sounds of wildlife, even the silence of the woods all create a tranquil atmosphere for quiet moments of introspection.

In this design the strong linear axis structuring the plan begins from an important vantage point inside the house. Notice that the lines of the axial corridor narrow as they get farther away from the deck. This design technique, called forced perspective, creates the illusion of greater distance between two points in space.

The view from the elevated deck of the residence to a space carved from the wooded area surrounding the house is dramatic. A raised reflection pool occupies the center of the circular garden space and serves as a focal element at the end of the visual axis. A sculpture with a botanical or ecological theme would serve the same design function. The focus is strongly framed on either side of the corridor between the deck and the clearing by layered heights of naturalized herbal plants.

The lowest vegetative layer consists of herbal wildflowers that are encouraged to naturalize and spill into the center footpath area. The earth-colored stepping stones of the center path blend with the wildflowers. Suggested native herbal plants for this low, naturalized layer include wild ginger (*Asarum canadense*), liverleaf (*Hepatica americana*), wintergreen or teaberry (*Gaultheria procumbens*), periwinkle (*Vinca minor*), autumn crocus (*Colchicum autumnale*), cinnamon fern (*Osmunda cinnamomea*), snow trillium (*Trillium grandiflorum*), and jonquil varieties (*Narcissus jonquilla*).

Herbal native shrubs are planted for the second layer and could include summersweet (*Clethra alnifolia*), wild senna (*Cassia marilandica*), highbush blueberry (*Vaccinium corymbosum*), red osier (*Cornus sericea*), bottlebrush buckeye (*Aesculus parviflora*), or the tall, showy devil's walking stick (*Aralia spinosa*).

The next layer consists of small, flowering, native herbal trees, such as sourwood or lily-of-the-valley tree (*Oxydendrum arboreum*), sweet bay magnolia (*Magnolia virginiana*), Washington hawthorn (*Crataegus phaenopyrum*), fringe tree (*Chionanthus virginicus*), and eastern redbud (*Cercis canadensis*). American holly (*Ilex opaca*) is an excellent evergreen tree for this planting zone, since it maintains the framing effect in winter.

For the round and regular planting arrangement of the trees, shrubs, and wildflowers that define the circular garden area, choose a simple palette of your favorite natives. Consider using aromatic plants to perfume the atmosphere of this special haven.

———————————————— L E G E N D ————————————————

1 Raised, stone reflection pool in circular clearing

2 Stepping stone footpath

3 Deck stairs

4 Low, native herbal wildflowers

5 Native herbal shrubs

6 Small, native herbal evergreen and flowering trees

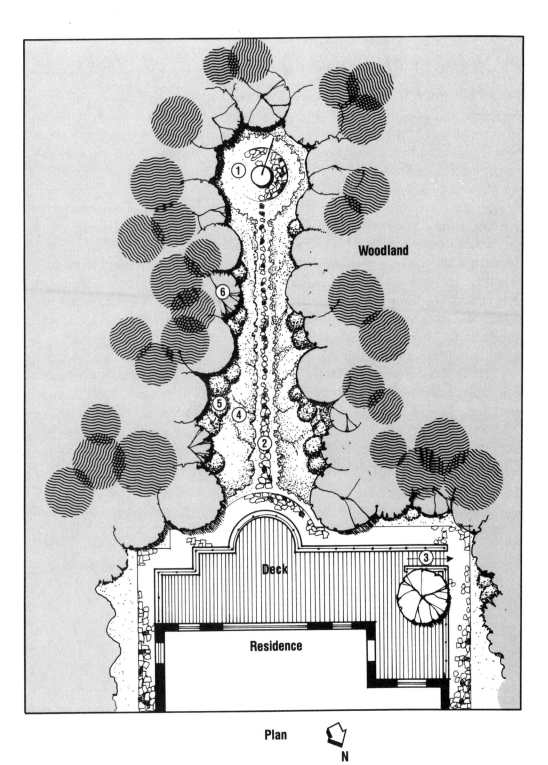

Plan

N

A Planting of Native and Naturalized Herbs

Native and naturalized herbs can be used to make an attractive planting. Serviceberry or shadblow is an ornamental indigenous tree with white blossoms in early spring. As the growing season ends, it produces red or purple berries, which attract birds, and has lovely fall foliage. With its light gray bark and slender branching habit, this tree is effective planted in front of evergreens. It will do well in sun or shade.

Sweet cicely is known as the fern of herbs, although its anise-scented leaves are more intricate and delicate than the fronds of most ferns. It has lovely, lacy white flowers. Sweet woodruff is a beautiful ground cover for shade. The six-inch-high plant has small shiny leaves arranged in whorls around its stem and delicate, white flower clusters. Bloodroot is another low-growing wildflower with appealing white flowers. Sweet violets add charm and fragrance to this or any naturalized planting. All of these herbaceous herbal plants bloom in early spring. They require partial shade to shade and a moist to moderately moist, well-drained, acid soil.

These plants are beautiful selections for a variety of naturalized garden situations such as border plantings along a woodland edge or as island bed plantings for lawn or patio areas. The tremendous potential for using native and naturalized herbal plants for home and public landscaping and gardening has only begun to be explored. Use these plants in your own landscape, and begin to discover the beauty and function of a naturalized herbal planting.

LEGEND

A *Amelanchier arborea*, serviceberry or shadblow

B *Myrrhis odorata*, sweet cicely

C *Galium odoratum*, sweet woodruff

D *Sanguinaria canadensis*, bloodroot

E *Viola odorata*, sweet violet

A Rock Garden and Steps

Herbs are a beautiful solution for steep embankments, which can be difficult to landscape. A dry, sunny, steep grade is a familiar environment for the many herbs found in similar conditions in their native land. Many of the herbs chosen for the illustrated rock garden trace their origins to the hot, gravelly slopes of the Mediterranean. These plants do well with the sharp drainage that occurs naturally on an embankment, and they are sun-loving and tolerant of drought.

In this design, stone slabs function as steps to accommodate the steep grade. The curve in the stair adds interest. A few stone pavers on the level areas at the top and bottom of the stair suggest continued movement; they signal the grade change and the approaching steps as well.

Gray santolina is an accent plant near the stairs. Its attractive, silvery gray foliage and intricate, corallike texture lead the eye in an ascent of the stairs. The mounding upright form contrasts with the low-growing and creeping thymes selected for areas immediately adjacent to the steps. Allow the creeping thyme varieties to spill onto the steps to soften the hard edges. Thyme can tolerate light foot traffic; its lovely fragrance, released when trod upon, is an added pleasure.

The foliage colors—blue, silver, and gray—and the repetition of creeping and mounding forms tie this planting composition into a unified whole. The rich diversity of foliage texture and the white, blue, yellow, and pink flowers enliven the garden canvas. Rocks with blue and gray coloring would blend nicely with this herbal painting.

An important principle of environmental gardening is illustrated in this design: the prevention of soil erosion from a steep bank. Without a proper ground covering, valuable topsoil may be washed away during a heavy rain, especially when the soil may already be saturated. The roots of established plants help hold topsoil in place, and the vegetative growth itself slows the velocity of water pouring down the embankment.

When you install new rock garden plants on a steep bank, consider using a geotextile netting to reduce erosion and keep the transplants in place until the roots have taken hold. These netting materials are literally pinned to the soil. They are usually biodegradable and decompose within a few years.

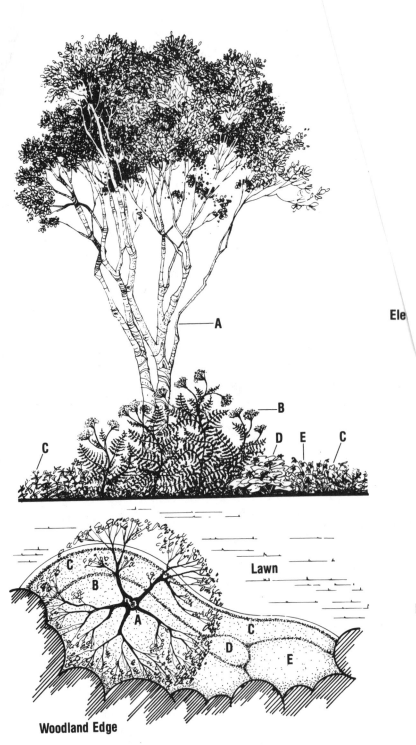

A

B

D E C

C

Ele

Lawn

Plan

C

B

A

C

D

E

Woodland Edge

A Rock Garden and Steps

Herbs are a beautiful solution for steep embankments, which can be difficult to landscape. A dry, sunny, steep grade is a familiar environment for the many herbs found in similar conditions in their native land. Many of the herbs chosen for the illustrated rock garden trace their origins to the hot, gravelly slopes of the Mediterranean. These plants do well with the sharp drainage that occurs naturally on an embankment, and they are sun-loving and tolerant of drought.

In this design, stone slabs function as steps to accommodate the steep grade. The curve in the stair adds interest. A few stone pavers on the level areas at the top and bottom of the stair suggest continued movement; they signal the grade change and the approaching steps as well.

Gray santolina is an accent plant near the stairs. Its attractive, silvery gray foliage and intricate, corallike texture lead the eye in an ascent of the stairs. The mounding upright form contrasts with the low-growing and creeping thymes selected for areas immediately adjacent to the steps. Allow the creeping thyme varieties to spill onto the steps to soften the hard edges. Thyme can tolerate light foot traffic; its lovely fragrance, released when trod upon, is an added pleasure.

The foliage colors—blue, silver, and gray—and the repetition of creeping and mounding forms tie this planting composition into a unified whole. The rich diversity of foliage texture and the white, blue, yellow, and pink flowers enliven the garden canvas. Rocks with blue and gray coloring would blend nicely with this herbal painting.

An important principle of environmental gardening is illustrated in this design: the prevention of soil erosion from a steep bank. Without a proper ground covering, valuable topsoil may be washed away during a heavy rain, especially when the soil may already be saturated. The roots of established plants help hold topsoil in place, and the vegetative growth itself slows the velocity of water pouring down the embankment.

When you install new rock garden plants on a steep bank, consider using a geotextile netting to reduce erosion and keep the transplants in place until the roots have taken hold. These netting materials are literally pinned to the soil. They are usually biodegradable and decompose within a few years.

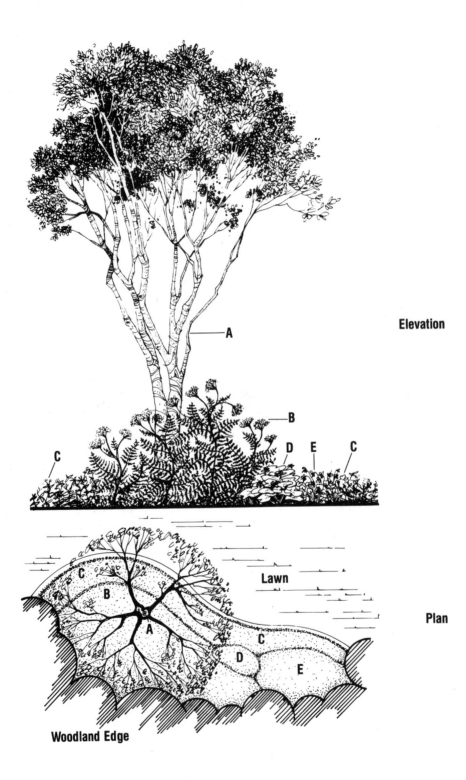

Elevation

Plan

Lawn

Woodland Edge

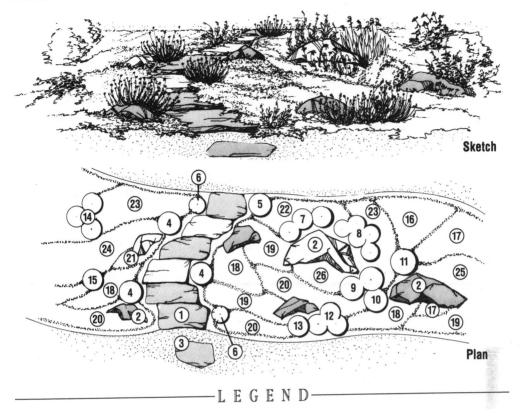

Sketch

Plan

L E G E N D

1 Stone steps

2 Boulder

3 Stone pavers

4 *Santolina chamaecyparissus*, lavender cotton or gray santolina

5 *Santolina chamaecyparissus* 'Nana', dwarf lavender cotton

6 *Salvia officinalis* 'Tricolor', tricolor sage

7 *Salvia officinalis*, garden sage

8 *Iris × germanica* var. *florentina*, orris or florentina iris

9 *Ruta graveolens* 'Blue Mound', 'Blue Mound' compact rue

10 *Ruta graveolens* 'Variegata', variegated rue

11 *Artemisia abrotanum*, southernwood

12 *Santolina virens*, green santolina

13 *Santolina ericoides*, compact green santolina

14 *Artemisia absinthium* 'Lambrook Silver', 'Lambrook Silver' wormwood

15 *Melissa officinalis*, lemon balm

16 *Chrysanthemum parthenium*, feverfew

17 *Origanum vulgare*, wild oregano

18 *Thymus vulgaris* 'Argenteus', silver thyme

19 *Thymus praecox arcticus* 'Albus', white-flowering creeping thyme

20 *Thymus praecox arcticus* 'Coccineus', red-flowering creeping thyme

21 *Thymus nitidus*, tiny-leaf thyme

22 *Thymus × citriodorus* 'Aureus', golden lemon thyme

23 *Thymus pseudolanuginosus*, woolly thyme

24 *Thymus praecox arcticus*, mother-of-thyme

25 *Thymus vulgaris*, common thyme

26 Small spring-flowering bulbs

A Knot Garden for a Small Space

The beauty of this knot garden design is that it can be easily sculpted into small, nook-and-cranny planting spaces, which are often difficult areas to landscape. The illustrated garden is 9½ feet square.

This design is a clever solution for a small exterior corner alongside the house. A floor-to-ceiling window allows a full view of the colorful, patterned design from indoors. The garden is also enjoyed from the terrace area bordering it on the other side.

The microclimate of the protected corner allows some borderline tender herbs to be planted farther north than usual. These include the fig tree, the dwarf edging boxwood, the rosemary, and the germander. The espaliered fig tree softens the bare brick wall of the house and creates the effect of a wall sculpture.

Germander is a traditional knot-garden plant with small delicate leaves, rose-colored flowers, and a compact form with a dense branching habit. The reddish purple foliage of the dwarf Japanese barberry is an excellent complement to the germander. Both plants respond well to close clipping, a requirement for knot plants. They must be maintained at a height of approximately six to eight inches, thus requiring trimming as often as every few weeks during the growing season.

Knot gardens are typically located in open areas. This garden could be used in a planting bed carved out of a paved terrace, or in an open lawn area. It would also be a gorgeous center jewel for a larger garden design.

LEGEND

1 *Teucrium chamaedrys*, germander
2 *Berberis thunbergii* 'Crimson Pigmy', dwarf red Japanese barberry
3 *Buxus sempervirons* 'Suffruticosa', dwarf edging boxwood
4 *Thymus praecox arcticus* 'Albus', white-flowering creeping thyme
5 *Thymus praecox arcticus* 'Coccineus', red-flowering creeping thyme
6 *Thymus herba-barona*, caraway thyme
7 *Salvia officinalis* 'Purpurascens', purple sage

8 *Lavandula angustifolia* subsp. *angustifolia* 'Munstead', dwarf lavender
9 *Rosmarinus officinalis*, rosemary
10 *Salvia officinalis* 'Tricolor', tricolor sage
11 *Ficus* 'Brown Turkey', espaliered fig tree
12 Cocoa or pecan shell mulch
13 Raised brick edge

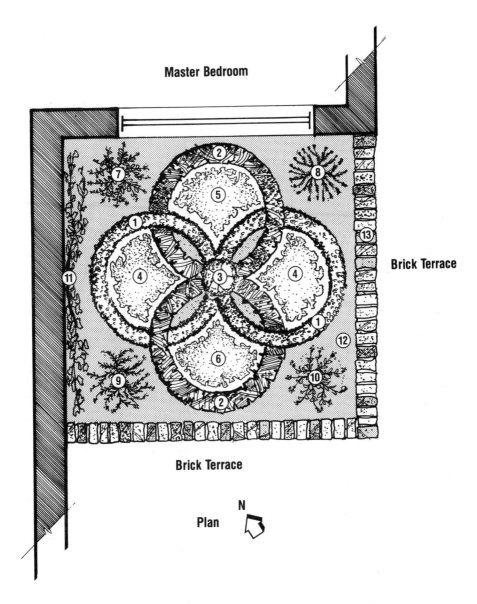

Master Bedroom

Brick Terrace

Brick Terrace

Plan

N

Sources of Supply

CARROLL GARDENS
444 East Main Street
P.O. Box 310
Westminster, MD 21157
Herb plants and perennials.

CATNIP ACRES FARM
67 Christian Street
Oxford, CT 06483
Specialty herb seeds and plants. Good
source for collectibles. Plants
available in spring only.

COMPANION PLANTS
7247 North Coolville Ridge
Athens, OH 45701
Herb plants and seeds.

GILBERTIE'S HERB GARDENS
Sylvan Avenue
Westport, CT 06880
Extensive collection of common and
specialty herb plants. Good source
for quantity.

THE HERBFARM
32804 Issaquah-Fall City Road
Fall City, WA 98024
Herb plants and seeds.

HUDSON, J. L., SEEDSMAN
P.O. Box 1058
Redwood City, CA 94064
Rare and unusual herb seeds.

LOGEE'S GREENHOUSES
55 North Street
Danielson, CT 06239
Unusual herb plants, scented
geraniums, fragrant plants.

NICHOLS GARDEN NURSERY
1190 North Pacific Highway
Albany, OR 97321
Herb and unusual vegetable seeds.

PARK, GEORGE W., SEED
COMPANY
P.O. Box 31
Greenwood, SC 29647
Herb seeds.

REDWOOD CITY SEED
COMPANY
Box 361
Redwood City, CA 94064
Rare and unusual herb seeds from
Japan, Europe, and the United States.

RICHTER, OTTO AND SONS
Box 26
Goodwood, Ontario
Canada L0C 1A0
Herb, gourmet vegetable, and
wildflower seeds.

ROSEMARY HOUSE
120 South Market Street
Mechanicsburg, PA 17055
Unusual herb seeds.

SANDY MUSH HERB NURSERY
Route 2
Surrett Cove Road
Leicester, NC 28748
Herb plants.

SUNNYBROOK FARMS
NURSERY
9448 Mayfield Road
P.O. Box 6
Chesterland, OH 44026
Specialty and common herb plants.
Good source for thyme varieties.

TAYLOR'S HERB GARDEN, INC.
1535 Lone Oak Road
Vista, CA 92084
Good source for specialty and
common herb plants.

TIDELAND GARDENS, INC.
P.O. Box 549
Chestertown, MD 21620
Field grown herb and perennial
plants. Common herb plants
available.

WELL-SWEEP HERB FARM
317 Mt. Bethel Road
Port Murray, NJ 07865
Good source for unusual herb plants.

WHITEFLOWER FARM
Litchfield, CT 06759
Herb plants and perennials.

WOODLANDERS, INC.
1128 Colleton Avenue
Aiken, SC 29801
Native southeastern United States
and unusual introduced plants.

BIBLIOGRAPHY

Bachelard, Gaston. *The Poetics of Space*. Boston: Beacon Press, 1960.

Bailey Hortorium, Liberty Hyde, staff of. *Hortus Third: A Concise Dictionary of Plants Cultivated in the United States and Canada*. New York: MacMillan, 1977.

Brooklyn Botanical Garden. *Herbs and Their Ornamental Uses*. BBG, 1972. (Black and white photos of herb plants.)

Buchanan, Rita. *A Weaver's Garden*. Loveland, CO: Interweave, 1987. (Well-researched book on herbal dye gardens, lovely illustrations.)

Bush-Brown, James and Louise. *America's Garden Book*. New York: C. Scribner's and Sons, 1980.

Ching, Francis, D.K., *Architecture: Form, Space, and Order*. Van Nostrand Reinhold, 1979.

Crockett, James U., and Ogden Tanner, and eds. *Herbs: The Time-Life Encyclopedia of Gardening*. Morristown, NJ: Time-Life, 1977.

Everett, Thomas H. *The New York Botanical Garden Illustrated Encyclopedia of Horticulture*. Garland Pub., 1980.

Favretti, Rudy J., and Joy P. *Landscapes and Gardens for Historic Buildings—A Handbook for Reproducing and Creating Authentic Landscape Settings*. Nashville, TN: The American Association for State and Local History, 1978.

Foster, Gertrude B., and Rosemary F. Louden. *Park's Success with Herbs*. Greenwood, S.C.: Geo. W. Park Seed Co., 1980. (Excellent reference for greenhouse seed propagation and growing herbs.)

Foster, Stephen. *Herbal Bounty*. Gibbs Smith, Inc., 1984. (Eloquently written book by a knowledgeable herb gardener and professional horticulturist.)

Gupton, Oscar W., and Fred C. Swope. *Wildflowers of the Shenandoah Valley and Blue Ridge Mountains*. U. of Virginia, 1981. (Color photos of wildflowers, many with herbal use.)

Herb Society of America, Dorothy Spencer, ed. "The Travelers Guide to Herb Gardens." HSA, 1986. (Booklet containing listings of over 400 herb gardens in the United States and Canada. Organized by state with maps, addresses, phone numbers, seasons, and descriptions of the gardens. Includes historical herb gardens. Write to H.S.A., Publications, 9019 Kirtland Chardon Road, Mentor, OH 44060.)

Hightshoe, Gary L. *Native Trees for Urban and Rural America.* Iowa State Univ. Research Fdtn., 1978. (Excellent graphic and chart information on native trees, many of which have herbal use.)

Hill, Madalene, and Gwen Barclay. *Southern Herb Growing.* Fredericksburg, TX: Shearer Publ., 1987. (Color photos of herb plants. Knowledgeable and experienced authors. Indispensable for herb growers in the South.)

Hobhouse, Penelope. *Color in the Garden.* Boston: Little, Brown, 1985. (Primarily about flowering perennials but color design principles are applicable to herbs.)

Hobhouse, Penelope, ed. *Gertrude Jekyll on Gardening.* New York: Random House, 1985.

Jellicoe, Geoffrey, and Susan, consulting eds., Patrick Goode and Michael Lancaster, executive eds. *The Oxford Companion to Gardens.* Oxford/New York: Oxford University Press, 1986.

Kowalchik, Claire, and William H. Hylton, eds. *Rodale's Illustrated Encyclopedia of Herbs.* Rodale Press, 1987. (Excellent reference on growing and using herbs.)

Lima, Patrick. *The Harrowsmith Illustrated Book of Herbs.* Camden House Publ., 1986. (Illustrations, photos, watercolors.)

Prest, John. *The Botanical Garden and the Re-creation of Paradise.* New Haven: Yale University Press, 1981.

Ransey, Charles G., and Harold R. Sleeper. *Architectural Graphic Standards,* 7th edition. Robert T. Packard, editor. New York: John Wiley & Sons, 1981.

Reppert, Bertha P. *A Heritage of Herbs.* Remembrance Press, 1976. (History, early gardening, old recipes, extensive list of native herbal plants.)

Shimizu, Holly Harmar. "Listing of Woody Plants with Herbal Use." Unpublished manuscript, 1984.

Spirn, Anne Whiston. *The Granite Garden: Urban Nature and Human Design.* Basic Books, 1984. (Author views the city as a living organism. Broadening concepts and practical information.)

Swanson, Faith H., and Rady, Virginia B. *Herb Garden Design.* U.P. of New England, 1984. (Beautiful herb garden design plans with plant lists.)

United States Department of Agriculture, The National Arboretum Herb Garden, friends of, and The Herb Society of America. *National Herb Garden.* 1985.

United States Department of the Interior, National Park Service, Patterson, James C. "Planting in Urban Soils." Ecological Services Bulletin #1. U.S. Government Printing Office: Washington, DC, 1974.

Verey, Rosemary, foreword by, and Guy Cooper, Gordon Taylor, and Clive Boursnell. *English Herb Gardens.* London: Widenfeld and Nicolson, 1986. (Photos and descriptions of many interesting English herb gardens.)

Whyte, William H. *The Social Life of Small Urban Spaces.* Washington, DC: Conservation Foundation, 1980. (Enlightening report on how people use or don't use small urban spaces.)

Wilder, Louise Beebe. *The Fragrant Garden.* Dover, 1974. (Very good book on growing plants for fragrance.)

Wilkinson, Elizabeth, and Marjorie Henderson, eds. *The House of Boughs: A Sourcebook of Garden Designs, Structures, and Suppliers.* New York: Viking, 1985.

Index